English Grammar in Use

A reference and practice book for intermediate students

Raymond Murphy

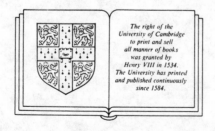

The right of the University of Cambridge to print and sell all manner of books was granted by Henry VIII in 1534. The University has printed and published continuously since 1584.

Cambridge University Press

Cambridge
New York   Port Chester
Melbourne   Sydney

Published by the Press Syndicate of the University of Cambridge
The Pitt Building, Trumpington Street, Cambridge CB2 1RP
40 West 20th Street, New York, NY 10011, USA
10 Stamford Road, Oakleigh, Melbourne 3166, Australia

© Cambridge University Press 1985, 1987

First published 1987
Fifth printing 1989

Book designed by Peter Ducker MSTD
Drawings by Leslie Marshall

Printed in Great Britain
at The Bath Press, Avon

British Library cataloguing in publication data

Murphy, Raymond

English grammar in use: a reference
and practice book for intermediate students.
– [2nd ed.]
1. English language – Grammar – Problems,
exercises, etc.
I. Title
428.2   PE1112

ISBN 0 521 33683 X

Contents

Prepositions

Thanks

I would like to thank all the students and teachers who have used the material which makes up this book. In particular I would like to express my thanks to my colleagues at the Swan School of English, Oxford, for their interest and encouragement.

Introduction

English Grammar in Use is a book for intermediate students of English who need to study and practise using the grammar of the language. It was originally conceived as a self-study reference and practice book but can also be incorporated into classroom teaching. It will be especially useful in cases where, in the teacher's view, existing course materials do not provide adequate coverage of grammar.

Level

The book is intended mainly for intermediate students (that is students who have already studied the basic structures of English). It concentrates on those structures which intermediate students want to use but which often cause difficulty. The book will probably be most useful at middle- and upper-intermediate levels (where all or nearly all of the material will be relevant), and can serve both as a basis for revision and as a means of practising new material. The book will also be useful for more advanced students who still make a lot of grammatical mistakes and who need a book for reference and practice.

The book is not intended to be used by elementary students.

How the book is organised

The book consists of 130 units, each of which concentrates on a particular point of grammar. Some areas (for example, the present perfect or the use of articles) are covered in more than one unit. In each unit there are explanations and examples (left-hand page) and exercises (right-hand page), except for Unit 117, which is a double unit.

At the beginning of the book the *Contents* pages provide a full list of units and there is a detailed *Index* at the end for easy reference.

There are also five *Appendices* at the end of the book: List of present and past tenses, Regular and irregular verbs, Spelling, Short forms and American English. It might be useful for the teacher to draw students' attention to these.

Using the book

It is certainly not intended that anyone should work through this book from beginning to end. It is for the teacher to decide what to teach and in what order to teach it, so the book is best used selectively and flexibly.

The book can be used with the whole class or with individual students. When using the book with the whole class, it is suggested that the teacher teaches the grammar points concerned in whatever way he/she wants. In this case the left-hand page is not used actively during the lesson but serves as a record of what has been taught and can be referred to by the student in the future. The exercises can then be done in class or as homework. Alternatively (and additionally), individual students can be directed to study certain units of the book by themselves if they have particular difficulties not shared by other students in their class.

UNIT 1   Present continuous (**I am doing**)

a) Study this example situation:

 Ann is in her car. She is on her way to work.

She **is driving** to work.

This means: she is driving now, at the time of speaking.

This is the *present continuous* tense:

$$\left.\begin{array}{l} \text{I } \textbf{am} \text{ (= I'm)} \\ \text{he/she/(it) } \textbf{is} \quad \text{(= he 's etc.)} \\ \text{we/they/you } \textbf{are} \text{ (= we're etc.)} \end{array}\right\} \textbf{driving}$$

We use the present continuous when we talk about something which is happening at the time of speaking:

  – Please don't make so much noise. **I'm studying.** (*not* 'I study')
  – 'Where is Margaret?'   'She**'s having** a bath.' (*not* 'she has')
  – Let's go out now. It **isn't raining** any more.
  – (*at a party*) Hello, Ann. **Are** you **enjoying** the party? (*not* 'do you enjoy')

b) We also use the present continuous when we talk about something which is happening around the time of speaking, but not necessarily exactly at the time of speaking. Study this example situation:

  – Tom and Ann are talking and drinking in a café. Tom says: '**I'm reading** an interesting book at the moment. I'll lend it to you when I've finished it.'

Tom is not reading the book at the time of speaking. He means that he has begun the book and hasn't finished it yet. He is in the middle of reading it. Here are some more examples:

  – Silvia **is learning** English at the moment. (*not* 'learns')
  – Have you heard about Tom? He **is building** his own house. (*not* 'builds')

But perhaps Silvia and Tom are not doing these things exactly at the time of speaking.

c) We often use the present continuous when we talk about a period around the present. For example: **today, this season** etc.:

  – 'You**'re working** hard **today**.'   'Yes, I have a lot to do.'
  – Tom **isn't playing** football **this season**. He wants to concentrate on his studies.

d) We use the present continuous when we talk about changing situations:

  – The population of the world **is rising** very fast. (*not* 'rises')
  – **Is** your English **getting** better? (*not* 'does ... get')

UNIT 1   Exercises

1.1 *In this exercise you have to put the verb into the correct form.*
  Examples: Please don't make so much noise. I ....**am studying**...... (study).
      Let's go out now. It ....**isn't raining**....... (not/rain) any more.
      Listen to those people. What language **are they speaking**. (they/speak) ?

  1 Please be quiet. I .... (try) to concentrate.
  2 Look! It .... (snow).
  3 Why .... (you/look) at me like that? Have I said something wrong?
  4 You .... (make) a lot of noise. Can you be a bit quieter?
  5 Excuse me, I .... (look) for a phone box. Is there one near here?
  6 (*in the cinema*) It's a good film, isn't it? .... (you/enjoy) it?
  7 Listen! Can you hear those people next door? They .... (shout) at each other again.
  8 Why .... (you/wear) your coat today? It's very warm.
  9 I .... (not/work) this week. I'm on holiday.
  10 I want to lose weight. I .... (not/eat) anything today.

1.2 *Complete these sentences using one of these verbs:*
  get   become   change   rise   improve   fall   increase
  You don't have to use all the verbs and you can use some of them more than once.
  Example: The population of the world ....**is rising**........... very fast.

  1 The number of people without jobs .... at the moment.
  2 He is still ill but he .... better slowly.
  3 These days food .... more and more expensive.
  4 The world .... Things never stay the same.
  5 The cost of living .... Every year things are dearer.
  6 George has gone to work in Spain. When he arrived, his Spanish wasn't very good but now it ....
  7 The economic situation is already very bad and it .... worse.

1.3 *Read this conversation between Brian and Steve. Put each verb into the correct form. The first one has already been done for you.*

  Brian and Steve meet in a restaurant:
  Brian: Hello, Steve. I haven't seen you for ages. What (1) .....**are you doing**..... (you/do) these days?
  Steve: I (2) .... (train) to be a shop manager.
  Brian: Really? (3) .... (you/enjoy) it?
  Steve: Yes, it's quite interesting. How about you?
  Brian: Well, I (4) .... (not/work) at the moment, but I'm very busy. I (5) .... (build) a house.
  Steve: Really? (6) .... (you/do) it alone?
  Brian: No, some friends of mine (7) .... (help) me.

UNIT 2   Present simple (**I do**)

a) Study this example situation:

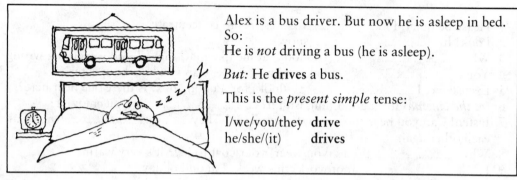

Alex is a bus driver. But now he is asleep in bed.
So:
He is *not* driving a bus (he is asleep).

But: He **drives** a bus.

This is the *present simple* tense:

I/we/you/they **drive**
he/she/(it)   **drives**

We use the present simple to talk about things in general. We are not thinking only about the present. We use it to say that something happens all the time or repeatedly, or that something is true in general. It is not important whether the action is happening at the time of speaking:

    — The earth **goes** round the sun.
    — Nurses **look** after patients in hospitals.
    — In Britain most of the shops **close** at 5.30 p.m.

Remember that we say **he/she/it** —s. Don't forget the **s**:
    — I **work** in a bank. Barry **works** in a shop.

b) We use **do/does** to make questions and negative sentences:

| **do** I/we/you/they } **work?** | I/we/you/they **don't** } **work** |
| **does** he/she/it | he/she/it **doesn't** |

    — Excuse me, **do** you **speak** English?
    — 'Would you like a cigarette?'   'No, thanks. I **don't smoke**.'
    — **What does** this word **mean**? (*not* 'What means this word?')
    — Rice **doesn't grow** in Britain.

For questions see also Unit 49.

c) We use the present simple when we say how often we do things:
    — I **get** up at 8 o'clock **every morning**. (*not* 'am getting')
    — **How often do** you **go** to the dentist?
    — Ann **doesn't often drink** tea.
    — In summer Tom **usually plays** tennis **twice a week**.

d) Note that we say 'Where **do** you **come** from?'(= Where are you from?):
    — Where **do** you **come** from? (*not* 'Where are you coming from?')
    — He **comes** from Japan. (*not* 'He is coming from Japan.')

e) When you make a *suggestion*, you can say **Why don't you ...?**:
    — 'I'm tired.'   '**Why don't you go** to bed early?'

4

UNIT 2   Exercises

2.1 *In this exercise you have to put the verb into the correct form.*
Examples: Water ....*boils*.............. (boil) at 100 degrees centigrade.
George ......*doesn't go*........ (not/go) to the cinema very often.
How many languages ....*do you speak*..... (you/speak)?

1 The swimming bath .... (open) at 9.00 and .... (close)
at 18.30 every day.
2 What time .... (the banks / close) in Britain?
3 I have a car but I .... (not/use) it very often.
4 How many cigarettes .... (you/smoke) a day?
5 'What .... (you/do)?' 'I'm an electrical engineer.'
6 'Where .... (your father / come) from?' 'He ....
(come) from Scotland.'
7 If you need money, why .... (you/not/get) a job?
8 I .... (play) the piano, but I .... (not/play) very well.
9 I don't understand the word 'deceive'. What .... ('deceive' / mean)?

2.2 *This time you have to read some sentences and correct them. The English is correct but the
information is wrong. Write two correct sentences each time.*
Example: The sun goes round the earth.   *The sun doesn't go round the earth.*
The earth goes round the sun.

1 The sun rises in the west.   ....
....

2 Mice catch cats.   ....
....

3 Carpenters make things from metal.   ....
....

4 The River Amazon flows into the Pacific Ocean.   ....
....

2.3 *Now you have to use these sentences to make questions. Begin your question with the
word(s) in brackets.*
Examples: Tom plays tennis. (How often?)   *How often does Tom play tennis?*
I get up in the morning. (What time / usually?)   *What time do you usually get up?*

1 Ann watches television. (How often?)   How often ....
2 I write to my parents. (How often?)   ....
3 I have dinner in the evening? (What time / usually?)   ....
4 Tom works. (Where?)   ....
5 I go to the cinema. (How often?)   ....
6 People do stupid things. (Why?)   ....
7 The car breaks down. (How often?)   ....

UNIT 3   Present continuous (**I am doing**) or present simple (**I do**)?

Before you study this unit, study Units 1 and 2.

a) Study this explanation and compare the examples:

Present continuous (**I am doing**) Use the present continuous to talk about something which is happening at or around the time of speaking:	*Present simple* (**I do**) Use the present simple to talk about things in general or things which happen repeatedly:
 I am doing ―――――――――――――― *past* *now* *future*	 ―――――――――― I do ―――――――――― *past* *now* *future*
The kettle **is boiling.** Can you turn it off, please?	Water **boils** at 100 degrees Celsius.
Listen to those people. What language **are** they **speaking?**	Excuse me, **do** you **speak** English?
'Where's Tom?' 'He**'s playing** tennis.'	Tom **plays** tennis every Saturday.
(*you find a stranger in your room*) What **are** you **doing** here?	What **do** you usually **do** at weekends? What **do** you **do?** (= What's your job?)
Silvia is in Britain for three months. She**'s learning** English.	Most people **learn** to swim when they are children.
Use the present continuous for a *temporary* situation:	Use the present simple for a *permanent* situation:
I**'m living** with some friends until I can find a flat.	My parents **live** in London. They have been there for 20 years.
That machine **isn't working.** It broke down this morning.	That machine **doesn't work.** It hasn't worked for years.

b) Some verbs are used only in *simple* tenses. For example, you cannot say 'I am knowing'. You can only say **I know.** Here is a list of verbs which are not normally used in *continuous* tenses (but there are exceptions):

want	like	belong	know	suppose	remember
need	love	see	realise	mean	forget
prefer	hate	hear	believe	understand	seem

have (when the meaning is 'possess' – see also Unit 24)
think (when the meaning is 'believe')

- **Do** you **like** London? (*not* 'are you liking')
- He **doesn't understand.** (*not* 'he isn't understanding')
- These shoes **belong** to me. (*not* 'are belonging')
- What **do** you **think** Tom will do? (= What do you believe he will do?)

but: What **are** you **thinking** about? (= What is going on in your mind?)

UNIT 3   Exercises

3.1 *In this exercise you have to decide whether the verbs in these sentences are right or wrong.*
Correct those which are wrong. The verb is underlined.
Examples: I don't know your telephone number.   RIGHT
              Please don't make so much noise. I study.   WRONG - am studying.

1 Look! Somebody is climbing up that tree over there.   ....
2 Can you hear those people? What do they talk about?   ....
3 Are you believing in God?   ....
4 Look! That man tries to open the door of your car.   ....
5 The moon goes round the earth.   ....
6 I'm thinking it would be a good idea to leave early.   ....
7 The government is worried because the number of
   people without jobs is increasing.   ....
8 I'm usually going to work by car.   ....

3.2 *Now you have to put the verb into the correct form, present continuous (**I am doing**) or*
*present simple (**I do**).*
Examples: Please don't make so much noise. I .....am studying......... (study).
              How many languages .....does Tom speak.... (Tom/speak)?
              This machine .....doesn't work....... (not/work). It hasn't worked for years.

1 I .... (not/belong) to a political party.
2 Hurry! The bus .... (come). I .... (not/want) to miss it.
3 The River Nile .... (flow) into the Mediterranean.
4 The river .... (flow) very fast today – much faster than usual.
5 .... (it/ever/snow) in India?
6 We usually .... (grow) vegetables in our garden but this year we
   .... (not/grow) any.
7 A: Can you drive?
   B: No, but I .... (learn). My father .... (teach) me.
8 You can borrow my umbrella. I .... (not/need) it at the moment.
9 (*at a party*) I usually .... (enjoy) parties but I .... (not/
   enjoy) this one very much.
10 George says he's 80 years old but I .... (not/believe) him.
11 Ron is in London at the moment. He .... (stay) at the Hilton Hotel.
   He usually .... (stay) at the Hilton Hotel when he's in London.

In these sentences think about whether the situation is temporary or permanent.

12 My parents .... (live) in Bristol. They were born there and have never
   lived anywhere else. Where .... (your parents / live)?
13 She .... (stay) with her sister at the moment until she finds somewhere
   to live.
14 A: What .... (your father / do)?
   B: He's a teacher, but he .... (not/work) at the moment.

7

UNIT 4   Present tenses (**I am doing** / **I do**) with a future meaning

a) *Present continuous* with a future meaning
Study this example situation:

This is Tom's diary for next week.

He **is playing** tennis on Monday afternoon.
He **is going** to the dentist on Tuesday morning.
He **is having** dinner with Ann on Friday.

In all these examples, Tom has already decided and arranged to do these things.

When you are talking about what you have already arranged to do, use the present continuous (**I am doing**). Do *not* use the present simple (**I do**).
  — A: What **are** you **doing** tomorrow evening? (*not* 'what do you do')
     B: I'm **going** to the theatre. (*not* 'I go')
  — A: **Are** you **playing** football tomorrow?
     B: Yes, but Tom **isn't playing.** He has hurt his leg.
  — A: Ann **is coming** tomorrow.
     B: Oh, **is** she? What time **is** she **arriving**?
     A: At 10.15.
     B: **Are** you **meeting** her at the station?
     A: I can't. I'm **working** tomorrow morning.
It is also possible to use **going to** (**do**) in these sentences:
  — What **are** you **going to do** tomorrow evening?
  — Tom **is going to play** tennis on Monday afternoon.
But the present continuous is usually more natural when you are talking about arrangements. See also Unit 5.

Do *not* use **will** to talk about what you have arranged to do:
  — What **are** you **doing** this evening? (*not* 'what will you do')
  — Alex **is getting** married next month. (*not* 'Alex will get')

b) *Present simple* with a future meaning
We use the present simple when we are talking about timetables, programmes etc. (for example, for public transport, cinemas):
  — What time **does** the film **begin?**
  — The train **leaves** Plymouth at 10.30 and **arrives** in London at 13.45.
  — The football match **starts** at 8 o'clock.
  — Tomorrow **is** Wednesday.
But we do not normally use the present simple for personal arrangements:
  — What time **are** you **meeting** Ann? (*not* 'do you meet')

UNIT 4   Exercises

4.1 *A friend of yours is planning to go on holiday very soon. You ask him about his plans. Use the words in brackets to make your questions.*
Example: (where / go?) Where are you going? ....

1 (how long /stay?) ....
2 (when / leave?) ....
3 (go / alone?) ....

4 (go / by car?) ....
5 (where / stay?) ....

4.2 *Ann is going on holiday. You have to write sentences about her holiday plans. Use the words in brackets to write your sentences.*
Example: (go / Scotland)   She is going to Scotland. ....

1 (leave / next Friday)   She ....
2 (stay / in Scotland for two weeks)   ....
3 (go / with a friend of hers)   ....
4 (stay / in a hotel)   They ....
5 (go / by train)   ....

4.3 *Tom wants you to visit him but you are very busy. Look at your diary for the next few days and explain to him why you can't come.*

Monday
Volleyball 7·30 pm
Tuesday
Work late (till 9 pm.)
Wednesday
theatre (with mother)
Thursday
meet Julia 8 p.m.
Friday
Saturday
Sunday
Notes

Tom: Can you come on Monday evening?
You: Sorry, I'd love to but I'm playing volleyball.
Tom: What about Tuesday evening then?
You: I can't I'm afraid. I (1)..............................
Tom: Well, what are you doing on Wednesday evening?
You: (2)..............................
Tom: I see. Well, are you free on Thursday evening?
You: I'm afraid not. (3)..............................

4.4 *Put the verb into the most suitable form, present continuous (**I am doing**) or present simple (**I do**).*
Examples: We ....are going........ (go) to the theatre this evening.
........Does the film begin........ (the film / begin) at 3.30 or 4.30?

1 We .... (have) a party next Saturday. Would you like to come?
2 I .... (not/go) away for my holidays next month because I haven't got enough money. .... (you/go) away?
3 The concert this evening .... (start) at 7.30.
4 George, is it true that you .... (get) married next week?
5 The art exhibition .... (open) on 3 May and .... (finish) on 15 July.
6 What time .... (the next train / leave)?
7 Ann, we .... (go) to town. .... (you/come) with us?

9

UNIT 5   Going to (I am going to do)

a) We use **going to (do)** when we say what we have already decided to do, what we intend to do in the future:

- A: There's a film on television tonight. **Are** you **going to watch** it?
  B: No, I'm too tired. **I'm going to have** an early night.
- A: I hear Ann has won a lot of money. What **is** she **going to do** with it?
  B: I've heard she**'s going to travel** round the world.
- A: Have you made the coffee yet?
  B: No, but **I'm** just **going to make** it. (just = just at this moment)

For the difference between **will** and **going to** see Unit 8.

b) We prefer to use the present continuous (**I am doing**) when we say what someone has *arranged* to do – for example, arranged to meet someone, arranged to travel somewhere. **Going to** is also possible:

- What time **are** you **meeting** Ann? (*or* 'are you **going to meet**')
- I'm **travelling** to Scotland on Monday. (*or* 'I'm **going to travel**')

See also Unit 4a.

c) We use **was/were going to** to say what someone intended to do in the past (but didn't do):

- We **were going to travel** by train but then we decided to go by car.
- A: Did Tom do the examination?
  B: No, he **was going to do** it but in the end he changed his mind.
- I **was** just **going to cross** the road when someone shouted 'Stop!'.

d) **Going to** also has another meaning. Study this example situation:

 The man can't see where he is going. There is a hole in front of him.

He **is going to fall** into the hole.

Here the speaker is saying what he thinks will happen. Of course he doesn't mean that the man intends to fall into the hole.

We use **going to** in this way when we say what we think will happen. Usually there is something in the present situation (the man walking towards the hole) that makes the speaker sure about what will happen.

- Look at those black clouds! **It's going to rain.** (the clouds are there now)
- Oh, I feel terrible. I think **I'm going to be** sick. (I feel terrible now)

10

UNIT 5 Exercises

5.1 *In this exercise you have to say when you are going to do something.*
    Examples: Have you cleaned the car? (tomorrow)   *Not yet. I'm going to clean it tomorrow.*
               Have you made the coffee? (just)   *Not yet. I'm just going to make it.*

1 Have you phoned Tom? (after lunch)   Not yet. I ....
2 Have you had dinner? (just)   Not yet. ....
3 Have you painted your flat? (soon)   Not ....
4 Have you repaired my bicycle? (just)   ....

5.2 *In this exercise you have to write questions with* **going to.**
    Example: I've won a lot of money. (what / with it?)   *What are you going to do with it?*

1 I'm going to a party tonight. (what / wear?)   ....
2 Tom has just bought a painting. (where / hang it?)   ....
3 I've decided to have a party. (who / invite?)   ....

5.3 *In this exercise you have to use* **was/were going to.**
    Example: Did you travel by train?
           No, I was going to travel by train but I changed my mind.

1 Did you buy that jacket you saw in the shop window?
   No, I .... but I changed my mind.
2 Did Sue get married?
   No, she .... but she ....
3 Did Tom resign from his job?
   No, ... but ....
4 Did Wayne and Sharon go to Greece for their holidays?
   No, ...
5 Did you play tennis yesterday?
   No, ...
6 Did you invite Ann to the party?
   No, ...

5.4 *Now you have to say what you think is going to happen in these situations.*
    Example: The sky is full of black clouds. (rain) *It's going to rain.*

1 Terry is doing his examinations tomorrow. He hasn't done any work for them and he is
   not very intelligent. (fail)   He ....
2 It is 8.30. Tom is leaving his house. He has to be at work at 8.45 but the journey takes 30
   minutes. (be late)   ....
3 There is a hole in the bottom of the boat. It is filling up with water very quickly. (sink)
   It ....
4 Ann is driving. There is very little petrol left in the tank. The nearest petrol station is a
   long way away. (run out of petrol)   ....

UNIT 6   Will (1)

a) We use **will** ('ll) when we decide to do something at the time of speaking:
- Oh, I've left the door open. I'**ll go** and shut it.
- 'What would you like to drink?'   'I'**ll have** a lemonade, please.'
- 'Did you phone Ann?'   'Oh no, I forgot. I'**ll do** it now.'
- I'm too tired to walk home. I think I'**ll get** a taxi.

You cannot use the present simple (**I do**) in these sentences.
- I'**ll go** and shut it. (*not* 'I go and shut it.')

Do not use **will** to say what someone has already decided to do or arranged to do:
- I can't meet you tomorrow because my parents **are coming** to see me.
  (*not* 'my parents will come')

The negative of **will** is **won't** (or **will not**):
- Receptionist: I'm afraid Mr Wood can't see you until 4 o'clock.
  You: Oh, in that case I **won't** wait.

We often use **I think I'll ...** or **I don't think I'll ...** when we decide to do something:
- I think I'**ll stay** at home this evening.
- I don't think I'**ll go** out tonight. I'm too tired.

b) We often use **will** in these situations:

> *Offering* to do something:
> - That bag looks heavy. I'**ll help** you with it. (*not* 'I help')
> - 'I need some money'.   'Don't worry. I'**ll lend** you some.'
>
> *Agreeing* or *refusing* to do something:
> - A: You know that book I lent you? Can I have it back?
>   B: Of course. I'**ll bring** it back this afternoon. (*not* 'I bring')
> - I've asked John to help me but he **won't**.
> - The car **won't** start. (= the car 'refuses' to start)
>
> *Promising* to do something:
> - Thank you for lending me the money. I'**ll pay** you back on Friday.
>   (*not* 'I pay')
> - I **won't tell** Tom what you said. I promise.
> - I promise I'**ll phone** you as soon as I arrive.
>
> *Asking* someone to do something (**Will you ...?**):
> - **Will you shut** the door, please?
> - **Will you** please **be** quiet? I'm trying to concentrate.

For **will** see also Unit 7. For **will** and **going to** see Unit 8.

UNIT 6   Exercises

6.1 *In this exercise you have to complete the sentences with* **I'll** + *a suitable verb.*
Example: I'm too tired to walk home. I think ....*I'll get*......... a taxi.

1 I feel a bit hungry. I think .... something to eat.
2 It's too late to telephone Tom now. .... him in the morning.
3 'It's a bit cold in this room.' 'Is it? .... on the heating then.'
4 'We haven't got any cigarettes.' 'Oh, haven't we? .... and get some.'
5 'Did you write that letter to Jack?' 'Oh, I forgot. Thanks for reminding me.
   .... it this evening.'
6 'Would you like tea or coffee?' '............................... coffee, please.'

6.2 *Now you have to use* **I think I'll ...** *or* **I don't think I'll ...** . *Read the situation and then write your sentence.*
Examples: It's cold. You decide to close the window.   *I think I'll close the window.*
    It's raining. You decide not to go out.   *I don't think I'll go out.*

1 You feel tired. You decide to go to bed.   I ....
2 A friend of yours offers you a lift in his car but you decide to walk.
   Thank you but ....
3 You arranged to play tennis. Now you decide that you don't want to play.
   ....
4 You were going to go swimming. Now you decide that you don't want to go.
   ....

6.3 *Now you have to offer to do things. Tom has a lot of things to do and in each case you offer to do them for him.*
Example: Tom: Oh, I must do the washing-up.   You: *No, it's all right. I'll do the washing-up.*

1 Tom: Oh, I must get the dinner ready. You: No, it's all right. I ....
2 Tom: Oh, I must do the shopping. You: No, ...
3 Tom: Oh, I must water the plants. You: ....

6.4 *This time you have to agree and promise to do things.*
Example: A: Can you clean the windows? B: Sure, ...*I'll clean them*..... this afternoon.
    A: Do you promise? B: *Yes, I promise I'll clean them this afternoon.*

1 A: Can you phone me later? B: Sure, ... tonight.
   A: Do you promise? B: Yes, ...
2 A: Can you repair the clock? B: Okay, ... tomorrow.
   A: Do .... ? B:
3 A: Please don't tell anyone. B: All right, I won't tell anyone.
   A: .... ? B: ....
4 A: Please don't hurt me. B: Don't worry, ...
   A: .... ? B: ....

UNIT 7   Will (2)

a) When we talk about the future, we often say what someone has arranged to do or intends to do. Do *not* use **will** in this situation:
>   – Tom **is playing** tennis on Monday. (*not* 'Tom will play')
>   – **Are** you **going to watch** television this evening? (*not* 'will you watch')

For arrangements and intentions see Units 4 and 5.

But often when we are talking about the future, we are not talking about arrangements or intentions. Study this example:

Tom: I'm very worried about my examination next week.
Ann: Don't worry, Tom. You'**ll pass.**

'You'll pass' is not an arrangement or an intention. Ann is just saying what will happen or what she thinks will happen; she is predicting the future. When we predict a future happening or a future situation, we use **will/won't.**

>   – When you return home, you'**ll notice** a lot of changes.
>   – This time next year I'**ll be** in Japan. Where **will** you **be?**
>   – When **will** you **know** your examination results?
>   – Tom **won't pass** his examination. He hasn't done any work for it.

We often use **will** with these words and expressions:

---

probably	I'**ll probably be** a bit late this evening.
(**I'm**) **sure**	You must meet Ann. **I'm sure** you'**ll like** her.
(**I**) **expect**	I expect Carol **will get** the job.
(**I**) **think**	**Do you think** we'**ll win** the match?

---

b) **Will** and **shall**

You can use **shall** or **will** with I and **we:**
>   – **We shall** (*or* **we will**) probably **go** to Scotland in June.

But in spoken English we normally use the short forms **I'll** and **we'll:**
>   – **We'll** probably **go** to Scotland in June.

The negative of **shall** is **shan't** (or **shall not**):
>   – **I shan't** (or **I won't**) be here tomorrow.

Do not use **shall** with **he/she/it/you/they.**

Note that we use **shall** (not **will**) in the questions **shall I ...?** and **shall we ...?** (for offers, suggestions etc.):
>   – **Shall I open** the window? (= Do you want me to open the window?)
>   – I've got no money. What **shall I do?** (= What do you suggest I do?)
>   – Where **shall we go** this evening?

For **will** see also Units 6, 8 and 9.

UNIT 7 Exercises

7.1 *Decide which form of the verb is correct (or more natural) in these sentences. Cross out the one which is wrong.*
Example: Tom isn't free on Saturday. He will work / is working.

1 I will go / am going to a party tomorrow night. Would you like to come too?
2 According to the weather forecast it will rain / is raining tomorrow.
3 I'm sure Tom will get / is getting the job. He has a lot of experience.
4 I can't meet you this evening. A friend of mine will come / is coming to see me.
5 A: Have you decided where to go for your holidays yet?
   B: Yes, we will go / are going to Italy.
6 Don't worry about the dog. It won't hurt / isn't hurting you.

7.2 *Answer these questions using the words in brackets.*
Example: When do you think he'll arrive? (expect / tonight) *I expect he'll arrive tonight.*

1 What do you think she'll say? (probably / nothing)   She ....
2 Where do you think she'll go? (expect / London)   I ....
3 When do you think she'll leave? (think / tomorrow)   I ....
4 How do you think she'll go there? (expect / by train)   I ....
5 When do you think she'll be back? (think / quite soon)   I ....
6 Do you think you'll miss her? (I'm sure / very much)   Yes, ...

7.3 *Now you have to read a situation and then write a sentence with* **shall I?** *In each situation you are talking to a friend.*
Example: It's very hot in the room. The window is shut.   *Shall I open the window?*

1 You've just tried on a jacket in a shop. You are not sure whether to buy it or not. Ask your friend for advice.   ....
2 You're going out. It's possible that it will rain and you're not sure whether to take an umbrella or not. Ask your friend for advice.   ....
3 It's Ann's birthday soon and you don't know what to give her. Ask your friend for advice.   What ....
4 Your friend wants you to phone him/her later. You don't know what time to phone. Ask him/her.   What ....

This time you have to make sentences with **shall we?**
Example: You and your friend haven't decided what to do this evening. You say:
   What shall we do this evening?

5 You and your friend haven't decided where to go for your holidays. You say:
   Where ....
6 You and your friend haven't decided what to have for dinner. You say:
   ....
7 You and your friend are going out. You haven't decided whether to go by car or to walk.
   You say: .... or ....

15

UNIT 8 Will or going to?

a) *Talking about future actions*

We use both **will** and **going to** to talk about our future actions but there is a clear difference. Study this example situation:

Helen's bicycle has a flat tyre. She tells her father.	**will:** We use **will** when we decide to do something at the time of speaking. The speaker has not decided before. Before Helen told her father, he didn't know about the flat tyre.
Helen: My bicycle has a flat tyre. Can you repair it for me?	
Father: Okay, but I can't do it now. **I'll repair** it tomorrow.	
Later, Helen's mother speaks to her husband.	**going to:** We use **going to** when we have already decided to do something. Helen's father had already decided to repair the bicycle before his wife spoke to him.
Mother: Can you repair Helen's bicycle? It has a flat tyre.	
Father: Yes, I know. She told me. **I'm going to repair** it tomorrow.	

Here is another example:

– Tom is cooking when he suddenly finds that there isn't any salt:
Tom: Ann, we haven't got any salt.
Ann: Oh, haven't we? **I'll get** some from the shop then. (*she decides at the time of speaking*)

Before going out, Ann talks to Jim:
Ann: **I'm going to get** some salt from the shop. (*she has already decided*) Can I get you anything, Jim?

b) *Saying what will happen (predicting future happenings)*

We use both **will** and **going to** to say what we think will happen in the future:

– Do you think Tom **will get** the job?
– Oh dear, it's already 4 o'clock. We're **going to be** late.

We use **going to** (not **will**) when there is something in the present situation that shows what will happen in the future (especially the near future). The speaker feels sure about what will happen because of the situation now (see also Unit 5d):

– Look at those black clouds. It's **going to rain**. (the clouds are there *now*)
– I feel terrible. I think **I'm going to be** sick. (I feel terrible *now*)

Do not use **will** in situations like these.

Otherwise, it is safer to use **will** (see also Unit 7):

– Ann **will** probably **arrive** at about 8 o'clock.
– I think Tom **will like** the present you bought for him.

UNIT 8   Exercises

8.1 *In this exercise you have to put the verb into the correct form using* **will** *or* **going to**.
  Examples: A: Why are you turning on the television?
          B: I *'m going to watch* .... (watch) the news.

          A: Oh, I've just realised – I haven't got any money.
          B: Don't worry – that's no problem. I *'ll lend* .... (lend) you some.

          Those clouds are very black, aren't they? I think it .... *is going to rain* ......(rain).

  1 A: I've got a terrible headache.
    B: Have you? Wait there and I .... (get) an aspirin for you.
  2 A: Why are you filling that bucket with water?
    B: I .... (wash) the car.
  3 A: I've decided to re-paint this room.
    B: Oh, have you? What colour .... (you/paint) it?
  4 A: Look! There's smoke coming out of that house. It's on fire!
    B: Good heavens! I .... (call) the fire-brigade immediately.
  5 A: The ceiling in this room doesn't look very safe, does it?
    B: No, it looks as if it .... (fall) down.
  6 A: Where are you going? Are you going shopping?
    B: Yes, I .... (buy) something for dinner.
  7 A: I can't work out how to use this camera.
    B: It's quite easy. I .... (show) you.
  8 A: What would you like to drink – tea or coffee?
    B: I .... (have) tea, please.
  9 A: Has George decided on what to do when he leaves school?
    B: Oh yes. Everything is planned. He .... (have) a holiday for a few
       weeks and then he .... (start) a computer programming course.
 10 A: Did you post that letter for me?
    B: Oh, I'm sorry. I completely forgot. I .... (do) it now.
 11 A: What shall we have for dinner?
    B: I don't know. I can't make up my mind.
    A: Come on, hurry up! Make a decision!
    B: Okay then. We .... (have) chicken.
 12 Jack: We need some bread for lunch.
    Ben: Oh, do we? I .... (go) to the shop and get some. I feel like a
          walk.
    Before he goes out, Ben talks to Jane:
    Ben: I .... (get) some bread. Do you want anything from the shop?
    Jane: Yes, I need some envelopes.
    Ben: Okay, I .... (get) you some.
 13 *John has to go to the airport to catch a plane. He hasn't got a car:*
    John: Alan, can you take me to the airport this evening?
    Alan: Of course I .... (take) you. I'd be delighted.
    Later that day Eric offers to take John to the airport.
    Eric: John, do you want me to take you to the airport?
    John: No thanks, Eric. Alan .... (take) me.

UNIT 9   **When** and **If** sentences (**When I do ... / If I do ...**)

a) Study this example:

> A: What time will you phone me tonight?
> B: I'll phone you **when I get** home from work.
>
> 'I'll phone you when I get home from work' is a sentence with two parts: 'I'll phone you' (the main part) and 'when I get home from work' (the **when** part). The sentence is future (*tonight*) but you cannot use **will** or **going to** in the **when** part of the sentence. Instead we use a present tense, usually present simple (**I do**).

— I'll send you a postcard **when I'm** on holiday. (*not* 'when I will be')
— **When** the rain **stops**, we'll go out. (*not* 'when the rain will stop')

The same thing happens after:

while   after   before   until/till   as soon as

— Can you look after the children **while I am** out? (*not* 'will be')
— **Before** you **leave**, you must visit the museum. (*not* 'will leave')
— Wait here **until** I **come** back. (*not* 'will come')

b) You can also use the present perfect (**I have done**) after **when/after/until** etc. to show that the first action will be finished before the second:

— **When I've read** this book, you can have it.
— Don't say anything while Tom is here. Wait here **until** he **has gone**.

It is often possible to use present simple or present perfect:

— I'll come **as soon as I finish.**   *or*   I'll come **as soon as I've finished.**
— You'll feel better **after you have**   *or*   You'll feel better **after you've had** something to eat.   something to eat.

c) After **if** we also use the present simple (**I do**) for the future:

— It's raining. We'll get wet **if** we **go** out. (*not* 'if we will go')
— Hurry up! **If** we **don't hurry**, we'll be late. (*not* 'if we won't hurry')

Be careful not to confuse **when** and **if**.
Use **when** for things which are *sure* to happen:

— *I'm going* shopping this afternoon. **When** I go shopping, I'll buy some food.

Use **if** (not **when**) for things which will *possibly* happen:

— *I might go* shopping this afternoon. If I go shopping, I'll buy some food.
— **If** it rains this evening, I won't go out. (*not* 'when it rains')
— Don't worry **if** I'm late tonight. (*not* 'when I'm late')
— **If** he doesn't come soon, I'm not going to wait. (*not* 'when he doesn't come')

UNIT 9   Exercises

9.1 *All the sentences in this exercise are about the future. Put the verbs into the correct form:* **will/won't** *or the present simple (**I do**).*
Example: When I ....see............(see) Tom tomorrow, I ....'ll invite......(invite) him to our party.

1 Before you .... (leave), don't forget to shut the windows.
2 I .... (phone) you as soon as I .... (arrive) in London.
3 Please don't touch anything before the police .... (come).
4 Everyone .... (be) very surprised if he .... (pass) the examination.
5 When you .... (see) Brian again, you .... (not / recognise) him.
6 We .... (not/start) dinner until Jack .... (arrive).
7 .... (you/be) lonely without me while I .... (be) away?
8 If I .... (need) any help, I .... (ask) you.
9 Come on! Hurry up! Ann .... (be) annoyed if we .... (be) late.

9.2 *This time you have to make one sentence from two sentences.*
Example: You are going to leave soon. You must visit the museum before that.
    You must visit the museum before *you leave.*................................

1 I'll find somewhere to live. Then I'll give you my address.
   I .... when ....
2 It's going to start raining. Let's go out before that.
   Let's .... before ....
3 I'm going to do the shopping. Then I'll come straight back home.
   .... after ....
4 You'll be in London next month. You must come and see me then.
   .... when ....
5 I'm going to finish reading this book. Then I'll get the dinner ready.
   .... when ....
6 We'll make our decision. Then we'll let you know.
   .... as soon as ....

9.3 *In this exercise you have to put in* **when** *or* **if**.
Example: .If........... it rains this evening, I won't go out.

1 I'm going to Paris next week. .... I'm there, I hope to visit a friend of mine.
2 Tom might phone this evening. .... he does, can you take a message?
3 I think he'll get the job. I'll be very surprised .... he doesn't get it.
4 I hope to be there by 10.30. But .... I'm not there, don't wait for me.
5 I'm going shopping. .... you want anything, I can get it for you.
6 I think I'll go home now. I'm feeling very tired. I think I'll go straight to bed .... I get home.
7 I'm going away for a few days. I'll phone you .... I get back.
8 I want you to come to the party but .... you don't want to come, you needn't.

19

UNIT 10   Will be doing and will have done

a) First study this example situation:

> Tom is a football fan and there is a football match on television this evening. The match begins at 7.30 and ends at 9.15. Ann wants to come and see Tom this evening and wants to know what time to come:
>
> Ann: Is it all right if I come at about 8.30?
> Tom: No, don't come then. **I'll be watching** the match on television.
> Ann: Oh. Well, what about 9.30?
> Tom: Yes, that'll be fine. The match **will have finished** by then.

b) We use **will be doing** (*future continuous*) to say that we will be in the middle of doing something at a certain time in the future. The football match begins at 7.30 and ends at 9.15. So during this time, for example at 8.30, Tom **will be watching** the match.
Here are some more examples:
- You'll recognise her when you see her. She**'ll be wearing** a yellow hat.
- This time next week I'll be on holiday. I'll probably **be lying** on a beautiful beach.

Compare **will be doing** with the other continuous forms:
Tom works every morning from 9 o'clock until midday. So:
- At 10 o'clock yesterday he **was working**. (*past continuous* – see Unit 12)
- It's 10 o'clock now. He **is working**. (*present continuous* – see Unit 1)
- At 10 o'clock tomorrow he **will be working**.

c) You can also use **will be doing** in another way: to talk about things which are already planned or decided:
- I'll **be going** to the city centre later. Can I get you anything?

With this meaning **will be doing** is similar to **am doing** (see Unit 4a):
- I'm **going** to the city centre later.

We often use **Will (you) be -ing?** to ask about people's plans, especially when we want something or want someone to do something:
- '**Will** you **be using** your bicycle this evening?' 'No, you can take it.'
- '**Will** you **be passing** the post office when you go out?' 'Yes, why?'

d) We use **will have done** (*future perfect*) to say that something will already have happened before a certain time in the future. Tom's football match ends at 9.15. So after this time, for example at 9.30, the match **will have finished**. Here are some more examples;
- Next year is Ted and Amy's 25th wedding anniversary. They **will have been** married for 25 years. (Now they have been married for 24 years.)
- We're late. I expect the film **will** already **have started** by the time we get to the cinema.

UNIT 10   Exercises

10.1 *In this exercise you have to make sentences with* **will be -ing.**
Example: I'm going to watch television from 9 until 10 o'clock this evening.
So at 9.30 I *will be watching television*.

1 Tomorrow afternoon I'm going to play tennis from 3 o'clock until 4.30.
   So at 4 o'clock tomorrow I ....
2 Jim is going to study from 7 o'clock until 10 o'clock this evening.
   So at 8.30 this evening he ....
3 We are going to clean the flat tomorrow. It will take from 9 until 11 o'clock.
   So at 10 o'clock tomorrow morning ....

10.2 *This time you have to write three sentences, one each about the past, present and future.*
Bob always reads the newspaper in the morning. It always takes him half an hour, from
8 o'clock until 8.30. So:

1 At 8.15 yesterday morning Bob ....
2 It's 8.15 now. He ....
3 At 8.15 tomorrow morning he ....

10.3 *This time you have to ask questions with* **Will you be -ing?**
Example: You want to borrow your friend's bicycle this evening.
   (you / use / your bicycle this evening?)   *Will you be using your bicycle this evening?*

1 You want your friend to give Tom a message this afternoon.
   (you / see / Tom this afternoon?) ....
2 You want to use your friend's typewriter tomorrow evening.
   (you / use / your typewriter tomorrow evening?) ....
   ....
3 Your friend is going shopping. You want him/her to buy some stamps for you at the
   post office. (you / pass / the post office when you're in town?) ....
   ....

10.4 *In this exercise you have to use* **will have done.**
Example: Tom and Ann are going to the cinema. The film begins at 7.30 and it is already
   7.20. And it will take them 20 minutes to get there.
   When they get there, (the film / already / start) *the film will have already started*.

1 Jim always goes to bed at 11 o'clock. Tom is going to visit him at 11.30 this evening.
   When Tom arrives, (Jim / go / to bed) ....
2 Tom is on holiday. He has very little money and he is spending too much too quickly.
   Before the end of his holiday, (he /spend / all his money)
   ....
3 Chuck came to Britain from the US nearly three years ago. Next Monday it will be
   exactly three years since he arrived. Next Monday (he / be / here / exactly three years)
   ....

21

UNIT 11 Past simple (**I did**)

a) Study this example:

> Tom: Look! It's raining again.
> Ann: Oh no, not again. It **rained** all day yesterday too.
>
> **Rained** is the *past simple* tense. We use the past simple to talk about actions or situations in the past.

- I very much **enjoyed** the party.
- Mr Edwards **died** ten years ago.
- When I **lived** in Manchester, I **worked** in a bank.

b) Very often the past simple ends in -ed:
- We invit**ed** them to our party but they decid**ed** not to come.
- The police stopp**ed** me on my way home last night.
- She pass**ed** her examination because she studi**ed** very hard.

For spelling rules see Appendix 3.
But many important verbs are *irregular*. This means that the past simple does *not* end in -ed. For example:

leave → **left**   We all **left** the party at 11 o'clock.
go   → **went**   Yesterday I **went** to London to see a friend of mine.
cost → **cost**   This house **cost** £35,000 in 1980.

The past of the verb **be** (**am/is/are**) is **was/were**:

> I/he/she/it **was**   we/you/they **were**
>
> I **was** angry because Tom and Ann **were** late.

For a list of irregular verbs see Appendix 2.

c) In past simple questions and negatives we use **did/didn't** + the infinitive (**do/open/rain** etc.):

> it rained   **did** it **rain**?   it **didn't rain**

- Ann: **Did** you **go** out last night, Tom?
  Tom: Yes, I went to the cinema. But I **didn't enjoy** the film.
- When **did** Mr Edwards **die**?
- What **did** you **do** at the week-end?
- We **didn't invite** her to the party, so she **didn't come**.
- Why **didn't** you **phone** me on Tuesday?

Note that we normally use **did/didn't** with **have**:
- **Did** you **have** time to write the letter?
- I **didn't have** enough money to buy anything to eat.

But we do *not* use **did** with the verb **be** (**was/were**):
- Why **were** you so angry?
- They **weren't** able to come because they were very busy.
- **Was** Tom at work yesterday?

For the past simple see also Units 12, 20, 21.

UNIT 11 Exercises

11.1 *In this exercise you have to read a sentence about the present and then write a sentence about the past.*
Example: Tom usually gets up at 7.30. Yesterday *he got up at 7.30.* ....

1 Tom usually wakes up early. Yesterday morning ....
2 Tom usually walks to work. Yesterday ....
3 Tom is usually late for work. Yesterday ....
4 Tom usually has a sandwich for lunch. Yesterday ....
5 Tom usually goes out in the evening. Yesterday evening ....
6 Tom usually sleeps very well. Last night ....

11.2 *This time you have to put one of these verbs in each sentence:*
hurt   teach   spend   sell   throw   fall   catch   buy   cost
Example: I was hungry, so I ....*bought*......... something to eat in the shop.

1 Tom's father .... him how to drive when he was 17.
2 Don .... down the stairs this morning and .... his leg.
3 We needed some money so we .... our car.
4 Ann .... a lot of money yesterday. She .... a dress which
  .... £50.
5 Jim .... the ball to Sue who .... it.

11.3 *In this exercise you have to write questions. A friend has just come back from holiday and you are asking him about it.*
Examples: where / go?   *Where did you go?* ....
           food / good?   *Was the food good?* ....

1 how long / stay there?   ....
2 stay in a hotel?   ....
3 go alone?   ....
4 how / travel?   ....
5 the weather / fine?   ....
6 what / do in the evenings?   ....
7 meet any interesting people?   ....

11.4 *This time you have to put the verb into the correct form. All the sentences are past.*
Example: I ......*didn't go*...... (not/go) to work yesterday because I ....*wasn't*...... (not/be)
        very well.

1 Tom .... (not/shave) this morning because he .... (not/have)
  time.
2 We .... (not/eat) anything because we .... (not/be) hungry.
3 I .... (not/rush) because I .... (not/be) in a hurry.
4 She .... (not/be) interested in the book because she ....
  (not/understand) it.

23

UNIT 12 Past continuous (**I was doing**)

a) Study this example situation:

Yesterday Tom and Jim played tennis. They began at 10 o'clock and finished at 11 o'clock.

What **were** they **doing** at 10.30?
They **were playing** tennis (at 10.30).

'They **were playing**' means that they were in the middle of playing tennis. They had started playing but they hadn't finished.

This is the *past continuous* tense:

I/he/she **was**
we/they/you **were** } playing

We use the past continuous to say that someone was in the middle of doing something at a certain time. The action or situation had already started before this time but hadn't finished:
   – This time last year I **was living** in Brazil.
   – What **were** you **doing** at 10 o'clock last night?

b) The past continuous does not tell us whether an action was finished or not. Perhaps it was finished, perhaps not. Compare:
   – Tom **was cooking** the dinner. (*past continuous*) = He was in the middle of cooking the dinner and we don't know whether he finished cooking it.
   – Tom **cooked** the dinner. (*past simple*) = He began and finished it.

c) We often use the past continuous (**I was doing**) and the past simple (**I did**) together to say that something happened in the middle of something else:
   – Tom **burnt** his hand when he **was cooking** the dinner.
   – I **saw** Jim in the park. He **was sitting** on the grass and **reading** a book.
   – It **was raining** when I **got** up.
   – While I **was working** in the garden, I **hurt** my back.
But to say that one thing happened *after* another, use the past simple:
   – Yesterday evening Tom was having a bath when the phone rang. He **got** out of the bath and **answered** the phone.
Compare:
   – When Tom arrived, we **were having** dinner. (*past continuous*) = We had already started dinner before Tom arrived.
   – When Tom arrived, we **had** dinner. (*past simple*) = Tom arrived and then we had dinner.

Note: There are some verbs (for example **know**) which are not normally used in continuous tenses. For a list of these verbs see Unit 3b.

24

UNIT 12 Exercises

12.1 *Here is a list of some things that Ann did yesterday (and the times at which she did them):*

1 8.45–9.15 had breakfast	4 12.45–1.30 had lunch
2 9.15–10.00 read the newspaper	5 2.30–3.30 washed some clothes
3 10.00–12.00 cleaned her flat	6 4.00–6.00 watched television

Now write sentences saying what she was doing at these times:

1 At 9 o'clock she was having breakfast.   4 At 1 o'clock ....
2 At 9.30 she ....   5 At 3 o'clock ....
3 At 11 o'clock ....   6 At 5 o'clock ....

12.2 *A group of people were staying in a hotel. One evening the fire alarm rang. Use the words in brackets to make sentences saying what each person was doing at the time.*
Example: (Don / have / a bath) Don was having a bath.................................

1 (Ann / write / a letter in her room) Ann ....
2 (George / get / ready to go out) George ....
3 (Carol and Dennis / have / dinner) Carol and Dennis ....
4 (Tom / make / a phone call) Tom ....

12.3 *Make sentences from the words in brackets. Put the verbs into the correct form, past simple (**I did**) or past continuous (**I was doing**).*
Example: (I / fall / asleep when I / watch / television) I fell asleep when I was watching television.

1 (the phone / ring / when I / have / a shower) The phone ....
2 (it / begin / to rain when I / walk / home) ....
3 (we / see / an accident when we / wait / for the bus) ....

12.4 *Put the verb into the correct form, past continuous or past simple.*
Example: While Tom ...was cooking.... (cook) the dinner, the phone ....rang.......... (ring).

1 George .... (fall) off the ladder while he .... (paint) the ceiling.
2 Last night I .... (read) in bed when suddenly I .... (hear) a scream.
3 .... (you/watch) television when I phoned you?
4 Ann .... (wait) for me when I .... (arrive).
5 I .... (not/drive) very fast when the accident .... (happen).
6 I .... (break) a plate last night. I .... (do) the washing-up when it .... (slip) out of my hand.
7 Tom .... (take) a photograph of me while I .... (not/look).
8 We .... (not/go) out because it .... (rain).
9 What .... (you/do) at this time yesterday?
10 I .... (see) Carol at the party. She .... (wear) a really beautiful dress.

UNIT 13   Present perfect (**I have done**) (1)

a) Study this example situation:

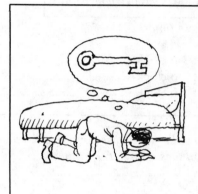

Tom is looking for his key. He can't find it.

He **has lost** his key.

'He **has lost** his key' means that he lost it a short time ago and he still hasn't got it.

This is the *present perfect (simple)* tense:

I/we/they/you **have** (= I've etc.)
he/she **has** (= he's etc.) } **lost**

I (etc.) **haven't**
he/she **hasn't** } **lost**   **have** you (etc.)
                                  has he/she } **lost?**

We form the present perfect with **have/has** + the *past participle*. The past participle often ends in **-ed** (opened, decided) but many important verbs are *irregular* (**lost, written, done** etc.). See Appendix 2.

b) When we use the present perfect there is a connection with the present:
- I've **lost** my key. (= I haven't got it *now*.)
- Jim **has gone** to Canada. (= He is in Canada or on his way there *now*.)
- Oh dear, I've **forgotten** her name. (= I can't remember it *now*.)
- **Have** you **washed** your hair? (= Is it clean *now*?)

c) We often use the present perfect to give new information or to announce a recent happening:
- I've **lost** my key. Can you help me look for it?
- Do you know about Jim? He's **gone** to Canada.
- Ow! I've **burnt** myself.

You can use the present perfect with **just** (= a short time ago):
- 'Would you like something to eat?' 'No, thanks. I've **just had** lunch.'
- Hello, **have** you **just arrived**?

You can use the present perfect with **already** to say that something has happened sooner than expected:
- 'Don't forget to post the letter, will you?' 'I've **already posted** it.'
- 'When is Tom going to start his new job?' 'He **has already started**.'

d) Study the difference between **gone to** and **been to**:
- Ann is on holiday. She **has gone** to Italy. (= She is there now or she is on her way there.)
- Tom is back in England now. He **has been** to Italy. (= He was there but now he has come back.)

(See also Unit 119.)

For the present perfect see also Units 14–19.
For the present perfect and past simple see Units 20–1.

26

UNIT 13   Exercises

13.1 *You are writing a letter to a friend and giving news about people you both know. Use the words given to make sentences and put the verb into the correct form.*
Example: Phil / find a new job   Phil has found a new job.

Dear Chris,
Lots of things have happened since I last wrote to you.
1 Charles / go / Brazil   Charles ....
2 Jack and Jill / decide / to get married   ....
3 Suzanne / have / a baby   ....
4 Monica / give up / smoking   ....
5 George / pass / his driving-test   ....

13.2 *In this exercise you have to read the situation and then write a suitable sentence. Use the verb given.*
Example: Tom is looking for his key. He can't find it. (lose)   He has lost his key.

1 Ann's hair was dirty. Now it is clean. (wash)   She ....
2 Tom was 80 kilograms. Now he weighs 70. (lose weight)   ....
3 The car has just stopped because there isn't any more petrol in the tank. (run out of petrol)   ....
4 Yesterday Bill was playing football. Now he can't walk and his leg is in plaster. (break)   ....

13.3 *This time you have to use* **just.** *Answer the questions using the words given.*
Example: Would you like something to eat. (no thank you / I / just / have / dinner)
   No thank you. I've just had dinner.

1 Have you seen John anywhere? (yes / I / just / see / him)   Yes ....
2 Has Ann phoned yet? (yes / she / just / phone)   ....
3 Would you like a cigarette? (no thanks / I / just / put / one out)   ....

13.4 *In this exercise you have to write sentences with* **already.**
Example: Don't forget to post that letter.   I've already posted it.

1 Don't forget to phone Tom.   I ....
2 Why don't you read the paper?   ....
3 Shall I pay the waiter?   No, I ....

13.5 *This time you have to put in* **been** *or* **gone.**
Example: 'Where's Ann?'   'She's on holiday. She has ....gone.... to Italy.'

1 Hello! I've just .... to the shops. Look! I've bought lots of things.
2 Jim isn't here at the moment. He's .... to the shops.
3 'Are you going to the bank?'   'No, I've already .... to the bank.'

UNIT 14   Present perfect (**I have done**) (2)

a) Study this example conversation:

> Dave: **Have** you **travelled** a lot, Nora?
> Nora: Yes, I've **been** to 47 different countries.
> Dave: Really? **Have** you ever **been** to China?
> Nora: Yes, I've **visited** China twice.
> Dave: What about India?
> Nora: No, I've never **been** to India.
>
>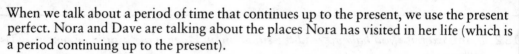
>
> When we talk about a period of time that continues up to the present, we use the present perfect. Nora and Dave are talking about the places Nora has visited in her life (which is a period continuing up to the present).

Here are some more examples:
  - 'Have you **read** *Hamlet*?' 'No, I **haven't read** any of Shakespeare's plays.'
  - How many times **have** you **been** to the United States?
  - Susan really loves that film. She's **seen** it eight times.
  - Sam **has lived** in Belfast all his life. (*or* Sam **has** always **lived** in Belfast.)
We often use **ever** and **never** with the present perfect:
  - **Have** you **ever eaten** caviar?
  - We **have never had** a car.
We often use the present perfect after a *superlative* (see Unit 104d):
  - What a boring film! It's **the most boring** film I've **ever seen**.

b) You have to use the present perfect with **This is the first time ...**, **It's the first time ...** etc. Study this example situation:
  - Ron is driving a car. He is very nervous and unsure because it's his first time behind the wheel of a car. You can say:
    This is the first time he **has driven** a car. (*not* 'drives')
  or: He **has never driven** a car **before**.
Here are some more examples:
  - Tom has lost his passport again. **It's the second time** he **has lost** it.
  - **Is this the first time** you've **been** in hospital?

c) Use the present perfect to say that you have never done something or that you haven't done something during a period of time which continues up to the present:
  - I **have never smoked**.
  - I **haven't smoked for three years**. (*not* 'I don't smoke for ...')
  - I **haven't smoked since September**. (*not* 'I don't smoke since ...')
  - Jill **hasn't written** to me **for nearly a month**.
  - Jill **has never driven** a car.
For the difference between **for** and **since** see Unit 19b.

28

UNIT 14 Exercises

14.1 *You are asking someone about things he has done in his life. Use the words in brackets to make your questions.*
Example: (you ever / be / to Italy?) Have you ever been to Italy?

1 (you ever / be / to South America?) ....
2 (you / read / any English books?) ....
3 (you / live / in this town all your life?) ....
4 (how many times / you / be / in love?) ....
5 (what's the most beautiful country you / ever / visit?) ....
   ....
6 (you ever / speak / to a famous person?) ....

14.2 *Complete the answers to these questions. Use the verb in brackets.*
Example: Is it a beautiful painting? (see) Yes, it's the most beautiful painting I've ever seen.

1 Is it a good film? (see) Yes, it's the best ....
2 Is it a long book? (read) Yes, it's the ....
3 Is she an interesting person? (meet) Yes, she's the most ....

14.3 *Now you have to write questions and answers as shown in the example.*
Example: Jack is driving a car but he's very nervous and not sure what to do.
   You ask: Is this the first time you've driven a car?
   Jack: Yes, I've never driven a car before.

1 Len is playing tennis. He's not very good and doesn't know the rules.
   You ask: Is this the first time ....
   Len: Yes, I've ....
2 Sue is riding a horse. She doesn't look very confident or comfortable.
   You ask: ....
   Sue: ....
3 Maria is in England. She's just arrived and it's very new for her.
   You ask: ....
   Maria: ....

14.4 *Answer these questions using the words in brackets.*
Example: When did you last smoke? (for two years) I haven't smoked for two years.

1 When did it last rain? (for ages) It .... for ages.
2 When did they last visit you? (since June) They ....
3 When did you last play tennis? (for a long time) ....
4 When did you last eat caviar? (never) ....
5 When did you last drive? (for six months) ....
6 When did you last go to Spain? (never) ....
7 When did she last write to you? (since last summer) ....

UNIT 15   Present perfect (**I have done**) (3)

a) Study this example:

> Tom: **Have** you **heard** from George?
> Ann: No, he **hasn't written** to me recently.
>
> We use the present perfect when we talk about a
> period of time that continues up to the present. Tom
> and Ann are talking about the period between a
> short time ago and now. So they say '**have** you
> **heard**' and 'he **hasn't written**'.

RECENTLY

past ———————————— *present*

Here are some more examples:
- **Have** you **seen** my dog? I can't find him anywhere.
- Everything is going fine. We **haven't had** any problems **so far**.
- We'**ve met** a lot of interesting people **in the last few days**.
- Fred **has been** ill a lot **in the past few years**, hasn't he?
- I **haven't seen** George **recently**. **Have** you?

For sentences with **for** and **since** see Unit 18.

b) We often use the present perfect with **yet** (see also Unit 107). **Yet** shows that the speaker is
expecting something to happen. Use **yet** only in questions and negative sentences:
- **Has** it **stopped** raining yet? (*not* 'did it stop')
- I **haven't told** them about the accident yet. (*not* 'I didn't tell')

c) We use the present perfect with **this morning / this evening / today / this week / this term** etc.
(when these periods are not finished at the time of speaking):
- I'**ve smoked** ten cigarettes **today**. (perhaps
  I'll smoke more before today finishes)
- **Has** Ann **had** a holiday **this year**?
- I **haven't seen** Tom **this morning**. **Have** you?
- Ron **hasn't studied** very much **this term**.
- Bill is phoning his girl-friend again. That's
  the third time he'**s phoned** her **this evening**.

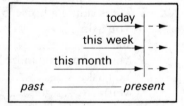

d) We also use the *present perfect continuous* (**I have been doing**) when we talk about a period
of time continuing up to the present:
- I **haven't been feeling** very well **recently**.

For the present perfect continuous see Units 16–18.

For the present perfect and past simple see Units 20–1.

30

UNIT 15   Exercises

15.1 *In this exercise you have to make questions with the words given.*
Example: (you / hear / from George recently?)   <u>Have you heard from George recently?</u>

1 (you / read / a newspaper recently?)   ....
2 (you / see / Tom in the past few days?)   ....
3 (you / play / tennis recently?)   ....
4 (you / eat / anything today?)   ....
5 (you / see / any good films recently?)   ....
6 (you / have / a holiday this year yet?)   ....

15.2 *This time answer the questions in the way shown. Use* **yet.**
Example: Have you seen the new film at the local cinema?
   <u>I haven't seen it yet</u> .... but <u>I'm going to see it.</u> ....

1 Have you eaten at the new Italian restaurant?
   I .... yet but I'm ....
2 Have you bought a car?
   I .... but I ....
3 Has Gerry asked Diana to marry him?
   He ....

15.3 *This time you have to complete the sentence. Use* **so far.**
Examples: I saw Tom yesterday but ....<u>I haven't seen him so far</u>.... today.
   It rained a lot last week but <u>it hasn't rained much so far</u> this week.

1 We ate a lot yesterday but we .... much so far today.
2 It snowed a lot last winter but it .... so far this winter.
3 I played tennis a lot last year but .... this year.
4 She worked hard last term but .... this term.
5 I watched television yesterday evening .... this evening.
6 My favourite football team won a lot of matches last season but they ....
   .... many matches so far this season.

15.4 *In this exercise you have to read the situation and then finish a sentence.*
Example: Ron is phoning Jill again. He has already phoned her twice this evening.
   It's the third <u>time he has phoned her this evening.</u> ....

1 You're late again. You've already been late once this week.
   It's the second .... this week.
2 The car has broken down. It has already broken down twice this month.
   It's the ....
3 Ann has just finished drinking a cup of tea. She has already had four cups this morning.
   It's the fifth ....

UNIT 16   Present perfect continuous (**I have been doing**)

a) Study this example situation:

Is it raining?
No, it isn't but the ground is wet.

It **has been raining**.

This is the *present perfect continuous* tense:

I/we/they/you **have** (= I've etc.)
he/she/it **has** (= he's etc.) } **been doing**

We use the present perfect continuous when we talk about an action (quite a long action) which began in the past and has recently stopped or just stopped. Here are some examples:
- – You're out of breath. **Have** you **been running**?
- – That man over there is bright red. I think he**'s been sunbathing**.
- – Why are your clothes so dirty? What **have** you **been doing**?
- – I've **been talking** to Tom about your problem and he thinks ...

b) We also use the present perfect continuous to ask or say how long something has been happening. This time the action or situation began in the past and is still happening or has just stopped. Study this example:

It is raining now. It began to rain two hours ago and it is still raining.

It **has been raining for two hours**.

We often use the present perfect continuous in this way, especially with **how long, for** and **since**.

Here are some more examples:
- – **How long have** you **been learning** English?
- – They've **been waiting** here **for over an hour**.
- – I've **been watching** television **since 2 o'clock**.
- – George **hasn't been feeling** very well **recently**.
- – **Have** you **been working** hard **today**?

You can also use the present perfect continuous (with **how long, for** and **since**) for actions repeated over a period of time:
- – She **has been playing** tennis **since she was eight**.
- – **How long have** you **been smoking**?

For more information about the present perfect + **since/for**, see Units 18–19.
For the difference between the present perfect simple and continuous, see Units 17–18.

UNIT 16   Exercises

16.1 *In this exercise you have to read the situation and then write a sentence with the present perfect continuous (**I have been doing**).*
Example: Tom is out of breath. (he / run)   <u>He has been running.</u>...

1 Ann is very tired. (she / work / hard)   ....
2 Bob has a black eye and Bill has a cut lip. (Bob and Bill / fight)   ....
3 George has just come back from the beach. He is very red. (he / lie / in the sun)
   ....
4 Janet is hot and tired. (she / play / tennis)   ....

16.2 *This time you have to ask a question for each situation.*
Example: Your friend's hands are covered in oil. (you / work / on the car?)
   <u>Have you been working on the car?</u>...

1 You see a little boy. His eyes are red and watery. (you / cry?)
   ....
2 You have just arrived to meet your friend who is waiting for you. (you / wait / long?)
   ....
3 Your friend comes in. His face and hands are very dirty. (what / you / do?)
   ....

16.3 *Now you have to say how long something has been happening.*
Example: It is raining now. It began raining two hours ago.
   <u>It has been raining</u>............... for two hours.

1 Kevin is studying. He began studying three hours ago.
   He .... for three hours.
2 I'm learning Spanish. I started learning Spanish in December.
   I .... since December.
3 Ann is looking for a job. She began looking six months ago.
   .... for six months.
4 Mary is working in London. She started working there on 18 January.
   .... since 18 January.
5 George smokes. He started smoking five years ago.
   .... for five years.

16.4 *In this exercise you have to ask questions with **how long**.*
Example: It is raining. <u>How long has it been raining?</u>.......................................

1 My foot is hurting.   How long ....
2 Mike plays chess.   How ....
3 Jim sells washing machines. ....
4 Tom is living in High Street. ....

UNIT 17 Present perfect continuous (**I have been doing**) or present perfect simple (**I have done**)?

a) Study these example situations:

Ann's clothes are covered in paint. She **has been painting** the ceiling.

Has been painting is the *present perfect continuous* tense.

We are interested in the action. It does not matter whether something has been finished or not. In the example, the action has not been finished.

The ceiling was white. Now it's blue. She **has painted** the ceiling.

Has painted is the *present perfect simple* tense.

This time, the important thing is that something has been finished. We are interested in the result of the action, not in the action itself.

Here are some pairs of examples:

Tom's hands are very dirty. He **has been repairing** the car.
You'**ve been smoking** too much recently. You should smoke less.

The car is going again now. Tom **has repaired** it.
Somebody **has smoked** all my cigarettes. The packet is empty.

b)

We use the *continuous* form to say how long something has been happening:

Ann **has been writing** letters **all day.**
How long have you **been reading** that book?
Jim **has been playing** tennis **since 2 o'clock.**

We use the *simple* form to say how much we have done, how many things we have done, or how many times we have done something:

Ann **has written ten letters** today.

How many pages of that book **have** you **read?**
Jim **has played** tennis **three times** this week.

See Unit 18 for more information about the present perfect and **how long?**.

c) Some verbs are not used in the continuous form, for example **know**. You have to say **have known** (*not* 'have been knowing'). For a list of these verbs see Unit 3b.

UNIT 17   Exercises

17.1 *In this exercise you have to read the situation and then write two sentences, one with the present perfect simple (**I have done**) and one with the present perfect continuous (**I have been doing**).*
Example: Tom is reading a book. He started two hours ago and he is on page 53.
         (he / read / for two hours) *He has been reading for two hours.*
         (he / read / 53 pages so far) *He has read 53 pages so far.*

  1 Linda is from Australia. Now she is travelling round Europe. She began her tour three months ago.
     (she / travel / around Europe for three months) ....
     (she / visit / six countries so far) ....
  2 Jimmy is a tennis champion. He began playing tennis when he was 11 years old. Now he has just won the national championship for the fourth time.
     (he / play / tennis since he was 11) ....
     (he / win / the national championship four times) ....
  3 Bill and Andy make films. They started making films together when they left college.
     (they / make / films since they left college) ....
     (they / make / ten films since they left college) ....

17.2 *This time you have to imagine that you are talking to a friend. Read the situation and ask a question beginning in the way shown.*
Example: Your friend is learning Arabic.   How long *have you been learning Arabic?*

  1 Your friend is waiting for you.   How long ....
  2 Your friend writes books.   How many books ....
  3 Your friend writes books.   How long ....
  4 Your friend plays football for his country.   How many times ....
....

17.3 *In this exercise you have to put the verb into the correct form, present perfect simple (**I have done**) or continuous (**I have been doing**).*
Examples: I ....*have lost*............ (lost) my key. Can you help me look for it?
         You look tired. ......*Have you been working*...... (you/work) hard?

  1 Look! Somebody .... (break) that window.
  2 I .... (read) the book you gave me but I ....
     .... (not/finish) it yet.
  3 'Sorry I'm late.' 'That's all right. I .... (not/wait) long.'
  4 Hello! I .... (clean) the windows. So far I
     .... (clean) five of them and there are two more to do.
  5 There's a strange smell in here. .... (you/cook) something?
  6 My brother is an actor. He .... (appear) in several films.

UNIT 18   Present perfect (**I have done / I have been doing**) with **how long, for** and **since**

a) Study this example situation:

Bob and Alice are married. They got married exactly 20 years ago. So today is their 20th wedding anniversary.

They **have been** married **for 20 years.**

We use the present perfect to say how long something has existed or how long something has been happening.

They **are** married. $\left\{\begin{array}{l}\text{How long have they been married?}\\ \text{They } \textbf{have been} \text{ married } \textbf{for}\\ \textbf{20 years.}\end{array}\right.$

b) We use the present perfect continuous (**I have been doing**) to say how long something has been happening. Note that the action is still happening now:
- I've **been learning** English **for a long time.**
- Sorry I'm late. **Have** you **been waiting long?**
- It's **been raining since I got up** this morning.

Sometimes the action is a repeated action (see also Unit 16b):
- Tom **has been driving for ten years.**
- **How long have** you **been smoking?**

The continuous (**I have been doing**) or the simple (**I have done**) can be used for actions repeated over a long period:
- I've **been collecting** / I've **collected** stamps since I was a child.

c) We use the simple (**I have done**) for situations that exist for a long time (especially if we say **always**). Note that the situation still exists now:
- My father **has always worked** hard. (*not* 'has always been working')

We use the continuous for situations over a shorter time. Compare:
- John **has been living** in London **since January.**
- John **has always lived** in London.

d) Some verbs (for example **be, have, know**) are not normally used in the continuous (see Unit 3b for a list and Unit 24 for **have**):
- How long **have** Bob and Alice **been** married?
- Tom **has had** a cold for the past week. (*not* 'has been having')
- Tom and I **have known** each other since we were at school.

e) Do not use the present simple (**I do**) or continuous (**I am doing**) to say how long something has been happening:
- I've **been waiting** here for an hour. (*not* 'I am waiting')
- How long **have** you **known** Tom? (*not* 'do you know')

UNIT 18   Exercises

18.1 *Are these sentences right or wrong? Correct the ones which are wrong.*
   Examples: How long have Bob and Alice been married?   RIGHT
           I know Bob for five years.   WRONG - have known

   1 Sue and Alan are married since July.   ....
   2 It is raining all day.   ....
   3 How long has George been unemployed?   ....
   4 Have you always been living in this house?   ....
   5 How long has Ken a beard?   ....
   6 How long do you know Ann?   ....
   7 She has been ill for quite a long time.   ....

18.2 *This time you have to write questions with* **how long?**
   Examples: Jim is learning Chinese. How long has he been learning Chinese?
           I know Bob. How long have you known Bob?

   1 My sister is married.   How long ....
   2 Boris is on holiday.   How long ....
   3 I live in Glasgow.   ....
   4 It is snowing.   ....
   5 Jack smokes.   ....
   6 I know about her problem.   ....
   7 Jack and Jill are looking for a flat.   ....
   8 Diana teaches English in Germany.   ....
   9 Dennis is in love with Margaret.   ....
   10 Colin has a car.   ....

18.3 *In this exercise you have to read a sentence and then write another sentence with* **since** *or* **for**.
   Example: I know Bob. (for five years)   I have known Bob for five years.

   1 Jack lives in Bolton. (since he was born)   Jack ....
   2 Bill is unemployed. (since April)   Bill ....
   3 Ann has a bad cold. (for the last few days)   ....
   4 I want to go to the moon. (since I was a child)   ....

   ....

   5 My brother is studying languages at university. (for two years)   ....

   ....

   6 Tim and Jane are working in Sheffield. (since February)   ....

   ....

   7 My cousin is in the army. (since he was 17)   ....

   ....

   8 They are waiting for us. (for half an hour)   ....

   ....

UNIT 19   Present perfect with **how long** and past simple with **when**
Since and **for**

a) Use the *past simple* (**I did**) to ask or say *when* something happened:
- A: **When did** it **start** raining?
- B: It **started** raining *at one o'clock / an hour ago.*
- A: **When did** Tom and Ann first **meet**?
- B: They first **met** *when they were at school / a long time ago.*

Use the *present perfect* (**I have done / I have been doing**) to ask or say *how long* something has been happening (up to the present):
- A: **How long has** it **been raining?**
- B: It's **been raining** *since one o'clock / for an hour.*
- A: **How long have** Tom and Ann **known** each other?
- B: They've **known** each other *since they were at school / for a long time.*

b) **Since** and **for**
We use both **since** and **for** to say how long something has been happening:
- I've been waiting for you **since 8 o'clock**.
- I've been waiting for you **for two hours**.

We use **since** when we say the beginning of the period (**8 o'clock**).
We use **for** when we say the period of time (**two hours**).

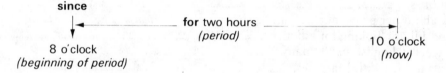

since

for two hours
(period)

8 o'clock
(beginning of period)

10 o'clock
(now)

since		for	
8 o'clock	1977	two hours	a week
Monday	Christmas	ten minutes	five years
12 May	lunchtime	three days	a long time
April	we arrived	six months	ages

- She's been working here **since April**. (= from April until now)
  She's been working here **for six months**. (*not* 'since six months')
- I haven't seen Tom **since Monday**. (= from Monday until now)
  I haven't seen Tom **for three days**. (*not* 'since three days')

We do not use **for** in expressions with **all** (**all day / all morning / all week / all my life** etc.):
- I've lived here **all my life**. (*not* 'for all my life')

c) Note the structure **How long is it since ...?**:
- A: **How long is it since** you had a holiday?
- B: **It's two years since** I had a holiday. (= I haven't had a holiday for two years.)
- **It's ages since** Tom visited us. (= He hasn't visited us for ages.)

38

UNIT 19 Exercises

19.1 *In this exercise you have to write questions with* **how long** *and* **when**.
Example: It is raining. (how long / it / rain?) *How long has it been raining?*
(when / it / start / raining?) *When did it start raining?*

   1 Ann is learning Italian.
      (how long / she / learn / Italian?) ....
      (when / she / begin / learning Italian?) ....
   2 I know Tom.
      (how long / you / know / Tom?) ....
      (when / you / first / meet / Tom?) ....
   3 Bob and Alice are married.
      (how long / they / be / married?) ....
      (when / they / get / married?) ....

19.2 *In this exercise you have to put in* **since** *or* **for**.
Example: Tom and I have known each other ......*for*...... six months.

   1 It's been raining .... I got up this morning.
   2 Tom's father has been a policeman .... 20 years.
   3 Have you been learning English .... a long time?
   4 .... Christmas, the weather has been quite mild.
   5 Ann has been on holiday .... three days.
   6 That's a very old car. I've had it .... ages.

19.3 *This time you have to make a new sentence beginning in the way shown.*
Examples: I know Tom. I first met him six months ago. I have *known him for six months.*
It's been raining since 2 o'clock. It started *raining at two o'clock.*

   1 Tom's ill. He became ill three days ago. He has ....
   2 We have been married for five years. We got ....
   3 Jim has a beard. He grew it ten years ago. He has ....
   4 He has been in France for three weeks. He went ....
   5 He has had his new car since February. He bought ....

19.4 *In this exercise you have to imagine that two people are talking. You have to make*
sentences with **It's ... since ...**
Example: A: Do you often go on holiday? (no / five years)
        B: *No, it's five years since I went on holiday.*

   1 A: Do you often eat in restaurants? (no / six months)
      B: No, it ....
   2 A: Does it often snow here? (no / years)
      B: No, ...
   3 A: Do you often play cards? (no / a long time)
      B: ....

UNIT 20   Present perfect (**I have done**) or past simple (**I did**)? (1)

a) Study this example situation:

This is Tom. He is looking for his key. He can't find it.

He **has lost** his key. (*present perfect*)

This means that he hasn't got his key now.

Five minutes later:

Now Tom **has found** his key.

This means that he has got his key now.

Has he **lost** his key? (*present perfect*)
No, he **hasn't**. He **has found** it.

Did he **lose** his key? (*past simple*)
Yes, he **did**.

He **lost** (*past simple*) his key but now he **has found** (*present perfect*) it.

The present perfect (**has lost**) always tells us something about the present. 'He **has lost** his key' tells us that he hasn't got it now (see Unit 13). The past simple (**lost**) tells us only about the past. If we say 'He **lost** his key', we don't know whether he has it now or not. We only know that he lost it at some time in the past. Here are some more examples:
  – He **grew** a beard but now he **has shaved** it off. (= He hasn't got a beard now.)
  – Prices **fell** but now they **have risen** again. (= They are high now.)

b) Do not use the present perfect (**I have done**) for happenings or actions which are not connected with the present (for example, historical events):
  – The Chinese **invented** printing. (*not* 'have invented')
  – Shakespeare **wrote** *Hamlet*. (*not* 'has written')
  – How many symphonies **did** Beethoven **compose**? (*not* 'has ... composed')

c) We use the present perfect (**I have done**) to give new information or to announce a recent happening (see Unit 13). But if we continue to talk about it, we normally use the past simple (**I did**):
  – A: Ow! I've **burnt** myself!
     B: How **did** you **do** that? (*not* 'have you done')
     A: I **touched** a hot dish. (*not* 'have touched')
  – A: Look! Somebody **has spilt** milk on the carpet.
     B: Well, it **wasn't** me. I **didn't do** it. (*not* 'hasn't been ... haven't done')
     A: I wonder who it **was** then. (*not* 'who it has been')
For more information about the present perfect and past simple see Unit 21.

UNIT 20   Exercises

20.1 *In this exercise you have to read the situation and then write a sentence. Use the verbs given in brackets. Read the example carefully first.*
Example: Ten minutes ago Tom lost his key. Now he has it in his hand.
(lose / find) *Tom lost his key but now he has found it.*

1 I lost a lot of weight but now I am too heavy again.
(lose weight / put on weight)   I .... but now I ....
2 She went to Australia but now she is back in Britain again.
(go / come back)   She .... but now ....
3 Last year Kevin bought a car. Now it belongs to someone else.
(buy / sell) ....
4 The police arrested the man but now he is at home again.
(arrest / release) ....
5 Bill cut his hair. Now it is long again.
(cut / grow) ....
6 The prisoner escaped from the prison. Now he is back in prison.
(escape / be caught) ....

20.2 *Are the underlined parts of these sentences right or wrong? Correct the ones which are wrong.*
Examples: Have you heard? Suzanne has got married!   *RIGHT*
The Chinese have invented printing.   *WRONG – invented*

1 Who has written the play *Hamlet*?   ....
2 Aristotle has been a Greek philosopher.   ....
3 Ow! I've cut my finger. It's bleeding.   ....
4 Look at George! He had a haircut.   ....
5 My grandparents got married in London.   ....
6 Einstein was the physicist who has developed the theory
of relativity.   ....

20.3 *In this exercise you have to put the verb into the correct form.*
Example: A: Look! Somebody .....*has spilt*..... (spill) milk on the carpet.
B: Well, it ....*wasn't*....... (not/be) me. I .....*didn't do*..... (not/do) it.
A: I wonder who it ....*was*........... (be) then.

1 A: Your hair looks different. .... (you/have) a haircut?
B: Yes.
A: .... (you/cut) it yourself?
B: No, Ann .... (cut) it for me.
2 A: Did you hear about Ben? He .... (break) his leg.
B: Really? How .... (that/happen)?
A: He .... (fall) off a ladder.

UNIT 21 Present perfect (**I have done**) or past simple (**I did**)? (2)

a) Do not use the present perfect (**I have done**) when you are talking about a finished time in the past (for example: **yesterday, two years ago, in 1979, when I was a child**). Use a *past* tense:

- Tom **lost** his key **yesterday**. (*not* 'has lost')
- **Did** you **see** the film on television **last night**? (*not* 'have you seen')
- Mr Greaves **retired** from his job **two years ago**. (*not* 'has retired')
- I **ate** a lot of sweets **when I was a child**. (*not* 'have eaten')

Use a past tense to ask when something happened:

- **What time did** they **arrive**? (*not* 'have they arrived')
- **When were** you **born**? (*not* 'have you been born')

Compare:

- Tom **has lost** his key. (*present perfect*)

Here we are not thinking of the past action; we are thinking of the present result of the action: he is without his key now. ·

- Tom **lost** his key **yesterday**. (*past simple*)

Here we are thinking of the action in the past. We don't know whether Tom is still without his key.

b) Now compare these sentences:

Present perfect (**I have done**)	*Past simple* (**I did**)
I've smoked 20 cigarettes **today**.	I smoked 20 cigarettes **yesterday**.
Today is a period of time which continues up to the present. It is not a finished time. So we use the present perfect.	**Yesterday** is a finished time in the past. So we use the past simple.

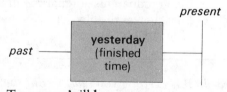

Tom **hasn't been** ill **this year**. **Have** you **seen** Ann **this morning**? (It is still morning.) **Have** you **seen** Ann **recently**? We've **been waiting** for an hour. (We are still waiting.) Ian **has lived** in London for six years. (He still lives there.) I **have never played** golf (in my life).	Tom **wasn't** ill **last year**. **Did** you **see** Ann **this morning**? (It is now afternoon.) **Did** you **see** Ann **last week**? We **waited** (or **were waiting**) for an hour. (We are no longer waiting.) Ian **lived** in Scotland for ten years. (He no longer lives there.) I **didn't play** golf **when I was on holiday last summer**.
The present perfect always has a connection with the present. See Units 13–20.	The past simple tells us only about the past. See Units 11, 12 and 20.

Unit 21 Exercises

21.1 *In this exercise you have to put the verb into the correct form, present perfect (**I have done**) or past simple (**I did**).*
Examples: I .... *have lost* .... (lose) my key. I can't find it anywhere.
.... *Did you see* .... (you/see) the film on television last night?

1 Jill .... (buy) a new car two weeks ago.
2 His hair is very short. He .... (have) a haircut.
3 Last night I .... (arrive) home at half past twelve. I
.... (have) a bath and then I .... (go) to bed.
4 .... (you/visit) many museums when you were in Paris?
5 My bicycle isn't here any more. Somebody .... (take) it.
6 When .... (you/give) up smoking?
7 I .... (not/eat) anything yesterday because I ....
(not/feel) hungry.
8 Why .... (Jim/not/want) to play tennis last Friday?
9 The car looks very clean. .... (you/wash) it?
10 Brian: Hello, Susan. Is Alan here?
Susan: No, I'm afraid he .... (go) out.
Brian: Oh, what a pity! When exactly .... (he/go) out?
Susan: About ten minutes ago.

21.2 *This time you have to make sentences using the words given.*
Examples: (I / smoke / 20 cigarettes yesterday) *I smoked 20 cigarettes yesterday.*
(how many cigarettes / you / smoke / today?)
How many cigarettes have you smoked today?

1 (I / be / ill twice so far this year) I ....
2 (how many times / be / you / ill last year?) How many times ....
3 (I / not / drink / any coffee so far today) ....
4 (he / be / late three times this week) ....
5 (how many games / the team / win / last season?) ....

6 (how many games / the team / win / so far this season?) ....
....

21.3 *Put the verb into the correct form, present perfect (**I have done**) or past simple (**I did**).*
Example: I .... *didn't play* .... (not/play) golf when I was on holiday last summer.

1 Mr Clark .... (work) in a bank for 15 years. Then he gave it up.
2 Molly lives in Dublin. She .... (live) there all her life.
3 Bob and Alice are married. They .... (be) married for 20 years.
4 When we were on holiday, the weather .... (be) awful.
5 The weather .... (be) very nice recently, don't you think?
6 My grandfather died 30 years ago. I .... (never/meet) him.
7 I don't know Carol's husband. I .... (never/meet) him.

UNIT 22   Past perfect (**I had done**)

a) Study this example situation:

At 10.30 — (Bye!) — Tom
Half an hour later — Me

I went to a party last week. Tom went to the party too. Tom went home at 10.30. So, when I arrived at 11 o'clock, Tom wasn't there.

When I arrived at the party, Tom wasn't there. He **had gone** home.

This is the *past perfect (simple)* tense:

I/he/she (etc.) **had** (= I'**d**/he'**d**/she'**d** etc.) **gone**
I/he/she (etc.) **hadn't gone**
had you/he/she (etc.) **gone?**

We form the past perfect with **had** + the *past participle* (**gone/opened/written** etc.). For irregular past participles see Appendix 2.

Sometimes we talk about something that happened in the past:
  – I **arrived** at the party.
We use the past perfect to say that something had already happened before this time:
  – **When I arrived** at the party, Tom **had** already **gone** home.
Here are some more examples:
  – When I got home, I found that someone **had broken** into my flat and **had stolen** my fur coat.
  – George didn't want to come to the cinema with us because he **had** already **seen** the film twice.
  – It was my first time in an aeroplane. I was very nervous because I **hadn't flown** before.

b) The past perfect (**I had done**) is the past of the present perfect (**I have done**). Compare these situations:

Present	*Past*
I'm not hungry. I've just **had** lunch.	I wasn't hungry. I'd just **had** lunch.
The house is dirty. We **haven't** cleaned it for weeks.	The house was dirty. We **hadn't** cleaned it for weeks.

c) Compare the past perfect (**I had done**) and the past simple (**I did**):
  – 'Was Tom there when you arrived?' 'No, he **had** already **gone** home.'
  but: 'Was Tom there when you arrived?' 'Yes, but he **went** home soon afterwards.'
  – Ann **wasn't** in when I **phoned** her. She **was** in London.
  but: Ann **had** just **got** home when I **phoned** her. She **had been** in London.

For the past perfect continuous see Unit 23.

UNIT 22   Exercises

22.1 *Complete these sentences using the verbs in brackets. You went back to your home town after many years and you found that many things were different.*
Example: Most of my friends were no longer there. They ....*had left*........ (leave).

1 My best friend, Kevin, was no longer there. He .... (go) away.
2 The local cinema was no longer open. It .... (close) down.
3 Mr Johnson was no longer alive. He .... (die).
4 I didn't recognise Mrs Johnson. She .... (change) a lot.
5 Bill no longer had his car. He .... (sell) it.

22.2 *Complete these sentences as in the example. Use the verb in brackets.*
Example: Mr and Mrs Davis were in an aeroplane. They were very nervous as the plane
took off because they (fly) *had never flown before.* ....

1 The woman was a complete stranger to me. (see)   I .... before.
2 Margaret was late for work. Her boss was very surprised. (be / late)   She ....
   ....
3 Jane played tennis yesterday – at least she tried to play tennis. She wasn't very good at
   it because she (play) ....
4 It was Keith's first driving lesson. He was very nervous and didn't know what to do.
   (drive)   He ....

22.3 *Now you have to make sentences using the words in brackets.*
Example: I wasn't hungry. (I / just / have / lunch) *I had just had lunch.* ....

1 Tom wasn't at home when I arrived. (he / just / go / out)   ....
2 We arrived at the cinema late. (the film / already / begin)   ....
3 They weren't eating when I went to see them. (they / just / finish / their dinner)
   ....
4 I invited Ann to dinner last night but she couldn't come. (she / already / arrange / to do
   something else)   ....
5 I was very pleased to see Nora again after such a long time. (I / not / see / her for five
   years)   ....

22.4 *Put the verb into the correct form, past perfect (**I had done**) or past simple (**I did**).*
Examples: 'Was Tom there when you arrived?'   'No, he ....*had gone*....... (go) home.'
            'Was Tom there when you arrived?'   'Yes, but he ....*went*........... (go) home
            soon afterwards.'

1 The house was very quiet when I got home. Everybody .... (go) to bed.
2 I felt very tired when I got home, so I .... (go) straight to bed.
3 Sorry I'm late. The car .... (break) down on my way here.
4 There was a car by the side of the road. It ....(break) down and the driver
   was trying to repair it. So we .... (stop) to see if we could help.

45

UNIT 23   Past perfect continuous (**I had been doing**)

a) Study this example situation:

yesterday morning

Yesterday morning I got up and looked out of the window. The sun was shining but the ground was very wet.

It **had been raining**.

It wasn't raining when I looked out of the window; the sun was shining. But it **had been raining**. That's why the ground was wet.

Had been raining is the *past perfect continuous* tense:

I/he/she (etc.) **had** (= I'd / he'd / she'd etc.) **been doing**

Here are some more examples:

      — When the boys came into the house, their clothes were dirty, their hair was untidy and one had a black eye. They **had been fighting**.

      — I was very tired when I arrived home. **I'd been working** hard all day.

b) You can use the past perfect continuous to say how long something had been happening before something else happened:

      — The football match had to be stopped. They **had been playing** for half an hour when there was a terrible storm.

      — Ken **had been smoking** for 30 years when he finally gave it up.

c) The past perfect continuous (**I had been doing**) is the past of the present perfect continuous (**I have been doing**). Compare:

Present	*Past*
How long **have** you **been waiting**? (until now)	How long **had** you **been waiting** when the bus finally came?
He's out of breath. He **has been running**.	He was out of breath. He **had been running**.

d) Compare the past perfect continuous (**I had been doing**) and the past continuous (**I was doing**):

      — When I looked out of the window, it **had been raining**. (= It wasn't raining when I looked out; it had stopped.)

      — When I looked out of the window, it **was raining**. (= Rain was falling at the time I looked out.)

e) Some verbs (for example **know**) cannot be used in the continuous form. See Unit 3b for a list of these verbs.

For the past perfect simple see Unit 22.

UNIT 23 Exercises

23.1 *In this exercise you have to read a situation and then write a sentence.*
Example: The two boys came into the house. One had a black eye and the other had a cut
lip. (they / fight) <u>They had been fighting.</u>

1 Tom was watching television. He was feeling very tired.
  (he / study / hard all day) He ....
2 When I walked into the room, it was empty. But there was a smell of cigarettes.
  (somebody / smoke / in the room) Somebody ....
3 When Mary came back from the beach, she looked very red from the sun.
  (she / lie / in the sun too long) ....
4 The two boys came into the house. They had a football and they were both very tired.
  (they / play / football) ....
5 Ann woke up in the middle of the night. She was frightened and she didn't know where
  she was. (she / dream) ....

23.2 *In this exercise you have to read a situation and then write a sentence.*
Example: We began playing football. After half an hour there was a terrible storm.
  We <u>had been playing for half an hour</u> when <u>there was a terrible storm</u>.

1 The orchestra began playing at the concert. After about ten minutes a man in the
  audience suddenly began shouting.
  The orchestra .... for about ten minutes when ....
  ....
2 I had arranged to meet Tom in a restaurant. I arrived and began waiting. After 20
  minutes I realised that I had come to the wrong restaurant.
  I .... when I ....
3 Mr and Mrs Jenkins went to live in the south of France. Six months later Mr Jenkins
  died. They .... when ....

23.3 *Put the verb into the correct form, past perfect continuous (**I had been doing**) or past
continuous (**I was doing**).*
Examples: Tom was leaning against the wall, out of breath. He <u>had been running</u> (run).
  I tried to catch Tom but I couldn't. He <u>was running</u> (run) very fast.

1 Jim was on his hands and knees on the floor. He .... (look) for his
  cigarette lighter.
2 We .... (walk) along the road for about 20 minutes when a car
  stopped and the driver offered us a lift.
3 When I arrived, everyone was sitting round the table with their mouths full. They
  .... (eat).
4 When I arrived, everyone was sitting round the table and talking. Their mouths were
  empty but their stomachs were full. They .... (eat).
5 When I arrived, Ann .... (wait) for me. She was rather annoyed with
  me because I was late and she .... (wait) for a very long time.

UNIT 24   Have and have got

a) Have and **have got**

We often use **have got / has got** rather than **have/has** alone. So you can say:
- We've got a new car.   *or*   We **have** a new car.
- Tom's got (= Tom **has got**) a headache.   *or*   Tom **has** a headache.

In questions and negative sentences there are three possible forms:

Have you got any money? **Do you have** any money? **Have you** any money? (*less usual*)	I **haven't got** any money. I **don't have** any money. I **haven't** any money.
Has she got a car? **Does she have** a car? **Has she** a car? (*less usual*)	She **hasn't got** a car. She **doesn't have** a car. She **hasn't** a car.

In the past we do *not* normally use **got**:
- When she was a child, she **had** long fair hair. (*not* 'she had got')

In past questions and negative sentences we normally use **did/didn't**:
- **Did** you **have** a car when you lived in London? (*not* 'had you')
- I wanted to phone you, but I **didn't have** your number. (*not* 'I hadn't')
- He **didn't have** a watch, so he didn't know what time it was.

b) Have for *actions*

We also use **have** for a number of actions. For example:

have breakfast / lunch / dinner / a meal / a drink / a cup of coffee / a cigarette etc. **have** a swim / a walk / a rest / a holiday / a party / a good time etc. **have** a bath / a shower / a wash **have** a look (at something) **have** a baby (= give birth to a baby) **have** a chat (with someone)

'Have got' is *not* possible in these expressions:
- I usually **have** a big breakfast in the morning. (*not* 'have got')

Compare:
- I **have** a bath every morning. (= I take a bath – *this is an action.*)
- I've **got** a bath. (= There is a bath in my house.)

When you use **have** for actions, you can use continuous forms (**is having / are having / was having** etc.):
- 'Where's Tom?' 'He's **having** a bath.'

In questions and negative sentences you must use **do/does/did**:
- I **don't** usually **have** a big breakfast. (*not* 'I usually haven't')
- What time **does** Ann **have** lunch? (*not* 'has Ann lunch')
- **Did** you **have** a swim this morning? (*not* 'had you a swim')

48

UNIT 24   Exercises

24.1 *In this exercise you have to make negative sentences with* **have**. *Some sentences are present* (**can't**) *and some past* (**couldn't**).

Examples: I can't make a phone call. (any change)   *I haven't got any change.*
              I couldn't read the notice. (my glasses)   *I didn't have my glasses.*

1 I can't climb up onto the roof. (a ladder)   I ....
2 We couldn't visit the museum. (enough time)   We ....
3 He couldn't find his way to our house. (a map) ....
4 She can't pay her bills. (any money) ....
5 I couldn't make an omelette. (any eggs) ....
6 I can't get into the house. (my key) ....
7 They couldn't take any photographs. (a camera) ....
8 We couldn't go out in the rain. (an umbrella) ....

24.2 *Complete these questions with* **have**. *Some are present and some are past.*

Examples: Excuse me, ... *have you got* ...... a light, please?
              Did you have .... a lot of friends when you lived in London?

1 Why are you holding your mouth like that? .... a toothache?
2 .... enough time to answer all the questions in the exam last week?
3 I need a stamp for this letter. .... any?
4 'It started to rain when I was walking home.' 'Did it? .... an umbrella?'
5 '................................ the time, please?' 'Yes, it's ten past seven.'
6 .... a beard before you joined the army?

24.3 *Complete these sentences using the most suitable expressions from the box. Put the verb into the correct form where necessary.*

have a baby	~~have a swim~~	have a nice time	have a bath
have a party	have a chat	have a good flight	have a rest
have a cigarette	have a look	~~have a nice meal~~	

1 Jack likes to keep fit, so he .... *has a swim* .... every day.
2 Tom and Ann have just come back from the restaurant. You say:
    Hello, *did you have a nice meal* ?
3 We .... last Friday. It was great – we invited lots of people.
4 'How often .... ?' 'Not often. I don't like washing.'
5 Suzanne gave up her job six months ago when she ....
6 Excuse me, can I .... at your newspaper, please?
7 You meet Tom at the airport. He has just arrived. You say:
    Hello, Tom! .... ?
8 'Where's Jim?' 'He .... in his room. He is very tired.'
9 I met Ann in the street yesterday. We stopped and ....
10 I haven't seen you since you came back from holiday. .... ?
11 I don't usually smoke. But I felt nervous, so I ....

UNIT 25 Used to (I used to do)

a) Study this example situation:

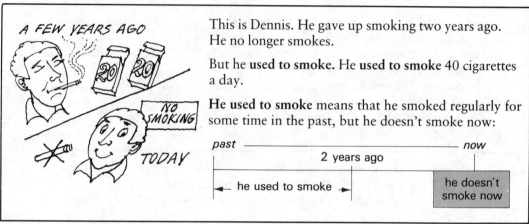

This is Dennis. He gave up smoking two years ago. He no longer smokes.

But he **used to smoke**. He **used to smoke** 40 cigarettes a day.

He used to smoke means that he smoked regularly for some time in the past, but he doesn't smoke now:

past ——————————————————————— now

2 years ago

◄— he used to smoke —►   he doesn't smoke now

We use **used to** with the *infinitive* (**used to do** / **used to smoke** etc.) to say that something regularly happened in the past but no longer happens:
- I **used to play** tennis a lot, but now I'm too lazy.
- 'Do you go to the cinema very often?'   'Not now, but **I used to**.'
- Tom **used to travel** a lot. These days he doesn't go away very often.

We also use **used to** for past situations (which no longer exist):
- We **used to live** in a small village but now we live in London.
- This building is now a furniture shop. It **used to be** a cinema.
- Do you see that hill over there? There **used to be** a castle on that hill.
- I've started drinking coffee recently. I never **used to like** it before.
- Ann **used to have** long hair but she cut it some time ago.

b) **Used to** + infinitive is always past. There is no present. You cannot say 'I use to do'. For the present, use the present simple (**I do**). Compare the present and past:

past	he **used to smoke**	we **used to live**	there **used to be**
present	he **smokes**	we **live**	there **is**

c) The normal question form is **did ... use to ...?**:
- **Did** you **use to eat** a lot of sweets when you were a child?

The negative form is **didn't use to ...** (*or* 'used not to')
- Jack **didn't use to go** out very often until he met Jill.

d) Be careful not to confuse **I used to do** and **I am used to doing** (see Unit 62). The structures and meanings are different:
- **I used to live** alone. (= I lived alone but I no longer live alone.)
- **I am** used to **living** alone. (= I live alone and don't find it strange or new because I've been living alone for some time.)

UNIT 25 Exercises

25.1 *In this exercise you have to complete the sentence with* **used to ...**
Example: Dennis doesn't smoke any more but he ....*used to smoke*.... 40 cigarettes a day.

1 The baby doesn't cry so much now but she.. every night.
2 She .... my best friend but we aren't friends any longer.
3 We live in Nottingham now but we .... in Leeds.
4 Now there's only one shop in the village but there .... three.
5 When I was a child I .... ice-cream, but I don't like it now.
6 Now Tom has got a car. He .... a motor-cycle.

25.2 *This time you have to write some sentences about a man who changed his life-style. Ron stopped doing some things and started doing other things:*

He stopped { studying hard / going to bed early / running three miles every morning }

He started { smoking / going out every evening / spending a lot of money }

Make sentences like these:
Examples: He used to study hard.
He never used to smoke. or He didn't use to smoke.

1 ....
2 ....
3 ....
4 ....

25.3 *Now you have to write some sentences about the present. Remember that there is no present tense of* **used to.**
Examples: Ron used to study hard but now he doesn't study very hard.
Ron didn't use to smoke but now he smokes.

1 Tom used to play tennis a lot but now ....
2 Ann never used to drink coffee but now ....
3 Jill didn't use to be fat but now ....
4 Jack didn't use to go out much but now ....

25.4 *Now you have to ask questions. Mr Ford is an old man now. You are asking someone what he used to do when he was younger.*
Example: I know he doesn't smoke now but did he use to smoke .... ?

1 I know he doesn't play the piano now but .... ?
2 I know he isn't very rich now but .... ?
3 I know he doesn't go out very often these days but .... ?
4 I know he doesn't dance these days but .... ?
5 I know he hasn't got many friends now but .... ?

UNIT 26   Can, could and be able to

a) We use **can (do)** to say that something is possible or that someone has the ability to do something. The negative is **can't** (**cannot**).

    – You **can see** the sea from our bedroom window.
    – **Can** you **speak** any foreign languages?
    – I'm afraid I **can't come** to your party next Friday.

Be able to is possible instead of **can**, but **can** is more usual:

    – **Are** you **able to speak** any foreign languages?

But **can** has only two forms: **can** (*present*) and **could** (*past*). So sometimes you have to use **be able to**:

    – I **haven't been able to sleep** recently. (**can** has no present perfect)
    – Tom might not **be able to come** tomorrow. (**can** has no infinitive)

b) **Could** and **was able to**

Sometimes **could** is the past of **can**. We use **could** especially with these verbs:

see   hear   smell   taste   feel   remember   understand

    – When we went into the house, we **could smell** burning.
    – She spoke in a low voice but I **could understand** what she was saying.

We also use **could** to say that someone had the general ability to do something:

    – My grandfather **could speak** five languages.
    – When Tom was 16, he **could run** 100 metres in 11 seconds.

But if you mean that someone *managed* to do something *in one particular situation*, you have to use **was/were able to** (not **could**):

    The fire spread through the building very quickly but everyone **was able** (= managed) **to escape**. (*not* 'could escape')
    – They didn't want to come with us at first but in the end we **were able** (= managed) **to persuade** them. (*not* 'could persuade')

Compare **could** and **was able to** in this example:

    – Jack was an excellent tennis player. He **could** beat anybody. (= He had the ability to beat anybody.)
    – But once he had a difficult game against Alf. Alf played very well but in the end Jack **was able to** beat him. (= He managed to beat him *in this particular game*.)

The negative **couldn't** is possible in all situations:

    – My grandfather **couldn't swim**.
    – We tried hard but we **couldn't persuade** them to come with us.

For **can** see also Unit 31. For **could** see also Units 27 and 31.

UNIT 26   Exercises

26.1   *In this exercise you have to use* **can** *or* **be able to***. Sometimes it is possible to use either; sometimes only* **be able to** *is possible.*
  Examples: George has travelled a lot. He .....can. (or. is able to) speak four languages.
  I haven't ......been able to........ sleep very well recently.

1 Tom .... drive but he hasn't got a car.
2 I can't understand Martin. I've never .... understand him.
3 I used to .... stand on my head but I can't do it now.
4 Ask Ann about your problem. She should .... help you.

26.2   *In this exercise you have to complete the sentence with* **could ...**
  Example: I can't sing now but I ....could. sing......... very well when I was a child.

1 He can't play tennis very well now but he .... quite well when he was younger.
2 She can't run very fast now but when she was at school she .... faster than anyone else.
3 I can't swim very far these days but ten years ago I .... from one side of the lake to the other.

26.3   *This time you have to answer the questions with* **was/were able to***.*
  Example: Did you persuade them?
      Yes. It was difficult but we were able to persuade them..................................

1 Did they find your house?
   Yes. It took them a long time but they ....
2 Did you win the match?
   Yes. It wasn't easy but I ....
3 Did the thief escape?
   Yes. The policeman chased the thief but he ....

26.4   *Now you have to complete a sentence with* **could, was/were able to** *or* **couldn't***.*
  Examples: My grandfather was very clever. He could (or was able to) speak five languages.
      I looked everywhere for the book but I ....couldn't......... find it.
      The fire spread quickly but everyone ....was able to.... escape.

1 He had hurt his leg, so he .... walk very well.
2 She wasn't at home when I phoned but I .... contact her at her office.
3 I looked very carefully and I .... see a figure in the distance.
4 They didn't have any tomatoes in the first shop I went to, but I .... get some in the next shop.
5 My grandmother loved music. She .... play the piano very well.
6 The boy fell into the river but fortunately we .... rescue him.

UNIT 27   Could (do) and could have (done)

a) We use **could** (do) in a number of ways. Sometimes it is the past of **can** (do) (see Unit 26), but sometimes it has a *present* or *future* meaning. For example, we sometimes use **could** to talk about possible future actions, especially when we make suggestions:

   – 'What shall we do this evening?'   'We **could go** to the cinema.'
   – When you go to New York, you **could stay** with Linda.

Can is also possible in these sentences. ('We **can** go to the cinema.'). **Could** is more unsure than **can.**

We also use **could** to talk about possible future happenings:

   – There **could be** another rise in the price of petrol soon. (= It is possible that there will be.)

Sometimes **could** means **would be able to:**

   – Why doesn't Tom apply for the job? He **could get** it.
   – I don't know how she works 14 hours a day. I **couldn't do** it.

b) The past of **could** (do) is **could have** (done). We use **could have** (done) to say that we had the ability or the opportunity to do something but did *not* do it:

   – We didn't go out last night. We **could have gone** to the cinema but we decided to stay at home. (We had the opportunity to go out but we didn't.)
   – Why did you stay at a hotel in New York? You **could have stayed** with Linda. (You had the opportunity to stay with her but you didn't.)
   – Why didn't Tom apply for the job? He **could have got** it. (He had the ability to get it.)

We also use **could have** (done) to say something was a possibility but *didn't* happen:

   – He was lucky when he fell off the ladder. He **could have hurt** himself.

c) Now here are some examples of **couldn't have** (done). 'I **couldn't have done** something' = I wouldn't have been able to do it if I had wanted or tried to do it:

   – When I went to New York last year, I decided not to stay with Linda. Later I found out that she was away while I was there, so I **couldn't have stayed** with her anyway.
   – The football match was cancelled last week. Tom **couldn't have played** anyway because he was ill.
   – Ann did really well to pass the examination. It was really difficult. I'm sure I **couldn't have passed** it.

For **could/couldn't** see also Units 26, 28b, 29c, 31.
For **could** in **if** sentences see Units 36–8.

54

UNIT 27   Exercises

27.1 *In this exercise you have to make suggestions. Use* **could.**
Example: Where shall we go for our holidays? (Scotland)   We could go to Scotland.

1 What shall we have for dinner tonight? (fish)   ....
2 When shall we go and see Tom? (on Friday)   ....
3 What shall I give Ann for her birthday? (a book)   ....

27.2 *This time you have to use* **could have.** *Answer the questions in the way shown.*
Example: 'Did you go to the cinema?'
'No. We   could have gone to the cinema but we decided not to .... ,

1 'Did you go to the concert last night?'   'No. We   .... ,
2 'Did John take the examination?'   'No. He   .... ,
3 'Did you buy a new car?'   'No. I   .... ,

27.3 *In this exercise you have to write sentences with* **could** *or* **could have.**
Examples: She doesn't want to stay with Linda.   But she could stay with Linda.
She didn't want to stay with Linda.   But she could have stayed with Linda.

1 He didn't want to help us.   But he   ....
2 He doesn't want to help us.   But   ....
3 They don't want to lend us any money.   But   ....
4 She didn't want to have anything to eat.   ....

27.4 *In this exercise first read this information about Ken:*

Ken doesn't know any Spanish.   Ken doesn't know anything about machines.
Ken is very rich and generous.   Ken can't drive.
Ken was ill on Friday night.   Ken was free on Monday afternoon.

A lot of people wanted Ken to do different things last week but they couldn't contact him.
So he didn't do any of these things. You have to say whether he could have done or
couldn't have done these things (if he had known).
Example: His aunt wanted him to drive her to the station.
He couldn't have driven her to the station (because he can't drive).

1 Ann wanted him to come to a party on Friday night.
He   .... because   ....
2 Jim wanted him to play tennis on Monday afternoon.
He   ....
3 Sue wanted him to translate a Spanish newspaper article into English.
.... because   ....
4 Jack wanted Ken to lend him £20.
....
5 Ken's mother wanted him to repair her washing machine.
....

UNIT 28   Must (have) and can't (have)

a) Study this example situation:

> Alf is a very good tennis player and not many players beat him. But yesterday he played against Bill and Bill won. So:
>
> Bill **must be** a very good player (otherwise he wouldn't have won).

We use **must** to say we are sure that something is true:
  - You've been travelling all day. You **must be** tired. (= I am sure that you are tired.)
  - I hear that your examinations are next week. You **must be studying** very hard at the moment. (= I am sure that you are studying.)
  - Carol knows a lot about films. She **must go** to the cinema a lot.
    (= I am sure she goes to the cinema a lot.)

We use **can't** to say that we think something is impossible:
  - You've only just had dinner. You **can't be** hungry already. (= It is impossible that you are hungry.)
  - Tom said that he would be here ten minutes ago and he is never late. He **can't be coming**.

Study the structure:

I/you/he (etc.)	must / can't	be tired/hungry etc. be studying/waiting/coming etc. go/do/play etc.

b) For the past we use **must have (done)** and **can't have (done)**. Study this example:

> We went to Roy's house last night and rang the doorbell. There was no answer.
> **He must have gone** out (otherwise he would have answered).

  - The phone rang but I didn't hear it. **I must have been** asleep.
  - I made a lot of noise when I came home. You **must have heard** me.
  - She passed me in the street without speaking. She **can't have seen** me.
  - Tom walked straight into the wall. He **can't have been looking** where he was going.

Study the structure:

I/you/he (etc.)	must / can't	have	been asleep/tired etc. been looking/waiting etc. gone/done/seen/heard etc.

'**Couldn't** have (done)' is possible instead of '**can't** have (done)':
  - She **couldn't have seen** me.
  - He **couldn't have been looking** where he was going.

For other meanings of **must** and **can't** see Units 26, 31 and 32.

UNIT 28   Exercises

28.1 *Complete these sentences using* **must (have) ...** *or* **can't (have) ...**
Examples: 'Is he British?'   'Yes, *he must be British.* ,
   'Did she see you?'   'No, *she can't have seen me.* ,

1 'Are they married?'   'Yes, they must .... ,
2 'Is he serious?'   'No, he can't .... ,
3 'Were they in a hurry?'   'Yes, they .... ,
4 'Does Ann know a lot of people?'   'Yes, she .... ,
5 'Did Tom know about the plan?'   'Yes, he .... ,
6 'Do they have much money?'   'No, they .... ,
7 'Was he driving carefully?'   'No, he .... ,
8 'Are they waiting for somebody?'   'Yes, they .... ,

28.2 *Complete these sentences with* **must** *or* **can't** + *a suitable verb.*
Example: You've been travelling all day. You ....*must be*........ very tired.

1 Brian has got three houses, six cars, a yacht and a helicopter. He .... a lot of money.
2 (*The doorbell rings.*) I wonder who that is. It .... Jim. He said he would come after 7 o'clock and it's only 6.30 now.
3 I wonder why Tom isn't at work today. I suppose he .... ill.
4 John seems to know a lot about history. He .... a lot of books.
5 Jack's putting on his hat and coat. He .... out.

28.3 *Now you have to read a situation and write a sentence with* **must have** *or* **can't have**. *Use the words in brackets.*
Example: The phone rang but I didn't hear it. (I must / be / asleep)
   I must have been asleep. ....

1 That dress you bought is very good quality. (it must / be / very expensive)
   It must ....
2 I haven't seen Jim for ages. (he must / go / away)   He ....
3 I wonder where my umbrella is. (you must / leave / it on the train) ....
   ....
4 Don passed the examination. He didn't study very much for it. (the exam can't / be / very difficult) ....
5 She knew everything about our plans. (she must / listen /to our conversation)
   ....
6 Dennis did the opposite of what I asked him to do. (he can't / understand / what I said) ....
7 When I woke up this morning, the light was on. (I must / forget / to turn it off)
   ....
8 I don't understand how the accident happened. (the driver can't / see / the red light)
   ....

UNIT 29   May (have) and might (have)

a) Study this example situation:

> You are looking for Jack. Nobody knows for sure where he is but you get some suggestions:
>
> He **may be** in his office. (= perhaps he is in his office)
> He **might be having** lunch. (= perhaps he is having lunch)
> Ask Ann. She **might know**. (= perhaps Ann knows)

We use **may** and **might** to say that something is possible. There is no important difference between **may** and **might**. You can say:
> – He **may** be in his office.   *or*   He **might** be in his office.

The negative is **may not** and **might not** (or **mightn't**):
> – Jack **might not be** in his office. (= perhaps he isn't in his office)
> – I'm not sure whether I can lend you any money. I **may not have** enough.
>   (= perhaps I don't have enough)

Study the structure:

I/you/he (etc.)	may / might	(not)	be in his office / be having/waiting etc. / know/have/do etc.

b) To say what was possible in the past, we use **may have (done)** and **might have (done)**:
> – A: I wonder why Ann didn't answer the doorbell.
>   B: Well, I suppose she **may have been** in the bath. (= perhaps she **was** in the bath)
> – A: Why didn't he say hello when he passed us in the street?
>   B: He **might have been day-dreaming**. (= perhaps he **was day-dreaming**)
> – A: I can't find my bag anywhere.
>   B: You **might have left** it in the shop. (= perhaps you **left** it)
> – A: I wonder why Ann didn't come to the meeting.
>   B: She **might not have known** about it. (= perhaps she **didn't know**)

Study the structure:

I/you/he (etc.)	may / might	(not)	have	been in the bath / been day-dreaming/waiting etc. / known/left/had etc.

c) You can use **could** instead of **may** or **might**. But with **could** the possibility is smaller:
> – 'Where's Jack?' 'I'm not sure. He **could be** in his office, I suppose, but he's not usually there at this time.'

For **may** and **might** see also Units 30 and 31.

Unit 29   Exercises

29.1 *In this exercise you have to make sentences with **may** or **might**. The first four sentences are present.*
Examples: 'Do you know if Jack is in his office?'   ' *I'm not sure. He may be in his office...* '
            'Do you know if Ann likes ice-cream?'   ' *I'm not sure. She might like ice-cream.* '

1 'Do you know if they are married?' 'I'm not sure. They .... '
2 'Do you know if she wants to go?' 'I'm not sure .... '
3 'Do you know if he's telling the truth?' 'I'm .... '
4 'Do you know if he has a car? 'I .... '

The next three sentences are past.
Examples: 'Do you know if he was serious?' ' *I'm not sure. He might have been serious.....* '
            'Do you know if they were looking?' ' *I'm not sure. They may have been looking.* '

5 'Do you know if she was ill?' 'I'm not sure. She .... '
6 'Do you know if she told anybody?' 'I .... '
7 'Do you know if they were listening?' ' .... '

*And now you have to use **may not** or **might not**.*
Example: 'Is Jack in his office?' ' *I'm not sure. He might not be in his office.* .... '

8 'Does she want to go?' ' .... '
9 'Is he telling the truth?' ' .... '
10 'Are they ready?' ' .... '

29.2 *This time you have to write sentences to explain each situation. Use the words in brackets to make your sentences.*
Example: I can't find George anywhere. I wonder where he is.
            a) (he might / go / shopping)   *He might have gone shopping.* ....
            b) (he could / play / tennis)   *He could be playing tennis.* ....

1 Look! Sue's going out. I wonder where she's going.
   a) (she may / go / to the theatre) ....
   b) (she could / go / to a party) ....
2 Why didn't Tom answer the doorbell? I'm sure he was in the house at the time.
   a) (he may / go / to bed early) ....
   b) (he might not / hear / the bell) ....
   c) (he could / be / in the bath) ....
3 How do you think the fire started?
   a) (someone may / drop / a cigarette) ....
   b) (it could / be / an electrical fault) ....
4 I wonder where Tom was going when you saw him.
   a) (he might / go / to work) ....
   b) (he may / go / shopping) ....
5 George didn't come to the party. I wonder why not.
   a) (he might / have / to go somewhere else) ....
   b) (he may not / know / about it) ....

UNIT 30   May and might (future)

a) We use **may** or **might** to talk about possible happenings or possible actions in the future. Study these examples:

- I'm not sure where to go for my holidays but I **may go** to Italy.
  (= perhaps I will go)
- The weather forecast is not very good. It **might rain** this afternoon.
  (= perhaps it will rain)
- I can't help you. Why don't you ask Tom? He **might be** able to help you.
  (= perhaps he will be able to help)

The negative form is **may not** or **might not (mightn't)**:

- Ann **may not come** to the party tonight. She isn't feeling well.
  (= perhaps she won't come)
- There **might not be** a meeting on Friday because the director is ill.
  (= perhaps there won't be a meeting.)

It doesn't matter whether you use **may** or **might**. You can say:

- I **may** go to Italy.   *or*   I **might** go to Italy.

b) There is also a continuous form: **may/might be doing**. Compare this with **will be doing** (see Unit 10a,b):

- Don't phone at 8.30. **I'll be watching** the football match on television.
- Don't phone at 8.30. I **may** (or **might**) **be watching** the football match on television. (= perhaps I'll be in the middle of watching it)

You can also use the continuous (**may/might be doing**) when you are talking about possible plans. Compare:

- **I'm going** to Italy in July. (for sure)
- I **may** (or **might**) **be going** to Italy in July. (it's possible)

But you can also say: I **may/might go** to Italy in July.

c) **May as well, might as well**
Study this example:

> A: What shall we do this evening?
> B: I don't know. Any ideas?
> A: Well, there's a film on television. It sounds quite interesting.
> B: **We might as well watch it** then. There's nothing else to do.
>
> We use **may/might as well** to say that we should do something but only because there is no reason not to do it and because there is nothing better to do. **We might as well watch it** means 'Why not watch it? There's nothing better to do.'

- You'll have to wait an hour for the next bus, so **you might as well walk**.
- **We may as well go** to the party. We've nothing else to do.
- 'Shall we have dinner now?'   '**We might as well.**'

For **may** and **might** see also Units 29 and 36c. For **may** only, see Unit 31.

60

UNIT 30   Exercises

30.1 *In this exercise you have to talk about your (and other people's) future plans. But you are not sure what is going to happen. Use* **may** *or* **might**.
Example: Where are you going for your holidays? (to Italy???)
I haven't finally decided but *I may (or might) go to Italy.*

1 What sort of car are you going to buy? (a Mercedes???)
I'm not sure yet but I ....
2 What are you doing this weekend? (go to London???)
I don't know for sure but ....
3 Where are you going to hang that picture? (in the dining-room???)
I haven't made up my mind yet but ....
4 When is Tom coming to see us? (tomorrow evening???)
I'm not sure but ....
5 What's Jill going to do when she leaves school? (a secretarial course???)
She hasn't decided yet but ....

30.2 *This time you have to talk about possible happenings. Use the word(s) in brackets.*
Examples: Do you think it will rain this afternoon? (may)   *It may rain this afternoon.*
Do you think Ann will come to the party? (might not)
She might not come to the party.

1 Do you think Tom will be late? (may)   He ....
2 Do you think Ann will be able to find our house? (might not)   She ....
....
3 Do you think there'll be an election this year? (might)   There ....
....
4 Do you think Tony will pass the exam? (may not)   ....
5 Do you think they'll be waiting for us when we arrive? (might)   ....
....
6 Do you think it'll snow later? (may)   ....

30.3 *Now you have to read these situations and make sentences with* **may/might** *as well.*
Example: A friend has invited you to a party. You're not very keen to go but there isn't anything else to do. So you think you should go.
You say: *I might as well go. There isn't anything else to do.*

1 You're in a café with a friend. You've just finished your drinks. You're not in a hurry, so you think you should both have another drink.
You say: We .... What would you like?
2 Someone has given you a free ticket for a concert. You're not very keen on the concert, but you think you should go because you have a free ticket.
You say: I .... It's a pity to waste a free ticket.
3 You've invited some friends to dinner but they haven't come. The dinner has been ready for half an hour and you think you should begin without them.
You say: We .... I don't think they are coming.

UNIT 31 Can, could, may and would: requests, permission, offers and invitations

a) *Asking people to do things* (requests)

We often use **can** or **could** when we ask someone to do something:

Can you wait a moment, please?
Ann, **can you** do me a favour?
Excuse me. **Could you** tell me how to get to the station?
Do you think you could lend me some money?
I wonder if you could help me.

To ask for something you can say **Can I have ...? / Could I have ...? / May I have ...?**:
 — (*in a shop*) **Can I have** these postcards, please?
 — (*at table*) **Could I have** the salt, please?

b) *Asking for and giving permission*
We often use **can, could** or **may** to ask permission to do something:
 — (*on the telephone*) Hello, **can I** speak to Tom, please?
 — '**Could I** use your telephone?' 'Yes, of course.'
 — '**Do you think I could** borrow your bicycle?' 'Yes, help yourself.'
 — '**May I** come in?' 'Yes, please do.'
To give permission, we use **can** or **may** (but *not* **could**):
 — You **can** (*or* **may**) smoke if you like.
Use **can/can't** to talk about what is *already allowed or not allowed*:
 — You **can drive** for a year in Britain with an international licence.
 — If you're under 17, you **can't drive** a car in Britain.

c) We sometimes use **can** when we *offer* to do things:
 — '**Can I get you** a cup of coffee?' 'That's very nice of you.'
 — (*in a shop*) '**Can I help you,** madam?' 'No thank you. I'm being served.'

d) For *offering* and *inviting* we use **Would you like ...?** (*not* 'do you like'):
 — **Would you like** a cup of coffee? (*not* 'do you like')
 — **Would you like to come** to the cinema with us tomorrow evening? (*not* 'do you like to come')

I'd like (= **I would like**) is a polite way of saying what you want, or what you want to do:
 — **I'd like** some information about hotels, please.
 — **I'd like to try** on this jacket, please.

UNIT 31 Exercises

31.1 *Read the situation and write what you would say. Use the words given in brackets.*
Example: You've got a pound note but you need some change. You ask somebody to help
you. (Can you ...?) *Can you change a pound?*

1 You want to borrow your friend's camera. What do you say to him/her? (Could I ...?)

2 You have a car and you want to give somebody a lift. What do you say? (Can I ...?)

3 You have to go to the airport but you don't know how to get there. You ask a passer-by.
(Could you ...?)

4 You are telephoning the owner of a flat which was advertised in a newspaper. You are
interested in the flat and you want to come and see it today. (Do you think I ...?)

5 You are at an interview. You want to smoke a cigarette. What do you ask first?
(May I ...?)

6 You want to leave work early because you have some important things to do. What do
you ask your boss? (Do you think I ...?)

7 You want to invite someone to come and stay with you for the weekend. (Would you like
...?)

8 The person in the next room has some music on very loud. How do you ask him politely
to turn it down? (Do you think you ...?)

31.2 *This time you have to decide how to say what you want to say.*
Example: You have to carry some heavy boxes upstairs. Ask someone to help you.
Do you think you could give me a hand with these boxes?

1 A friend has just come to see you in your flat. Offer him something to drink.

2 You want your friend to show you how to change the film in your camera. What do you
say to him/her?

3 You're on a train. The woman next to you has finished reading her newspaper. Now you
want to have a look at it. What do you say?

4 You need a match to light your cigarette. You haven't got any but the man sitting next to
you has some. What do you ask him?

5 There is a concert on tonight and you are going with some friends. You think Tom would
enjoy it too. Invite him.

6 You're in the post office. You want three stamps for Japan. What do you say?

7 You are sitting in a crowded bus. There is an old lady standing. Offer her your seat.

8 You're in a car with a friend, who is driving. He is going to park the car but there is a No
Parking sign. You see the sign and say:

UNIT 32   Must and have to

a) We use **must** (do) and **have to** (do) to say that it is necessary to do something. Often it doesn't matter which you use:

- Oh dear, it's later than I thought. I $\left\{ \begin{array}{l} \textbf{must} \\ \textbf{have to} \end{array} \right\}$ go now.

- You $\left\{ \begin{array}{l} \textbf{must} \\ \textbf{have to} \end{array} \right\}$ have a passport to visit most foreign countries.

There is sometimes a difference between **must** and **have to**. With **must** the speaker is giving his own feelings, saying what *he* thinks is necessary:

- I **must** write to Ann. I haven't written to her for ages. (= The speaker personally feels that he must write to Ann.)
- The government really **must** do something about unemployment. (= The speaker personally feels that the government must do something.)

With **have to** the speaker is not giving his own feelings. He is just giving facts. For example:

- Ann's eyes are not very good. She **has to** wear glasses for reading.
- I can't meet you on Friday. I **have to** work.

b) You can only use **must** to talk about the *present* and *future*:

- We **must** go now.
- **Must** you leave tomorrow?

Have to can be used in all forms. For example:

- I **had to** go to hospital. (*past*)
- I might **have to** go to hospital. (*infinitive*)
- **Have** you ever **had to** go to hospital. (*present perfect*)

Note that we use **do/does/did** with **have to** in present and past questions and negative sentences:

- What **do I have to** do to get a driving licence? (*not* 'have I to do')
- Why **did** you **have to** go to hospital? (*not* 'had you to go')
- Tom **doesn't have to** work on Saturdays. (*not* 'hasn't to work')

c) **Mustn't** and **don't have to** are completely different. 'You **mustn't** do something' means: 'it is necessary that you do *not* do it':

- You **mustn't** tell anyone what I said. (= Don't tell anyone.)
- I promised I'd be on time. I **mustn't** be late. (= I must be on time.)

See also Unit 33a.

'You **don't have to** do something' means: 'it is not necessary to do it; you don't need to do it':

- I **don't have to** wear a suit to work but I usually do.
- She stayed in bed this morning because she **didn't have to** go to work.

d) You can use 'have **got** to' instead of **have to**. So you can say:

- I've **got to** work tomorrow   *or*   I **have to** work tomorrow.
- When **has** Tom **got to** leave?   *or*   When **does** Tom **have to** leave?

UNIT 32   Exercises

32.1 *Complete these sentences with* **must** *or* **have to** *(in its correct form). Sometimes it is possible to use either; sometimes only* **have to** *is possible.*
Examples: Well, it's 10 o'clock. I .....*must (or have to)*... go now.
Ann was feeling ill last night. She ....*had to*........... leave the party early.

1 You really .... work harder if you want to pass that examination.
2 Many children in Britain .... wear uniform when they go to school.
3 Last night Don suddenly became ill. We .... call the doctor.
4 Ann has .... wear glasses since she was eight years old.
5 I'm afraid I can't come tomorrow. I .... work late.
6 I'm sorry I couldn't come yesterday. I .... work late.
7 Tom may .... go away next week.
8 We couldn't repair the car ourselves. We .... take it to a garage.
9 When you come to London again, you .... come and see us.

32.2 *Now make questions with* **have to.**
Example: 'Tom had to go to the police station.'
   'Why *did he have to go to the police station?* .... '

1 'Ann has to leave tomorrow.'   'What time exactly .... '
2 'We had to answer a lot of questions in the examination.'
 'How many questions .... '
3 'George had to pay a parking fine.'   'How much .... '
4 'I have to get up early tomorrow.'   'Why .... '

32.3 *This time make negative sentences with* **have to.**
Example: 'Did they change trains?'
   'No, it was a through train so *they didn't have to change (trains).* .... '

1 'Did you pay to get into the concert?'
 'No, we had free tickets so we .... '
2 'Does Jack shave?'   'No, he's got a beard so .... '
3 'Did you get up early this morning?'
 'No, it's my day off so .... '
4 'Do you work?'   'No, I'm extremely rich so .... '

32.4 *Complete these sentences with* **mustn't** *or* **don't/doesn't have to.**
Examples: I don't want anyone to know. You ....*mustn't*....... tell anyone what I said.
   I ....*don't have to*....... wear a suit to work but I usually do.

1 I can stay in bed tomorrow morning because I .... work.
2 Whatever you do, you .... touch that switch. It's very dangerous.
3 You .... forget what I told you. It's very important.
4 She .... get up so early. She gets up early because she prefers to.
5 We .... leave yet. We've got plenty of time.

UNIT 33   Must, mustn't, needn't and needn't have

a) Must, mustn't, and needn't

> (You) **must** (**do**) means that it is necessary that you do something:
>
> You haven't got much time. You **must** hurry.
> You can tell Tom what I said but he **must** keep it a secret.
>
> (You) **mustn't** (**do**) means that it is necessary that you do *not* do something:
>
> The baby is asleep. You **mustn't** shout. (= It is necessary that you do *not* shout.)
> You can tell Tom what I said but he **mustn't** tell anybody else. (= It is necessary that he doesn't tell anybody else.)
>
> (You) **needn't** (**do**) means that it is *not necessary* to do something:
>
> You've got plenty of time. You **needn't** hurry. (= It is not necessary to hurry.)
> I can hear you quite clearly. You **needn't** shout. (= It is not necessary to shout.)

b) Instead of **needn't** you can use **don't/doesn't need to**:
   – You've got plenty of time. You **don't need to** hurry.
Remember we say 'don't need **to** hurry', but 'needn't hurry' (without **to**).

c) Needn't have (done)
Study this example situation:

> Tom wanted to catch a train. He left home late, so he hurried to the station. But the train was also late – it didn't leave until 20 minutes after Tom arrived at the station.
>
> Tom **needn't have hurried** (because the train was late).
>
> 'Tom **needn't have hurried**' means that he hurried *but it wasn't necessary*.

We use **needn't have** to say that someone did something but it wasn't necessary:
   – Ann bought some eggs but when she got home she found that she already had plenty of eggs. So she **needn't have bought** any eggs.
   – Thank you for doing the washing-up but you **needn't have done** it really. I was going to do it later.

d) Didn't need to is different from **needn't have**.
We use **didn't need to** (and 'didn't **have** to') to say that an action was unnecessary. This was known at the time of the action:
   – I **didn't need to go**, so I didn't go.
   – I **didn't need to go** but I decided to go anyway.
When we use **needn't have**, it was *not known* at the time that the action was not necessary:
   – I **needn't have gone**. (= I went – this was unnecessary, but I didn't know at the time that it was unnecessary.)

Unit 33   Exercises

33.1 *In this exercise you have to write a sentence with* **needn't**.
Example: Shall I do the shopping now? (no / this afternoon)
      No, you needn't do it now. You can do it this afternoon.

1 Shall I clean the windows today? (no / tomorrow)
  No, you .... You .... tomorrow.
2 Shall I type these letters now? (no / later)
  No, ... You ....
3 Shall I go to the bank this morning? (no / this afternoon)
  ....

33.2 *In this exercise you have to complete the sentences with* **must, mustn't** *or* **needn't**.
Examples: We haven't got much time. We .... *must* .... hurry.
         We've got plenty of time. We .... *needn't* ..... hurry.

1 'Do you want me to wait for you?'   'No, it's okay. You .... wait.'
2 Tom gave me a letter to post. I .... forget to post it.
3 You .... come if you don't want to but I hope you will.
4 'What sort of house do you want to buy? Something big?'   'Well, it .... be
  big – that's not important. But it .... have a nice garden – that's essential.'
5 We have enough food at home so we .... go shopping today.
6 This book is very valuable. You .... look after it very carefully and you
  .... lose it.

33.3 *This time you have to make a sentence with* **needn't have**.
Example: I don't know why we hurried.   *We needn't have hurried.*

1 I don't know why they left so early.   They ....
2 I don't know why she shouted at me like that.   She ....
3 I don't know why he read the whole book.   ....
4 I don't know why she cancelled her holiday.   ....

33.4 *Now read these situations and make sentences with* **needn't have**.
Example: Ann bought some eggs. When she got home, she found that she already had
     plenty of eggs.   *She needn't have bought any eggs.*

1 Tom went out and took an umbrella with him because he thought it was going to rain.
  But it didn't rain.   ....
2 Jack got very angry with Jill and threw a book at her. Later Jill said: 'I know you were
  very angry but .... ,'
3 Brian had no money, so he sold his car. A few days later he won a lot of money in a
  competition.   ....

67

UNIT 34 Should (1)

a) Study this example:

> Tom has just come back from the cinema:
>
> Ann: Hello, Tom. Did you enjoy the film?
> Tom: Yes, it was great. You **should go** and see it.
>
> Tom is advising Ann to go and see the film. 'You **should go**' means that it would be a good thing to do. We often use **should (do)** when we say what we think is a good thing to do or the right thing to do.

- The government **should do** something about the economy.
- '**Should** we **invite** Sue to the party?'   'Yes, I think we **should**.'

'You **shouldn't** do something' means that it is not a good thing to do:

- You've been coughing a lot recently. You **shouldn't smoke** so much.
- Tom **shouldn't drive** really. He is too tired.

Should is not as strong as **must**:

- You **should** stop smoking. (= It would be a good idea.)
- You **must** stop smoking. (= It is necessary that you stop.)

b) We often use **should** when we ask for or give an opinion about something. Often we use **I think / I don't think / do you think?**:

- **I think** the government **should do** something about the economy.
- **I don't think** you **should work** so hard.
- '**Do you think** I **should apply** for this job?'   ' Yes, **I think** you **should**.'

c) We also use **should** to say something is not 'right' or not what we expect:

- The price on this packet is wrong. It says 65 pence but it **should be** 50.
- Those children **shouldn't be playing**. They **should be** at school.
- That motor-cyclist **should be wearing** a crash helmet.

d) For the past, we use **should have (done)** to say that someone did the wrong thing:

- Hello, Ann. The party last night was great. You **should have come**. Why didn't you?
- I'm feeling sick. I **shouldn't have eaten** so much chocolate.
- Why were you at home yesterday? You **should have been** at work.
- She **shouldn't have been listening** to our conversation. It was private.

e) You can use **ought to** instead of **should** in the sentences in this unit:

- It's really a good film. You **ought to go** and see it.
- Tom **ought not to drive**. He is too tired.
- It was a great party. You **ought to have come**.

For more information about **should** see Unit 35.

UNIT 34   Exercises

34.1   *You are giving advice to a friend. Use* **should** *or* **shouldn't**.
  Example: Your friend is always coughing because he smokes too much. Advise him to
    stop smoking.   *You should stop smoking.*

  1   Your friend has a bad toothache. Advise him to go to the dentist.   You ....
      ....
  2   Your friend rides his bicycle at night without lights. You think this is dangerous. Advise
      him not to do it.   ....
  3   Your friend is going to visit Greece. Advise him to learn a few words of Greek before he
      goes.   ....

34.2   *This time you give your opinion about something. Use* **I think** / **I don't think** ...
  Example: Tom has just been offered a job. You think it would be a good idea for him to
    accept it.   *I think Tom should accept the job.*

  1   You think it would be a good idea for all motorists to wear seat-belts.
      I think   ....
  2   You don't think it would be a good idea for Jill and Sam to get married.
      I   ....
  3   Your friend has a bad cold. Tell him that you think it would be a good idea for him to
      stay at home this evening.

      ....

34.3   *Now you have to read the situations and write sentences with* **should** (**have**) *and* **shouldn't**
  (**have**). *Sometimes you have to use the present, sometimes the past.*
  Examples: The speed limit is 30 miles an hour but Tom is driving at 50.
      He shouldn't be driving so fast.
      When we got to the restaurant there were no free tables. We hadn't reserved
      one.   *We should have reserved a table.*

  1   It's very cold. Mr Taylor, who has been ill recently, is walking along the road without a
      coat.   He   ....
  2   We went for a walk. While we were walking, we got hungry but we hadn't brought
      anything with us to eat. We said: We   ....
  3   I went to Paris. Marcel lives in Paris but I didn't go to see him while I was there. When
      I saw him later, he said: You   ....
  4   The notice says that the shop is open every day from 8.30. It is now 9 o'clock but the
      shop isn't open.   ....
  5   The driver in front stopped suddenly without warning and I drove into the back of his
      car. It wasn't my fault.   ....
  6   The children normally go to bed at 9 o'clock. It is now 9.30. They are not in bed; they
      are watching television. (*two sentences*)   ....

      ....
  7   The accident happened because Tom was driving on the wrong side of the road.

      ....

UNIT 35   Should (2)

a) **Should** to say that something will probably happen:
- A: Do you think you'll be late home tonight?
  B: I don't think so. I **should be** home at the usual time.

Here, 'I **should be** home' means 'I will probably be home'. You can use **should** to say what will probably happen. **Ought to** can also be used with this meaning:
- She's been studying very hard, so she **should pass** her examination.
  (*or* 'she **ought to pass** her examination')

b) **If ... should ...**
- **If you should see** Tom this evening, can you tell him to phone me?

This is similar to 'If you see Tom' (without **should**). With **should** the speaker is less certain:
- **If it should rain**, can you bring in the washing from the garden?
- Don't worry **if I should be** late home tonight.

You can also begin with **should** (before the subject):
- **Should you see** Tom this evening, can you tell him to phone me?

c) You can use **should** after these verbs (other structures are possible too):

suggest   propose   recommend   insist   demand

- They **insisted** that we **should have** dinner with them.
or: They **insisted** that we **had** dinner with them.
- She **demanded** that I **should apologise** to her.
or: She **demanded** that I **apologised** to her.

Be careful with **suggest**. You cannot use the infinitive (to do / to play etc.) after **suggest**:

What do you **suggest we should do?**   *or*   What do you **suggest we do?**
  (but *not* 'What do you suggest us to do?')
Jim **suggested** (that) **I should buy** a car.   *or*   Jim **suggested** (that) **I bought** a car.
  (but *not* 'Jim suggested me to buy')

For **suggest -ing** see Unit 53.

---

d) You can use **should** after these adjectives:

important	strange	funny	natural	surprised
essential	odd	typical	interesting	surprising

- It's **strange** that he **should be** late. He's usually on time.
- I was **surprised** that he **should say** such a thing.

UNIT 35 Exercises

35.1 *In this exercise you have to use* **should** *to say that you think something will happen.*
Example: Do you think Margaret will pass the examination?
Well, ...*she should pass the examination*... She has studied very hard.

1 Do you think Ted will get the job he applied for?
   Well, ... He's got all the necessary qualifications.
2 Do you think Jim will win his tennis match against Tom?
   Well, ... He's a much better player than Tom.
3 Do you think £10 will be enough to do all the shopping?
   Well, it .... But take a bit more in case it isn't.

35.2 *In this exercise you have to use* **if ... should ...**
Example: I don't suppose you'll see Tom this evening but *if you should see him,*
can you ask him to phone me?

1 I don't think Ann will arrive before I get home but ....
   can you look after her until I come?
2 I don't think there will be any letters for me while I'm away but ....
   .... , can you send them on to this address?
3 I don't suppose you'll need any help but .... , just let me
   know.

35.3 *Now you have to write a sentence (beginning in the way shown) which means the same as*
the first sentence.
Example: 'I think it would be a good idea to see a specialist', the doctor said to me.
The doctor recommended that *I should see a specialist.*...

1 'You really must stay a little longer', she said to me.
   She insisted that ....
2 'Why don't you visit the museum after lunch?' I said to them.
   I suggested that ....
3 'You must pay the rent by Friday at the latest', he said to us.
   He demanded that ....
4 'Why don't you go away for a few days?' Jack suggested to me.
   Jack suggested that ....

35.4 *This time you have to put* **should** *in these sentences with one of these verbs:*
worry   listen   ~~be~~   leave   say
Example: It's strange that he ....*should be*........ late. He's usually on time.

1 It's funny that you .... that. I was going to say the same thing.
2 It's only natural that parents .... about their children.
3 Isn't it typical of him that he .... without saying goodbye?
4 It's very important that everyone .... very carefully.

UNIT 36   If sentences (present/future)

a) Compare these examples:

> Tom: I think I left my lighter in your house. Have you seen it?
> Ann: No, but I'll have a look. **If I find** it, I'll give it to you.
>
> In this example there is a real possibility that Ann will find the lighter. So she says: 'If I **find** ...
> I'll ...' (see also Unit 9c).
>
> Ann: **If I found** £100 in the street, I would keep it.
>
> This is a different type of situation. Ann is not thinking about a real possibility; she is
> imagining the situation. So she says: 'If I **found** ... I **would** ...' (*not* 'If I find ... I'll').

When you imagine a future happening like this, you use a *past* tense (**did/was/found** etc.)
after **if**. But the meaning is *not* past:
- What would you do if you **won** a million pounds?
- If we **didn't go** to their party next week, they would be very angry.
- Ann wouldn't lend me any money **if I asked** her.

b) We do not normally use **would** in the **if** part of the sentence:
- I'd be very frightened **if** someone **pointed** a gun at me. (*not* 'if someone
  would point')
- If we **didn't go** to their party next week, they would be angry. (*not* 'if we
  wouldn't go')

Sometimes it is possible to say **if ... would**, especially when you ask someone to do something
in a formal way:
- I would be very grateful **if** you **would** send me your brochure and price list
  as soon as possible. (*from a formal letter*)
- 'Shall I close the door?' 'Yes, please, **if** you **would**.'

c) In the other part of the sentence (not the **if** part) we use **would/wouldn't**. **Would** is often
shortened to **'d**, especially in spoken English:
- If you stopped smoking, you'd probably **feel** healthier.
- They **wouldn't come** to the party if you invited them.

You can also use **could** and **might**:
- They **might be** angry if I didn't visit them. (= perhaps they would be)
- If it stopped raining, we **could go** out. (= we would be able to go out)

d) Do not use **when** in sentences like the ones in this unit:
- Tom would be angry **if** I didn't visit him. (*not* 'when I didn't visit')
- What would you do **if** you were bitten by a snake? (*not* 'when you were')

See also Unit 9c.

For **if** sentences see also Units 37 and 38.

UNIT 36   Exercises

36.1 *In this exercise you have to put the verb into the correct form.*
Examples: If I found £100 in the street, I ....*would keep*....... (keep) it.
    They'd be rather angry if you ....*didn't visit*....... (not/visit) them.

1 If I was offered the job, I think I .... (take) it.
2 I'm sure Tom will lend you some money. I would be very surprised if he
   .... (refuse).
3 Many people would be out of work if that factory .... (close) down.
4 If she sold her car, she .... (not/get) much money for it.
5 They're expecting us. They would be disappointed if we .... (not/
   come).
6 Would George be angry if I .... (take) his bicycle without asking?
7 Ann gave me this ring. She .... (be) terribly upset if I lost it.
8 If someone .... (walk) in here with a gun, I'd be very frightened.
9 What would happen if you .... (not/go) to work tomorrow?
10 I'm sure she .... (understand) if you explained the situation to her.

36.2 *This time you have to make questions.*
Example: Perhaps one day somebody will give you a lot of money.
    What would you do if somebody gave you a lot of money?

1 Perhaps one day a millionaire will ask you to marry him/her.
   What would you do if ....
2 Perhaps one day you will lose your passport in a foreign country.
   What ....
3 Perhaps one day somebody will throw an egg at you.
   What ....
4 Perhaps one day your car will be stolen.
   What ....
5 Perhaps one day somebody will park his car on your foot.
   ....

36.3 *Now answer these questions in the way shown.*
Example: Are you going to catch the 10.30 train? (we / arrive too early)
    No. *If we caught the 10.30 train, we would arrive too early.*

1 Is he going to take the examination? (he / fail it)
   No. If he .... , he ....
2 Are you going to invite Bill to the party? (I / have to invite Linda too)
   No. If I ....
3 Are you going to bed now? (I / not / sleep)
   No. ....
4 Is she going to apply for the job? (she / not / get it)
   No. ....

UNIT 37   If and **wish** sentences (present)

a) Study this example situation:

> Tom wants to telephone Sue but he can't do this because he doesn't know her telephone number. He says:
>
> **If I knew** her number, **I would telephone** her.
>
> Tom says 'If I knew her number ...'. This tells us that he doesn't know her number. He is imagining the situation. The real situation is that he doesn't know her number.

When you imagine a situation like this, you use a *past* tense ('I **did** / I **was** / I **knew**' etc.) after **if**. But the meaning is present, not past:

- Tom would travel **if** he **had** more money. (but he doesn't have much money)
- **If** I **didn't want** to go, I wouldn't. (but I want to go)
- We wouldn't have any money **if** we **didn't work**. (but we work)

b) We also use the past for a present situation after **wish**. We use **wish** to say that we regret something, that something is not as we would like it to be:

I WISH I HAD AN UMBRELLA

> I wish I **knew** Sue's telephone number. (I don't know it.)
> **Do you** ever **wish** you **could** fly? (You can't fly.)
> I wish it **didn't rain** so much in England. (It rains a lot.)
> It's crowded here. **I wish** there **weren't** so many people. (There are a lot of people.)
> **I wish** I **didn't have** to work. (I have to work.)

c) In **if** sentences and after **wish** you can use **were** instead of **was**:

- If I **were** you, I wouldn't buy that coat. (*or* 'If I **was** you')
- I'd go out if it **weren't** raining. (*or* 'if it **wasn't** raining')
- I wish my room **were** larger. (*or* 'I wish my room **was** larger.')

d) Do not use **would** in the **if** part of the sentence or after **wish**:

- If I **were** rich, I would buy a castle. (*not* 'if I would be rich')
- I wish I **were** taller. (*not* 'I wish I would be taller.')

But sometimes **I wish ... would ...** is possible. See Unit 39.

Could sometimes means 'would be able to' and sometimes 'was able to':

- She **could** (= would be able to) get a job more easily if she **could** (= was able to) type.

For **if** sentences and **wish** see also Units 36, 38 and 39.

UNIT 37   Exercises

37.1 *In this exercise you have to put the verb into the correct form.*
Examples: If I ....*knew*............... (know) her number, I would telephone her.
I .....*wouldn't buy*..... (not/buy) that coat if I were you.

1 I .... (give) you a cigarette if I had one but I'm afraid I haven't.
2 This soup would taste better if it .... (have) more salt in it.
3 If you .... (not/go) to bed so late every night, you wouldn't be so tired
   all the time.
4 I wouldn't mind living in England if the weather .... (be) better.
5 I'd help you if I .... (can) but I'm afraid I can't.
6 If I were you, I .... (not/marry) him.
7 We would happily buy that house if it .... (not/be) so small.

37.2 *This time you have to read a situation and write a sentence with* **if.**
Example: We don't visit you very often because you live so far away.
But if *you didn't live so far away, we would visit you more often.*

1 People don't understand him because he doesn't speak very clearly.
   But if he .... , people ....
2 I'm not going to buy that book because it's too expensive.
   But if that book ....
3 She doesn't go out very often because she can't walk without help.
   But if ....
4 He's fat because he doesn't take any exercise.
   But ....
5 We can't have lunch in the garden because it's raining.
   ....
6 I can't meet you tomorrow evening because I have to work.
   ....

37.3 *Now you have to write sentences with* **I wish ...**
Example: I don't know many people (and I'm lonely).   *I wish I knew more people.*

1 I can't give up smoking (but I'd like to).   I wish I ....
2 I haven't any cigarettes (and I need one).   I wish ....
3 George isn't here (and I need him).   I wish George ....
4 It's cold (and I hate cold weather).   I wish ....
5 I live in London (and I hate London).   I ....
6 Tina can't come to the party (she's your best friend).   I ....
7 I have to work tomorrow (but I'd like to stay in bed).   ....
8 I don't know anything about cars (and my car has just broken down).
   ....
9 I'm not lying on a beautiful sunny beach (and that's a pity).
   ....

UNIT 38   If and **wish** sentences (past)

a) Study this example situation:

> Last month Ann was ill. Tom didn't know this, so he didn't go to see her. They met again after Ann got better. Tom said:
>
> **If I had known** that you were ill, **I would have gone** to see you.
>
> The real situation was that Tom didn't know that Ann was ill. So he says **If I had known ...** When you are talking about the past, you use the *past perfect* (**I had done / I had been / I had known** etc.) after **if**.

- **If I had seen** you when you passed me in the street, I would have said hello. (but I didn't see you)
- I would have gone out **if I hadn't been** so tired. (but I was too tired)
- **If he had been looking** where he was going, he wouldn't have walked into the wall. (but he wasn't looking)

Do not use **would** (**have**) in the **if** part of the sentence:

- If I had seen you, I would have said hello. (*not* 'if I would have seen')

Both **would** and **had** can be shortened to 'd:

- If I'd seen (= **had** seen) you, I'd have said (= **would** have said) hello.

b) You also have to use the *past perfect* (**I had done**) after **wish** when you say that you regret something that happened or didn't happen in the past:

- **I wish I had known** that Ann was ill. I would have gone to see her. (I didn't know that she was ill.)
- I feel sick. **I wish I hadn't eaten** so much. (I ate too much.)
- **Do you wish you had studied** science instead of languages? (You didn't study science.)
- The weather was awful. **I wish it had been** warmer. (It wasn't warm.)

You cannot use **would have** after **wish**:

- I wish it **had been** warmer. (*not* 'would have been')

c) **Would have** (**done**) is the past form of **would** (**do**):

- If I had gone to the party last night, I **would be** tired now. (I am not tired now – *present.*)
- If I had gone to the party last night, I **would have seen** Ann. (I didn't see Ann – *past.*)

Might have and **could have** are possible instead of **would have**:

- If we'd played better, we **might have won**. (= perhaps we would have won)
- We **could have gone** out if the weather hadn't been so bad. (= we would have been able to go out)

For **if** sentences and **wish** see also Units 36, 37 and 39.

UNIT 38   Exercises

38.1 *In this exercise you have to put the verb into the correct form.*
Examples: If I _____had known_____ (know) that you were ill last week, I'd have gone to see you.
Tom _wouldn't have entered_ (not/enter) for the examination if he had known that it would be so difficult.

1 Tom got to the station in time. If he .... (miss) the train, he would have been late for his interview.
2 It's good that Ann reminded me about Tom's birthday. I .... (forget) if she hadn't reminded me.
3 We might not have stayed at this hotel if George .... (not/recommend) it to us.
4 I'd have sent you a postcard while I was on holiday if I .... (have) your address.

38.2 *Now you have to read a situation and write a sentence with* **if**.
Example: She didn't eat anything because she wasn't hungry.
If _she had been hungry, she would have eaten something._ .

1 The accident happened because the driver in front stopped so suddenly.
If the driver in front ....
2 I didn't wake George because I didn't know he wanted to get up early.
If I ....
3 I was able to buy the car because Jim lent me the money.
If ....
4 She wasn't injured in the crash because she was wearing a seat-belt.
If ....
5 You're hungry now because you didn't have breakfast.
If ....
6 She didn't buy the coat because she didn't have enough money on her.
If ....

38.3 *This time you have to imagine that you are in a situation. For each situation, make a sentence with* **I wish ...**
Example: You've eaten too much and now you feel sick.
You say: _I wish I hadn't eaten so much._

1 You've just painted the door red. Now you decide that it doesn't look very nice.
You say: I wish I ....
2 You are walking in the country. You would like to take some photographs but you didn't bring your camera. You say: I ....
3 A good friend of yours visited your town but unfortunately you were away when he came. So you didn't see him. You say: ....
4 You've just come back from your holiday. Everything was fine except for the hotel, which wasn't very good. You say: ....

UNIT 39   Would

For **would** and **would have** in **if** sentences (*conditional*), see Units 36, 37 and 38.
For **would** in offers, invitations etc., see Unit 31. This unit explains some other
uses of **would**.

a)   Sometimes we use **would** after **I wish** .... Study this example:

I WISH IT WOULD STOP RAINING

It is raining. Tom wants to go out, but not in the
rain. He says:

I wish it **would stop** raining.

This means that Tom is complaining about the rain
and wants it to stop. We use **I wish ... would ...**
when we want something to happen or somebody
to do something. The speaker is complaining about
the present situation.

— **I wish** someone **would answer** that telephone. It's been ringing for about
  five minutes.
— The music next door is very loud. **I wish** they **would turn** it down.

We often use **I wish ... wouldn't** to complain about the way people do things:

— **I wish** you **wouldn't drive** so fast. It makes me nervous.

We use **I wish ... would** when we want something to change or somebody else to do
something. So you cannot say 'I wish *I* would ...'.
For more information about **wish**, see Units 37 and 38.

b)   **Would/wouldn't** is sometimes the past of **will/won't**:

present   Tom: I'll lend you some money, Ann.
   past   Tom said that he **would** lend Ann some money.

present   Ann: I promise I **won't** be late.
   past   Ann promised that she **wouldn't** be late.

present   Tom: Damn! The car **won't** start.
   past   Tom was angry because the car **wouldn't** start.

c)   You can also use **would** when you look back on the past and remember things that often
happened:

— When we were children, we lived by the sea. In summer, if the weather was
  fine, we **would** all **get up** early and **go** for a swim.
— Whenever Arthur was angry, he **would** just **walk** out of the room.

Used to is also possible in these sentences:

— ... we all **used to get up** early and **go** ...

See Unit 25 for **used to**.

78

UNIT 39   Exercises

39.1   *In this exercise you have to read a situation and then write a sentence with* **I wish ...**
would ...
Example: It's raining. You want to go out, but not in the rain. So you want it to stop
raining. What do you say?   *I wish it would stop raining.*

1   You're waiting for Tom. He's late and you're getting impatient. You want him to come.
What do you say?   I wish ....
2   A baby is crying and you're trying to sleep. You want the baby to stop crying. What do
you say?   I ....
3   You're looking for a job – so far without success. You want somebody to give you a
job. What do you say?   I wish somebody ....
4   Brian has been wearing the same old clothes for years. You think he needs some new
clothes and you want him to buy some. What do you say to him?   ....
....

39.2   *Now you have to use* **I wish ... wouldn't ...**
Example: Tom drives very fast. You don't like this. What do you say to him?
I wish you wouldn't drive so fast.

1   You are telling your friend about the man in the next flat. He often plays the piano in
the middle of the night and you don't like this. What do you say to your friend?
I ....
2   A lot of people drop litter in the street. You don't like this. What do you say?
I wish people ....
3   Jack always leaves the door open. You don't like this. What do you say to him?
I ....

39.3   *In this exercise you have to write a sentence with* **promised**.
Example: I wonder why she's late.   *She promised she wouldn't be late.*

1   I wonder why Tom hasn't written to me.   He promised ....
2   I wonder why Ann told Tom what I said.   She promised ....
3   I wonder why they haven't come.   They ....

39.4   *These sentences are about things that often happened in the past. You have to put in*
would *with one of these verbs:*   be   ~~walk~~   take   shake
Example: Whenever Arthur was angry, he ......*would walk*...... out of the room.

1   We used to live next to a railway line. Every time a train went past, the whole house
....
2   That cinema is nearly always empty now. I remember a few years ago it ....
crowded every night.
3   When he went out, Jack .... always .... an umbrella with him whether it
was raining or not.

UNIT 40   In case

a) Study this example situation:

Geoff is a football referee. He always wears two watches during a game because it is possible that one watch will stop.

He wears two watches **in case one of them stops.**

In case one of them stops = 'because it is possible that one of them will stop'.

Here are some more examples of **in case**:
- John might phone tonight. I don't want to go out **in case he phones.** (= because it is possible that he will phone)
- I'll draw a map for you **in case you can't find our house.** (= because it is possible that you won't be able to find it)

b) Do not use **will** after **in case**. Use a present tense when you are talking about the future:
- I don't want to go out tonight in case John **phones.** (*not* 'in case John will phone')

c) **In case** is not the same as **if.** Compare these sentences:
- We'll buy some more food **if** Tom comes. (= Perhaps Tom will come; if he comes, we'll buy some more food; if he doesn't come, we won't buy any more food.)
- We'll buy some more food **in case** Tom comes. (= Perhaps Tom will come; we'll buy some more food now, whether he comes or not; then we'll *already* have the food *if* he comes.)

Compare:
- This letter is for Ann. Can you **give** it to her **if** you see her?
- This letter is for Ann. Can you **take** it with you **in case** you see her?

d) You can use **in case** to say why someone did something in the past:
- We bought some more food **in case Tom came.** (= because it was possible that Tom would come)
- I drew a map for her **in case she couldn't find our house.**
- We rang the bell again **in case they hadn't heard the first time.**

e) 'In case of ... ' is different from **in case. In case of fire** means 'if there is a fire':
- **In case of fire,** please leave the building as quickly as possible.
- **In case of emergency,** telephone this number. (= if there is an emergency)

UNIT 40　Exercises

40.1 *Tom is going for a long walk in the country. He has decided to take these things with him: his camera, some chocolate, an umbrella, a towel, a map and some lemonade. He is taking these things because:*

perhaps he'll need a drink   perhaps he'll lose his way
perhaps he'll want to have a swim   perhaps it will rain
perhaps he'll want to take some photographs perhaps he'll get hungry

Now write sentences with **in case** *saying why Tom has decided to take these things.*
Example: He's going to take his camera in case he wants to take some photographs.

1　He's going to take some chocolate in case ....
2　He's going to take ....
3　..
4　..
5　..

40.2 *In this exercise you have to write sentences with* **in case.**
Example: It was possible that John would phone. So I didn't go out.
   I didn't go out in case John phoned. ....

1　It was possible that he would come to London one day. So I gave him my address.
 I gave him my address in case ....
2　It was possible that I wouldn't see her again. So I said goodbye.
 I said ....
3　It was possible that her parents were worried about her. So she phoned them.
 She ....
4　It was possible that I would forget the name of the street. So I wrote it down.
 ....
5　It was possible that they hadn't received my first letter. So I wrote them a second letter.
 ....

40.3 *This time you have to put* **in case** *or* **if** *in these sentences.*
Examples: John might phone tonight. I don't want to go out ...in case... he phones.
    Could you give this book to Tom ....if....... you see him?

1　I hope you'll come to London sometime. .... you come, you must visit us.
2　I've just painted the door. I'll put a Wet Paint notice next to it .... someone doesn't realise the paint is still wet.
3　We have fitted a burglar alarm to the house .... somebody tries to break in.
4　The alarm will ring .... somebody tries to break into the house.
5　Write your name and address on your bag .... you lose it.
6　Go to the lost property office .... you lose your bag.
7　I was advised to arrange insurance .... I needed medical treatment while I was on holiday abroad.

UNIT 41   Unless, as long as and provided/providing (that)

a) Unless
Study this example situation:

Joe can't hear very well. If you speak to him normally, he can't hear you. If you want him to hear you, you have to shout.

Joe can't hear **unless you shout.**

This means: 'Joe *can* hear *only if* you shout'. **Unless** means **except if.** We use **unless** to make an exception to something we say.

Here are some more examples of **unless:**
  - Don't tell Ann what I said **unless she asks you.** (= except if she asks you)
  - I'll come tomorrow **unless I have to work.** (= except if I have to work)
  - I wouldn't eat fish **unless I was extremely hungry.** (= except if I was extremely hungry)

We often use **unless** in warnings:
  - We'll be late **unless we hurry.** (= except if we hurry)
  - **Unless you work harder,** you're not going to pass the examination. (= except if you work harder)
  - The man said he would hit me **unless I told him where the money was.** (= except if I told him)

Instead of **unless** it is possible to say **if ... not:**
  - Don't tell Ann what I said **if she doesn't** ask you.
  - We'll be late **if we don't** hurry.

b) As long as   provided (that)   providing (that)
These expressions mean **but only if:**
  - You can use my car **as long as** (*or* ' so long as') **you drive carefully.** (= but only if you drive carefully)
  - Travelling by car is convenient **provided (that) you have somewhere to park.** (= but only if you have somewhere to park)
  - **Providing (that) she studies hard,** she should pass the examination. (= but only if she studies hard)

c) When you are talking about the future, do *not* use **will** with **unless, as long as, provided** or **providing.** Use a *present* tense:
  - We'll be late **unless** we **hurry.** (*not* 'unless we will hurry')
  - **Providing** she **studies** hard ... (*not* 'providing she will study')

See Unit 9 for more information about this rule.

Unit 41 Exercises

41.1 *In this exercise you have to read a sentence and then write a new sentence with the same meaning. Use* **unless** *in your sentences.*
Example: You must study more or you won't pass the examination.
You won't pass the examination unless you study more.

1 You must listen carefully or you won't know what to do.
You won't know what to do ....
2 We must hurry or we'll miss the train.
We'll ....
3 You must speak very slowly or he won't be able to understand you.
He ....
4 My salary must be increased or I'll look for another job.

   ....
5 She must apologise to me or I won't forgive her.

   ....

41.2 *Now you have to read a sentence with* **only if** *and then write a new sentence with* **unless**.
Example: Joe can hear only if you shout.   *Joe can't hear unless you shout.*

1 I'm going to the party only if you go too.
I'm not going to the party ....
2 You are allowed into the club only if you are a member.
You're not ....
3 The dog will attack you only if you move.
The dog ....
4 He'll speak to you only if you ask him a question.
He ....

41.3 *This time you have to choose the correct word or expression for each sentence.*

Example: You can use my car | ~~unless~~ / as long as | you drive carefully. ('as long as' is correct)

1 I'm playing tennis tomorrow | unless / providing | it's raining.

2 We're going to start painting the house tomorrow | unless / provided | it's not raining.

3 You can smoke in here | unless / as long as | you leave a window open to let the smoke out.

4 George doesn't trust anyone. He won't lend you any money | unless / as long as | you promise in writing to pay him back.

5 The children can stay here | unless / providing | they don't make too much noise.

6 I'm going now | unless / provided | you want me to stay.

7 I can't understand why he's late | unless / as long as | he didn't get our message.

83

UNIT 42 Passive (1) (be done / have been done)

a) *Active* and *passive* Study this example:

This house **was built** in 1895.

This is a *passive* sentence. Compare:

Somebody **built** this house in 1895. (*active*)

This house was built in 1895. (*passive*)

We often prefer the passive when it is not so important who or what did the action. In this example, it is not so important who built the house.

In a passive sentence, if you want to say who did or what caused the action, use **by**:
- This house was built **by my grandfather**. (= my grandfather built it)
- Have you ever been bitten **by a dog**? (= Has a dog ever bitten you?)

b) In passive sentences we use the correct form of **be** (**is/are/was/were/has been** etc.) + the *past participle*:

(be) done   (be) cleaned   (be) damaged   (be) built   (be) seen

For irregular past participles (**done/seen/written** etc.) see Appendix 2.
For the passive of the present and past tenses see Unit 43.

c) The *passive infinitive* is **be done / be cleaned / be built** etc. We use the infinitive after modal verbs (**will, can, must** etc.) and a number of other verbs (for example: **have to, be going to, want to**). Compare:

Active: We **can solve** this problem.

Passive: This problem **can be solved**.

- The new hotel **will be opened** next year.
- George **might be sent** to America by his company in August.
- The music at the party was very loud and **could be heard** from far away.
- This room **is going to be painted** next week.
- Go away! I **want to be left** alone.

There is a *past* infinitive form: **have been done / have been cleaned / have been built** etc.:

Active: Somebody **should have cleaned** the windows yesterday.

Passive: The windows **should have been cleaned** yesterday.

- My bicycle has disappeared. It **must have been stolen**.
- She **wouldn't have been injured** if she had been wearing a seat-belt.
- The weather was awful. The football match **ought to have been cancelled**.

84

UNIT 42 Exercises

42.1 *Complete these sentences with one of the following verbs (in the correct form):*
arrest   wake   knock   check   translate   find   drive   make
spend   ~~hear~~   carry
Example: The music at the party was very loud and could ...... *be heard* .... from far away.

1 A decision will not .... until the next meeting.
2 That building is dangerous. It ought to .... down before it falls down.
3 When you go through Customs, your luggage may .... by a customs officer.
4 I told the hotel receptionist that I wanted to .... up at 6.30.
5 Her new book will probably .... into a number of foreign languages.
6 If you kicked a policeman, you'd ....
7 Police are looking for the missing boy. He can't .... anywhere.
8 Do you think that less money should .... on arms?
9 The injured man couldn't walk and had to ....
10 I don't mind driving but I prefer to .... by other people.

42.2 *Here again you have to complete a sentence. This time use these verbs:*
must   ~~should~~   shouldn't   might   would
Example: Did anyone clean the windows?
No. They *should have been cleaned* but they weren't.

1 A: Did anyone invite Ann to the party?
    B: I don't know. She .... – I'm not sure.
2 A: Did anyone see you?
    B: No, but I .... if it hadn't been so dark.
3 A: Has someone repaired this machine?
    B: Well, it's working again so it ....
4 A: Did someone throw those old letters away?
    B: Yes, but it was a mistake. They ....

42.3 *Now you have to read a sentence and write another sentence with the same meaning:*
Example: We can solve the problem.   The problem *can be solved.* ....

1 People should send their complaints to the head office.
    Complaints ....
2 They had to postpone the meeting because of illness.
    The meeting ....
3 Somebody might have stolen your car if you had left the keys in it.
    Your car ....
4 An electrical fault could have caused the fire.
    The fire ....
5 They are going to hold next year's congress in San Francisco.
    Next year's congress ....
6 They shouldn't have played the football match in such bad weather.
    The football match ....

UNIT 43   Passive (2) (present and past tenses)

These are the passive forms of the present and past tenses:

Present simple   am/is/are + done/cleaned etc.
    Active: Somebody **cleans** | this room | every day.

    Passive: | This room | **is cleaned** every day.

Many accidents **are caused** by dangerous driving.
I'm not often **invited** to parties.
How many people **are injured** in road accidents every day?

Past simple   was/were + done/cleaned etc.
    Active: Somebody **cleaned** | this room | yesterday.

    Passive: | This room | **was cleaned** yesterday.

During the night we **were** all **woken** up by a loud explosion.
When **was** that castle **built**?
The house **wasn't damaged** in the storm but a tree **was blown** down.

Present continuous   am/is/are being + done/cleaned etc.
    Active: Somebody **is cleaning** | the room | at the moment.

    Passive: | The room | **is being cleaned** at the moment.

Look at those old houses! They **are being knocked** down.
(*shop assistant to customer*) **Are** you **being served**, madam?

Past continuous   was/were being + done/cleaned etc.
    Active: Somebody **was cleaning** | the room | when I arrived.

    Passive: | The room | **was being cleaned** when I arrived.

Suddenly I heard footsteps behind me. We **were being followed**.

Present perfect   have/has been + done/cleaned etc.
    Active: The room looks nice. Somebody **has cleaned** | it. |

    Passive: The room looks nice. | It | **has been cleaned**.

Have you heard the news? The president **has been shot**.
Have you ever **been bitten** by a dog?
I'm not going to the party. I **haven't been invited**.

Past perfect   had been + done/cleaned etc.
    Active: The room looked much better. Somebody **had cleaned** | it. |

    Passive: The room looked much better. | It | **had been cleaned**.

Jim didn't know about the change of plans. He **hadn't been told**.

UNIT 43   Exercises

43.1 *In this exercise you have to read a sentence and then write another sentence with the same meaning. Begin each sentence as shown.*
Examples: Somebody stole my bag in the shop.   My bag *was stolen in the shop.*
The police have arrested three men.
Three men *have been arrested by the police.*

1 The bill includes service.   Service .... in the bill.
2 People don't use this road very often.   This road ....
3 They cancelled all flights because of fog.   All flights ....
4 Somebody accused me of stealing the money.   I ....
5 They are building a new ring-road round the city.
   A new ring-road ....
6 I didn't realise that someone was recording our conversation.
   I didn't realise that our conversation ....
7 They have changed the date of the meeting.   The date of the meeting ....
8 Brian told me that somebody had attacked and robbed him in the street.
   Brian told me that he ....

43.2 *This time you have to make a passive sentence from the words in brackets.*
Examples: That church looks very old. (when / it / build?)   *When was it built?*
A: Is Margaret popular?
B: Yes. (she / like / by everybody)   *She is liked by everybody.*

1 This is a very popular television programme. (every week it / watch / by millions of people)   Every week it ....
2 What happens to the cars produced in this factory? (most of them / export?)
   ....
3 A: Was there any trouble at the demonstration?
   B: Yes. (about 20 people / arrest) ....
4 A: There is no longer military service in Britain.
   B: Really? (when / it / abolish?) ....
5 A: Did anybody call an ambulance to the scene of the accident?
   B: Yes. (but nobody / injure / so it / not / need) ....
6 A: Last night someone broke into our house.
   B: Oh dear. (anything / take?) ....
7 Mr Kelly can't use his office at the moment. (it / redecorate)
   ....
8 George didn't have his car yesterday. (it / service / at the garage)
   ....
9 Where's my bicycle? It's gone! (it / steal!) ....
10 The people next door disappeared six months ago. (they / not / see / since then)
   ....
11 This room looks different. (it / paint / since I was last here?)
   ....
12 A tree was lying across the road. (it / blow / down in the storm)
   ....

UNIT 44 Passive (3)

a) Some verbs can have two objects. For example **offer**:
They didn't offer **Ann the job**. (the two objects are **Ann** and **the job**)
So it is possible to make two different passive sentences:

- **Ann** wasn't offered the job.
- **The job** wasn't offered to Ann.

It is more usual for the passive sentence to begin with the person.
Other verbs like **offer** which can have two objects are:

ask   tell   give   send   show   teach   pay

Here are some examples of passive sentences with these verbs:

- **I was given** two hours to make my decision. (= they gave **me two hours**)
- **The men were paid** £800 to do the job. (= someone paid **the men £800**)
- **Have you been shown** the new machine? (= has anyone shown **you the new machine?**)

b) **Born:** remember that **be born** is a *passive* verb and is usually past:

- Where **were you born?** (*not* 'are you born') $\Big\}$ – *past simple*
- **I was born** in Chicago. (*not* 'I am born')
- How many babies **are born** in this hospital every day? – *present simple*

c) The passive **-ing** form is **being done / being cleaned** etc.:
Active: I don't like people **telling** me what to do.
Passive: I don't like **being told** what to do.

- I remember **being given** a toy drum on my fifth birthday. (= I remember someone giving me ...)
- Hurry up! You know Mr. Miller hates **being kept** waiting. (= he hates people keeping him waiting)
- He climbed over the wall without **being seen**. (= without anyone seeing him)

d) Sometimes you can use **get** instead of **be** in the passive:

- There was a fight at the party but nobody **got** hurt. (= nobody was hurt)
- **Did** Ann **get** offered the job? (= was Ann offered the job?)

You can use **get** in the passive to say that something happens to someone or something.
Often the action is not planned; it happens by chance:

- The dog **got** run over by a car. (= the dog was run over)

In other types of situation **get** is not usually possible:

- George **is** liked by everyone. (*not* 'gets liked')

Get is used mainly in informal spoken English. You can use **be** in all situations.

88

UNIT 44   Exercises

44.1 *In this exercise you have to read a sentence and then write a new sentence with the same meaning. Begin in the way shown each time.*
Example: They didn't offer Ann the job.   Ann wasn't offered the job.

1 They don't pay Jim very much.   Jim ....
2 They will ask you a lot of questions at the interview.   You ....
   ....
3 Nobody told me that George was ill.   I ....
4 His colleagues gave him a present when he retired.   He ....
   ....
5 We will send you your examination results as soon as they are ready.   You ....
   ....
6 They didn't ask me my name.   I ....
7 I think they should have offered Tom the job.   I think Tom ....
   ....

44.2 *When were these famous people born? You have to choose the right year for each person:*   1889   1770   1452   ~~1870~~   1564

1 Lenin was born in 1870.   4 Charlie Chaplin ....
2 Shakespeare ....   5 Beethoven ....
3 Leonardo da Vinci ....   6 And you? I ....

44.3 *This time you have to complete the sentences. Each time you have to use* **being** *with one of these verbs:*   ~~keep~~   pay   attack   give   invite   use   ask
Example: Mr Miller doesn't like ....being kept........ waiting.

1 He came to the party without ....
2 She won't go out alone after dark. She is afraid of ....
3 I don't like .... stupid questions.
4 Few people are prepared to work without ....
5 Mr Kelly doesn't like his phone .... by other people.
6 Most people like .... presents.

44.4 *Here too you have to complete the sentences. This time make a passive sentence with* **get** *and one of these verbs:*   break   catch   sting   use   damage   ~~hurt~~   steal
Example: There was a fight at the party but nobody got hurt.

1 Ted .... by a bee while he was sitting in the garden.
2 How did that window .... ?
3 Did any of these houses .... in the storm last night?
4 These tennis courts don't .... often. Not many people want to play.
5 If you want to break the law, make sure that you don't ....
6 I used to have a bicycle but it ....

UNIT 45 It is said that ... / He is said to ... etc. and supposed to

a) Study this example situation:

This is Henry. He is very old but nobody knows exactly how old he is. But:

It is said that [he] is 108 years old.

[He] is said to be 108 years old.

Both these sentences mean: 'People say that he is 108 years old.'
You can also use these structures with:

thought	believed	reported	understood
known	expected	alleged	considered

It is said that Henry eats ten eggs a day.   *or*   Henry is said to eat ten eggs a day.

It is believed that the wanted man is living in New York.   *or*   The wanted man is believed to be living in New York.

It is expected that the strike will begin tomorrow.   *or*   The strike is expected to begin tomorrow.

It is alleged that he stole £60.   *or*   He is alleged to have stolen £60.

It was alleged that he stole £60.   *or*   He was alleged to have stolen £60.

These structures are often used in news reports:

It is reported that two people were killed in the explosion.   *or*   Two people are reported to have been killed in the explosion.

b) Supposed to

Sometimes **(be) supposed to** means 'said to':
- Let's go and see that film. It's **supposed to be** very good. (= It is said to be very good; people say that it's very good.)
- He **is supposed to have stolen** £60. (= He is said to have stolen £60.)

But sometimes **supposed to** has a different meaning. You can use **supposed to** to say what is planned or arranged (and this is often different from what really happens):
- I'd better hurry. It's nearly 8 o'clock. **I'm supposed to be meeting** Tom at 8.15. (= I arranged to meet Tom; I said I would meet Tom.)
- The train **was supposed to arrive** at 11.30 but it was 40 minutes late. (= The train should have arrived at 11.30 according to the timetable.)
- You **were supposed to clean** the windows. Why didn't you do it?

We use **not supposed to** to say what is not allowed or not advisable:
- You're **not supposed to park** here. (= You aren't allowed to park here.)
- Mr Collins is much better after his illness but he's still **not supposed to do** any heavy work.

UNIT 45   Exercises

45.1 *In this exercise you have to read a sentence and then write another sentence with the same meaning.*
Example: It is believed that the wanted man is living in New York.
The wanted man *is believed to be living in New York.*

1 It is said that many people are homeless after the floods.
   Many people are said ....
2 It is known that the Prime Minister is in favour of the new law.
   The Prime Minister ....
3 It is expected that the government will lose the election.
   The government ....
4 It is thought that the prisoner escaped by climbing over the wall.
   The prisoner ....
5 It is believed that the thieves got in through the kitchen window.
   The thieves ....
6 It is alleged that he drove through the town at 90 miles an hour.
   He ....
7 It is reported that two people were seriously injured in the accident.
   Two people ....
8 It is said that three men were arrested after the explosion.
   Three men ....

45.2 *There are a lot of stories about Arthur but nobody knows whether they are true. Make sentences with* **supposed to**.
Example: People say that Arthur eats spiders.   *Arthur is supposed to eat spiders.*

1 People say that Arthur is very rich.   Arthur ....
2 People say that he has 22 children.   He ....
3 People say that he sleeps on a bed of nails.   He ....
4 People say that he won a lot of money gambling.   He ....
5 People say that he writes poetry.   He ....

45.3 *Now you have to use* **supposed to** *with its other meaning. In each example what happens is not what is supposed to happen. Use* **supposed to** *or* **not supposed to** *with one of these verbs:*   ~~clean~~   come   be   ~~smoke~~   phone   study   take
Examples: Tom, you're smoking! But you know you *are not supposed to smoke* in this room.
Why are the windows still dirty? You *were supposed to clean* them.

1 What are the children doing at home? They .... at school.
2 He .... in the evenings but he always goes out.
3 Don't put sugar in your tea. You know you .... sugar.
4 Oh dear! I .... Ann but I completely forgot.
5 They arrived very early – at 2.00. They .... until 3.30.

91

UNIT 46 Have something done

a) Study this example situation:

The roof of Jill's house was damaged in a storm, so she arranged for a workman to repair it. Yesterday the workman came and did the job.

Jill **had the roof repaired** yesterday.

This means: Jill didn't repair the roof herself. She arranged for someone else to do it for her.

Compare:

- Jill **repaired** the roof. (= she did it herself)
- Jill **had** the roof **repaired**. (= she arranged for someone else to do it)

Now study these sentences:

- Did Ann make that dress herself or **did she have it made**?
- Are you going to repair the car yourself or **are you going to have it repaired**?

To say that we arrange for someone else to do something for us, we use the structure **have something done**.

The word order is important: the *past participle* (**done/repaired** etc.) comes *after* the object (**the roof**):

	have +	*object*	+	*past participle*	
Jill	had	the roof		repaired	yesterday.
Where did you	have	your hair		done?	
We are	having	the house		painted	at the moment.
Tom has just	had	a telephone		installed	in his flat.
How often do you	have	your car		serviced?	
Why don't you	have	that coat		cleaned?	
I want to	have	my photograph		taken.	

b) 'Get something done' is possible instead of **have something done** (mainly in informal spoken English):

- I think you should **get your hair cut**. (= have your hair cut)

c) Have something done sometimes has a different meaning. For example:

- He **had all his money stolen** while he was on holiday.

This doesn't mean that he arranged for somebody to steal his money! 'He **had all his money stolen**' means only: 'All his money was stolen'.

With this meaning, we use **have something done** to say that something (often something not nice) happened to someone:

- George **had his nose broken** in a fight. (= his nose was broken)

92

UNIT 46   Exercises

46.1   *In this exercise you have to answer the questions in the way shown.*
Example: 'Did Ann make that dress herself?'   'No, she had it made   ,'

1 'Did you cut your hair yourself?'   'No, I .... ,'
2 'Did they paint the house themselves?'   'No, they   .... ,'
3 'Did Jim cut down that tree himself?'   'No, ... ,'
4 'Did Sue repair the car herself?'   'No, ... ,'

46.2   *This time you have to complete the sentences. Use the words in brackets.*
Examples: We ......are having the house painted...... (the house / paint) at the moment.
...........Did you have your hair cut........... (you / your hair / cut) last week?

1 Your hair is too long. I think you should .... (it / cut).
2 How often .... (you / your car / service)?
3 The engine in Tom's car couldn't be repaired, so he had to ....
.... (a new engine / fit).
4 .... (you / your newspaper / deliver) or do you go to the
shop yourself to buy it?
5 A: What are those workmen doing in your garden?
   B: Oh, I .... (a swimming pool / build).
6 A: Can I see those holiday photographs you took?
   B: I'm afraid not. I .... (not/the film/develop) yet.
7 Is it true that many years ago he .... (his portrait / paint) by a famous artist?

46.3   *Now you have to read a situation and then write a sentence with* **have something done**.
Example: Jill's coat was dirty so she took it to the cleaners. Now it is clean. What has Jill
   done?   She has had her coat cleaned.

1 Tom thinks his eyesight is getting worse, so he's going to the optician. What is Tom going
to do there?   He is ....
2 Sue is at the hairdresser's at the moment. A hairdresser is cutting her hair.
What is Sue doing?   ....
3 Ann's watch was broken, so she took it to a jeweller's. Now it's working again.
What has Ann done?   ....

46.4   *Now you have to use* **have something done** *with its second meaning (see section c).*
Example: George's nose was broken in a fight. What happened to George?
   He had his nose broken in a fight.

1 John's money was stolen on a train. What happened to John?
He ....
2 Fred's hat was blown off in the wind. What happened to Fred?
....
3 George's papers were taken from him at the police station. What happened to George?
....

UNIT 47   Reported speech (1)

a) Study this example situation:

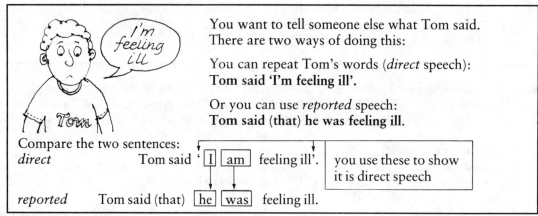

You want to tell someone else what Tom said. There are two ways of doing this:

You can repeat Tom's words (*direct* speech):
Tom said 'I'm feeling ill'.

Or you can use *reported* speech:
Tom said (that) he was feeling ill.

Compare the two sentences:

direct   Tom said ' I am feeling ill'.   │ you use these to show
                                                    │ it is direct speech

reported   Tom said (that) he was feeling ill.

b) When we use reported speech, we are usually talking about the past. So verbs usually change to the past in reported speech. For example:

am/is → **was**   are → **were**   have/has → **had**   will → **would**   can → **could**
do/want/know etc. → **did/wanted/knew** etc.

Study these examples. You met Tom. Here are some things he said to you:

My parents are very well.

Ann has bought a new car.

I want to go on holiday but I don't know where to go.

I'm going to give up my job.

I can't come to the party on Friday.

I'm going away for a few days. I'll phone you when I get back.

Now you tell someone else what Tom said (in reported speech):
  - Tom said (that) his parents **were** very well.
  - Tom said (that) he **was** going to give up his job.
  - Tom said (that) Ann **had** bought a new car.
  - Tom said (that) he **couldn't** come to the party on Friday.
  - Tom said (that) he **wanted** to go on holiday but he **didn't know** where to go.
  - Tom said (that) he **was** going away for a few days and **would** phone me when he **got** back.

c) The past simple (**I did**) can usually stay the same in reported speech, or you can change it to the past perfect (**I had done**): did → **did** *or* **had done**
direct   Tom said 'I **woke** up feeling ill and so I **stayed** in bed'.
reported   Tom said (that) he **woke** (*or* **had woken**) up feeling ill and so he **stayed** (*or* **had stayed**) in bed.

For reported speech see also Units 48 and 50b.

UNIT 47   Exercises

47.1 *Yesterday you met a friend of yours, Charlie. Charlie told you a lot of things. Here are some of the things he said to you:*

1 I'm thinking of going to live in Canada.

2 My father is in hospital.

3 Nora and Jim are getting married next month.

4 I haven't seen Bill for a while.

5 I've been playing tennis a lot recently.

6 Margaret has had a baby.

7 I don't know what Fred is doing.

8 I hardly ever go out these days.

9 I work 14 hours a day.

10 I'll tell Jim I saw you.

11 You can come and stay with me if you are ever in London.

12 Tom had an accident last week but he wasn't injured.

13 I saw Jack at a party a few months ago and he seemed fine.

Later that day you tell another friend what Charlie said. Use reported speech.

1 *Charlie said that he was thinking of going to live in Canada.*
2 Charlie said that ....
3 ....
4 ....
5 ....
6 ....
7 ....
8 ....
9 ....
10 ....
11 ....
12 ....
13 ....

47.2 *In this exercise someone says something to you which is the opposite of what they said before. You have to answer* **I thought you said ...**
Example: 'That restaurant is expensive.'   '*I thought you said it wasn't expensive.*'

1 'Ann is coming to the party.'   'I thought you said she .... '
2 'Bill passed his examination.'   'I thought you said .... '
3 'Ann likes Bill.'   'I thought .... '
4 'I've got many friends.'   'I thought you said you .... '
5 'Jack and Jill are going to get married.'   ' .... '
6 'Tom works very hard.'   ' .... '
7 'I want to be rich and famous.'   ' .... '
8 'I'll be here next week.'   ' .... '
9 'I can afford a holiday this year.'   ' .... '

UNIT 48   Reported speech (2)

a) It is not always necessary to change the verb when you use reported speech. If you are reporting something and you feel that it is still true, you do not need to change the tense of the verb:

direct   Tom said 'New York **is** bigger than London'.
reported Tom said (that) New York **is** (*or* **was**) bigger than London.
direct   Ann said 'I **want** to go to New York next year'.
reported Ann said (that) she **wants** (*or* **wanted**) to go to New York next year.

Notice that it is also correct to change the verb into the *past*.
But you *must* use a past tense when there is a difference between what was said and what is really true. Study this example situation:

> You met Ann. She said '**Jim is ill**'. (*direct speech*)
> Later that day you see Jim playing tennis and looking well. You say:
> 'I'm surprised to see you playing tennis, Jim. Ann said that you **were** ill'.
> (*not* 'that you are ill', because he isn't ill)

Must, might, could, would, should and **ought** stay the same in reported speech. **May** in direct speech normally changes to **might** in reported speech.

b) **Say** and **tell**
If you say *who* you are talking to, use **tell**:
          – Tom **told me** (that) he didn't like Brian. (*not* 'Tom said me ...')
Otherwise use **say**:
          – Tom **said** (that) he didn't like Brian. (*not* 'Tom told (that) he ...')
Also: you can't say 'Tom told about his trip to America'. You have to say:
          – Tom told **us** (*or* **me/them/Ann** etc.) about his trip to America.
If you don't say who he told, you have to say:
          – Tom **talked** (*or* **spoke**) about his trip to America. (*but not* 'said about')

c) We also use the *infinitive* (**to do** / **to stay** etc.) in reported speech, especially with **tell** and **ask** (for orders and requests):

direct   'Stay in bed for a few days', the doctor said to me.
reported The doctor **told me to stay** in bed for a few days.
direct   '**Don't shout**', I said to Jim.
reported I told Jim **not to shout**.
direct   'Please **don't tell** anyone what happened', Ann said to me.
reported Ann **asked me not to tell** anyone what (had) happened.
direct   '**Can you open** the door for me, Tom?' Ann asked.
reported Ann **asked Tom to open** the door for her.

Said is also possible with the infinitive:
          – The doctor **said to stay** in bed for a few days. (*but not* 'said me')

UNIT 48   Exercises

48.1   *In this exercise you have to write what you would say in these situations.*
Example: Ann says 'I'm tired'. Five minutes later she says 'Let's play tennis'. What do you
say?   *You said you were tired*.

1   Your friend says 'I'm hungry' so you go to a restaurant. When you get there he says 'I
don't want to eat'. What do you say?   You said ....
2   Tom tells you 'Ann has gone away'. Later that day you meet her. What do you say?
Tom told ....
3   George said 'I don't smoke'. A few days later you see him smoking a cigarette.
What do you say to him?   You said ....
4   You arranged to meet Jack. He said 'I won't be late'. At last he arrives – 20 minutes
late. What do you say?   You ....
5   Sue said 'I can't come to the party tonight'. That night you see her at the party. What do
you say to her?   ....
6   Ann says 'I'm working tomorrow evening'. Later that day she says 'Let's go out
tomorrow evening'. What do you say?   ....

48.2   *Now you have to complete these sentences with* **said, told** *or* **talked**.
Example: Tom ......*said*...... that he didn't like Brian.

1   Jack .... me that he was enjoying his new job.
2   Tom .... it was a nice restaurant but I didn't like it much.
3   The doctor .... that I would have to rest for at least a week.
4   Mrs Taylor .... us she wouldn't be able to come to the next meeting.
5   Ann .... Tom that she was going away.
6   George couldn't help me. He .... to ask Jack.
7   At the meeting the chairman .... about the problems facing the company.
8   Jill .... us all about her holiday in Australia.

48.3   *Now you have to read a sentence and write a new sentence with the same meaning.*
Examples: 'Listen carefully', he said to us. He told   *us to listen carefully.*
'Don't wait for me if I'm late', Ann said.
Ann said   *not to wait for her if she was late.*

1   'Eat more fruit and vegetables', the doctor said.
The doctor said ....
2   'Read the instructions before you switch on the machine', he said to me.
He told ....
3   'Shut the door but don't lock it', she said to us.
She told ....
4   'Can you speak more slowly? I can't understand', he said to me.
He asked .... because ....
5   'Don't come before 6 o'clock', I said to him.
I told ....

UNIT 49   Questions (1)

a) We usually make questions by changing the word order: we put the *auxiliary verb* (*AV*) before the *subject* (*S*):   S + AV   AV+ S

it	is	→ is	it? **Is it** raining?
you	can	→ can	you? When **can you** come and see us?
Tom	has	→ has	Tom? Where **has Tom** gone?

We make questions with the verb **be** in the same way:

they were → were they?   **Were they** surprised?

b) In *present simple* questions use **do/does**:
- **Do you like** music? (*not* 'like you')
- Where **does Jack live**? (*not* 'where lives Jack')

In *past simple* questions use **did**:
- When **did they get** married? (*not* 'when got they')
- Why **did Ann sell** her car? (*not* 'why sold Ann')

But be careful with **who/what/which** questions. If **who/what/which** is the *subject* of the sentence, do not use **do/does/did**. Compare:

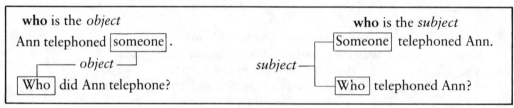

In these examples **who/what/which** is the *subject*:
- **Who wants** something to eat? (*not* 'who does want')
- **Who invented** the steam engine? (*not* 'who did invent')
- **What happened** to you last night? (*not* 'what did happen')
- **Which switch operates** this machine? (*not* 'which switch does operate')

c) *Negative questions*

> We use negative questions especially:
> *to show surprise*:
> **Didn't you hear** the bell? I rang it four times.
>
> *in exclamations*(*!*):
> **Doesn't that dress look** nice! (= that dress looks nice)
>
> *when we expect the listener to agree with us*:
> '**Haven't we met** somewhere before?'   'Yes, I think we have.'

Notice the meaning of **yes** and **no** in answers to negative questions:
- **Didn't Dave go** to Canada?⌈ **Yes.**   (= Yes, he went.)
                               ⌊ **No.**   (= No, he didn't go.)

Note the word order in negative questions with **Why ...?**:
- **Why didn't you lock** the door? (*not* 'why you didn't lock')
- **Why don't we go** out for a meal? (*not* 'why we don't go')

98

49.1 *In this exercise you have to ask questions about Ed and Liz.*
   Examples: (Ed and Liz / be / married?)   Are Ed and Liz married?   'Yes, they are.'
   (they / have / any children?)   Have they got any children?   'Yes, three.'

   1 (where / Ed and Liz live?)   ....   'In Nottingham.'
   2 (how long / they / be / married?)   ....   '15 years.'
   3 (they / go out very often?)   ....   'No, not very often.'
   4 (what / Ed do for a living?)   ....   'He's a policeman.'
   5 (he / enjoy his job?)   ....   'Yes, very much.'
   6 (he / arrest anyone yesterday?)   ....   'No.'
   7 (they / have / a car?)   ....   'Yes.'
   8 (when / they / buy it?)   ....   'A year ago.'
   9 (how much / it cost?)   ....   '£3,000.'
   10 (they / go / on holiday next summer?)   ....   'Yes.'
   11 (where / they / go?)   ....   'To Scotland.'

49.2 *This time you have to make questions with* **who** *or* **what**.
   Examples: 'Somebody hit me.' 'Who hit you ?'
   'I hit somebody.' 'Who did you hit ?'

   1 'Something happened.' 'What .... ?'
   2 'Someone lives in that house.' 'Who .... ?'
   3 'Somebody gave me this key.' 'Who .... ?'
   4 'Henry gave me something.' 'What .... ?'
   5 'Tom meets someone every day.' 'Who .... ?'
   6 'I fell over something.' 'What .... ?'
   7 'Something fell on the floor.' 'What .... ?'
   8 'This word means something.' 'What .... ?'

49.3 *Now you have to make negative questions. Each time you are surprised.*
   Example: 'We won't see Ann this evening.' 'Oh! (she / not / come / to the party tonight?)'
      Isn't she coming to the party tonight?

   1 'I hope we don't meet Brian tonight.' 'Why? (you / not / like him?)' ....
   ....
   2 'I'll have to borrow some money.' 'Why? (you / not / have / any?)' ....
   ....
   3 'Don't go and see that film.' 'Why? (it / not / be / good?)' ....
   ....

49.4 *In this exercise you have to make exclamations (!).*
   Example: You think that dress looks nice. Doesn't that dress look nice !

   1 You think it's a lovely day. .... !
   2 You think it was a good film. .... !
   3 You think everything is expensive these days. .... !
   4 You think Tom looked well. .... !

UNIT 50 Questions (2) (**Do you know where ...?** / **He asked me where ...**)

a) When we ask people for information, we sometimes begin our question with **Do you know ...?** or **Could you tell me ...?**. If you begin a question like this, the word order is different from a simple question:

> Compare: Where has Tom gone?   (*simple question*)
>
> **Do you know** where Tom has gone?

When the question (**Where has Tom gone?**) is part of a bigger sentence (**Do you know ...**), it loses the normal question word order. Compare:
- When **will Ann arrive?**   Have you any idea when **Ann will arrive?**
- What time **is it?**   Could you tell me what time **it is?**
- Why **are you laughing?**   Tell us why **you are laughing.**

Be careful with **do/does/did** questions:
- When **does the film begin?**   Do you know when **the film begins?**
- Why **did Ann leave** early?   I wonder why **Ann left** early.

Use **if** or **whether** where there is no other question word:
- Did he see you?   Do you know **if** (or **whether**) he saw you?

b) The same changes in word order happen in *reported* questions:

direct   The policeman said to us,   'Where   are you going ?'

reported   The policeman asked us   where   we were going .

direct   Tom said, 'What time   do the banks close ?'

reported   Tom wanted to know what time   the banks closed .

In reported questions the verb usually changes to the past (**were, closed**). For more information about this see Unit 47.

Now study these examples. Here are some of the questions you were asked at an interview for a job:

> How old are you?
>
> What do you do in your spare time?
>
> How long have you been working in your present job?
>
> Can you type?
>
> Why did you apply for the job?
>
> Have you got a driving licence?
>
> *you*

Now you tell a friend (in reported speech) what the interviewer asked you:
- She asked (me) how old **I was.**
- She enquired whether (*or* if) **I had** a driving licence. (*or* **had got**)
- She wanted to know whether (*or* if) **I could** type.
- She asked (me) what **I did** in my spare time.
- She wanted to know how long **I had been** working in my present job.
- She asked (me) why **I had applied** for the job. (*or* 'why **I applied**')

100

UNIT 50   Exercises

50.1   *In this exercise you have to make a new sentence from these questions.*
Example: Where has Tom gone?   Do you know <u>where Tom has gone</u> ?

  1   Where is the post office?   Could you tell me .... ?
  2   What does this word mean?   Do you know .... ?
  3   What's the time?   I wonder ....
  4   Where did you park your car?   Can't you remember .... ?
  5   Is Ann coming to the meeting?   I don't know ....
  6   Where does Jack live?   Have you any idea .... ?
  7   What time did he leave?   Do you know .... ?
  8   Where can I change some money?   Could you tell me .... ?
  9   What qualifications do I need?   I want to know ....
10   Why didn't Tom come to the party?   I don't know ....
11   How much does it cost to park here?   Do you know .... ?

50.2   *You are making a phone call. You want to speak to Sue but she isn't there. Someone else answers the phone. You want to know three things: (1)* **where has she gone?** *(2)* **when will she be back?** *and (3)* **did she go out alone?** *Complete the conversation:*

1   'Do you know .... ?'   ' Sorry. I've got no idea.'
2   'Never mind. I don't suppose you know ....'   'No, I'm afraid I don't.'
3   'One more thing. Do you happen to know .... ?'   'I'm afraid I didn't see her go out.'

50.3   *You have been away for a while and have just come back to your home town. You meet Gerry, a friend of yours. He asks you lots of questions:*

1 How are you?	5 Are you glad to be back?	6 Are you going away again?
2 How long have you been back?		7 Why did you come back?
3 What are you doing now?		8 Do you still smoke?
4 Where are you living?		9 Can you come to dinner on Friday?

Now you tell another friend what Gerry asked you. Use reported speech.

1   <u>He asked me how I was.</u>
2   He asked me ....
3   He asked ....
4   He ....
5   ....
6   ....
7   ....
8   ....
9   ....

UNIT 51   Auxiliary verbs in short answers, short questions etc.
So am I / Neither am I
I think so / I hope so etc.

a)

> **Can** you swim?   I **have** lost my key.   He **might** not come.

In these sentences **can, have** and **might** are *auxiliary* (= helping) verbs.
We often use auxiliary verbs when we don't want to repeat something:
  - 'Are you working tomorrow?'   'Yes, I **am**.' (= I am working tomorrow)
  - He could lend us the money but he **won't**. (= he won't lend us the money)
Use **do/does/did** for present and past simple short answers:
  - 'Does he smoke?'   'He **did** but he **doesn't** any more.'

b)   We use auxiliary verbs in short questions:
  - 'It rained every day during our holiday.'   '**Did** it?'
  - 'Ann isn't very well today.'   'Oh, **isn't** she?'
  - 'I've just seen Tom.'   'Oh, **have** you? How is he?'
These short questions (**Did it?, isn't she?, have you?**) are not real questions. We use them to show polite interest in what someone has said and they help to keep the conversation going.

Sometimes we use short questions to show surprise:
  - 'Jim and Nora are getting married.'   '**Are they?** Really?'

c)   We also use auxiliary verbs with **so** and **neither**:
  - 'I'm feeling tired.'   '**So am I.**' (= I am feeling tired too)
  - 'I never read newspapers.'   '**Neither do I.**' (= I never read them either)
Note the word order after **so** and **neither** (*verb* before *subject*):
  - I passed the exam and **so did Tom.** (*not* 'so Tom did')
Nor can be used instead of **neither**:
  - 'I can't remember his name.'   '**Nor** can I. / **Neither** can I.'
Not ... either can be used instead of **neither** and **nor**:
  - 'I haven't got any money.'   '**Neither** have I.' *or* 'I **haven't either.**'

d)   **I think so / hope so** etc.
We use **so** in this way after a number of verbs, especially **think, hope, expect, suppose** and **I'm afraid**:
  - 'Is she English?'   '**I think so.**'
  - 'Will Tom come?'   '**I expect so.**'
  - 'Has Ann been invited to the party?'   '**I suppose so.**'
The negative form depends on the verb:

I think so / I expect so   – **I don't think so / I don't expect so**
I hope so / I'm afraid so – **I hope not / I'm afraid not**
I suppose so   – **I don't suppose so** *or* **I suppose not**

  - 'Is she American?'   '**I don't think so.**'
  - 'Is it going to rain?'   '**I hope not.**' (*not* 'I don't hope so')

102

UNIT 51 Exercises

51.1 *In this exercise you are talking to someone. Answer him in the way shown.*
Examples: I'm hungry.   Are you? I'm not.
I'm not tired.   Aren't you? I am.

1 I like Brian. ....
2 I can't ride a horse. ....
3 I've got plenty of friends. ....
4 I didn't enjoy the film much. ....
5 I'd get married if I were in Tom's position. ....
6 I don't like living in the country. ....
7 I'm not going to have anything to eat. ....
8 I've never been to America. ....
9 I thought the exam was quite easy. ....

51.2 *Here too you are talking to someone. You have the same ideas, taste etc. as your friend. Use*
So ... *or* **Neither ...** *each time.*
Examples: I'm feeling tired.   So am I.   I don't like eggs.   Neither do I.

1 I need a holiday. ....
2 I don't like milk. ....
3 I couldn't get up this morning. ....
....
4 I'd love a cup of tea. ....
5 I've never been to Africa. ....

6 I was ill yesterday. ....
7 I should smoke less. ....
8 I spent the whole evening watching
television. ....
9 I didn't know that Ann was in
hospital. ....

51.3 *Now you have to answer with* **I think so, I hope not** *etc. You are B in each conversation. Read*
the information in brackets before you answer each question.
Example: (You hate rain.)   A: Is it going to rain?   B: (hope) I hope not.

1 (You need more money quickly.)
A: Do you think you'll get a pay increase soon?   B: (hope) ....
2 (You think Tom will probably get the job which he applied for.)
A: I wonder if Tom will get the job.   B: (expect) ....
3 (You're not sure whether Jill is married – probably not.)
A: Is Jill married?   B: (think) ....
4 (You haven't got any money.)
A: Can you lend me some money?   B: (afraid) ....
5 (Your friend's sister has been badly injured in an accident.)
A: Is she badly injured?   B: (afraid) ....
6 (Ann normally works every day, Monday to Friday – tomorrow is Wednesday.)
A: Is Ann working tomorrow?   B: (suppose) ....
7 (You're in a hurry to catch your train – it's important that you don't miss it.)
A: Do you think we're going to miss the train?   B: (hope) ....
8 (You're not sure but the concert probably begins at 7.30.)
A: Does the concert begin at 7.30?   B: (think) ....

UNIT 52   Question tags (**are you? doesn't he?** etc.)

a)

> You haven't got a car, **have you?**   It was a good film, **wasn't it?**

Have you? and **wasn't it?** are *question tags* (= mini-questions which we put on the end of a sentence). In question tags we use the auxiliary verb (see Unit 51a). For the present and past simple use **do/does/did**:

— They came by car, **didn't they?**

b) Normally we use a positive question tag with a negative sentence:

> *negative sentence +*   *positive tag*
> Tom **won't** be late,   **will he?**
> They **don't** like us,   **do they?**
> That **isn't** George over there,   **is it?**

And normally we use a negative question tag with a positive sentence:

> *positive sentence +*   *negative tag*
> Ann **will** be here soon,   **won't she?**
> Tom **should** pass his exam,   **shouldn't he?**
> They **were** very angry,   **weren't they?**

Notice the meaning of **yes** and **no** in answers to question tags:

— You're not going to work today, are you? $\begin{cases} \textbf{Yes.} \text{ (= I am going)} \\ \textbf{No.} \text{ (= I'm not going)} \end{cases}$

c) The meaning of a question tag depends on how you say it. If the voice goes *down*, you aren't really asking a question; you are only asking the other person to agree with you:

— 'Tom doesn't look very well today, does he?' 'No, he looks awful.'
— She's very attractive. She's got beautiful eyes, hasn't she?

But if the voice goes *up*, it is a real question:

— 'You haven't seen Ann today, have you?' 'No, I'm afraid not.'
  (= Have you seen Ann today?)

We often use a *negative sentence + positive tag* to ask for things or information, or to ask someone to do something. The voice goes up at the end of the tag in sentences like these:

— 'You haven't got a cigarette , have you?' 'Yes, here you are.'
— 'You couldn't do me a favour, could you?' 'It depends what it is.'
— 'You don't know where Ann is, do you?' 'Sorry, I've no idea.'

d) After **Let's ...** the question tag is **shall we?**:

— **Let's** go out for a walk, **shall we?**

After the imperative (**do/don't do** something) the tag is **will you?**:

— **Open** the door, **will you?**   — **Don't** be late, **will you?**

Notice that we say **aren't I?** (= am I not):

— I'm late, **aren't I?**

104

UNIT 52 Exercises

52.1 *In this exercise you have to put a question tag on the end of each sentence.*
Examples: Tom won't be late, ...*will he*........?   They were very angry, ...*weren't they*...?

1 Ann's on holiday, ...?
2 You weren't listening, ...?
3 Sue doesn't like onions, ...?
4 Jack's applied for the job, ...?
5 You've got a camera, ...?
6 You can type, ...?
7 He won't mind if I go early, ...?
8 Tom could help you, ...?
9 There are a lot of people here, ...?
10 Let's have dinner, ...?
11 This isn't very interesting, ...?
12 I'm too fat, ...?
13 You wouldn't tell anyone, ...?
14 Listen, ...?
15 I shouldn't have got angry, ...?
16 Don't drop it, ...?
17 They had to go home, ...?
18 He'd never seen you before, ...?

52.2 *This time you have to read a situation and then write a sentence with a question tag. In each example you are asking your listener to agree with you.*
Example: You are with a friend outside a restaurant. You are looking at the prices. It's very expensive. What do you say?   *It's very expensive, isn't it?*

1 You look out of the window. <u>It's a beautiful day.</u> What do you say to your friend?
It's ....
2 You've just come out of the cinema with your friend. You both really enjoyed the film. You thought <u>it was great.</u> What do you say?   The film ....
3 Tom's hair is much shorter. Clearly <u>he has had his hair cut.</u> What do you say to him?
You ....
4 You are shopping. You are trying on a jacket. You look in the mirror: <u>it doesn't look very nice.</u> What do you say to your friend?   It ....
5 You are talking about Bill. You know that <u>Bill works very hard.</u> Everyone knows this. What do you say about Bill?   Bill ....

52.3 *In these situations you are asking people for information, asking people to do things etc. Make sentences like those in section c.*
Example: You want a cigarette. Perhaps Tom has got one. Ask him.
Tom, you haven't got a cigarette, have you?

1 Jack is just going out. You want him to get some stamps. Ask him.
Jack, you ....
2 You're looking for Ann. Perhaps Tom knows where she is. Ask him.
Tom, you ....
3 You need a bicycle pump. Perhaps Tom has got one. Ask him.
Tom, ...
4 Ann has a car and you don't want to walk home. You want her to give you a lift. Ask her.
Ann, ...
5 You're looking for your purse. Perhaps Tom has seen it. Ask him.
....

UNIT 53   Verb +-ing

a)

stop	enjoy	fancy	admit	consider	miss
finish	mind	imagine	deny	involve	postpone
delay	suggest	regret	avoid	practise	risk

If these verbs are followed by another verb, the structure is usually *verb + -ing*:
- **Stop** talking!
- I'll do the shopping when I've **finished** cleaning the flat.
- I don't **fancy** going out this evening.
- Have you ever **considered** going to live in another country?
- I can't **imagine** George riding a motor-bike.
- When I'm on holiday, I **enjoy not** having to get up early.

The following expressions also take -ing:

give up (= stop)	**put off** (= postpone)	**keep** *or* **keep on** (= do something
go on (= continue)	**carry on** (= continue)	continuously or repeatedly)

- Are you going to **give up** smoking?
- She **kept** (**on**) interrupting me while I was speaking.

Note the *passive* form (**being done / being seen / being told** etc.):
- I don't mind **being told** what to do.

You cannot normally use the *infinitive* (**to do / to dance** etc.) after these verbs and expressions:
- I **enjoy** dancing. (*not* 'to dance')
- Would you **mind** closing the door? (*not* 'to close')
- Tom **suggested** going to the cinema. (*not* 'to go')

b) When you are talking about finished actions, you can also say **having done / having stolen** etc. But it is not necessary to use this form. You can also use the simple **-ing** form for finished actions:
- He admitted **stealing** (*or* **having stolen**) the money.
- They now regret **getting** (*or* **having got**) married.

c) With some of the verbs in this unit (especially **admit, deny, regret** and **suggest**) you can also use a **that ...** structure:
- He **denied that** he had stolen the money. (*or* **denied** stealing)
- Tom **suggested that** we went to the cinema. (*or* **suggested** going)

For **suggest** see also Unit 35c.

For verbs +-**ing** see also Units 56 and 57.

UNIT 53   Exercises

53.1 *In this exercise you have to complete the sentences with these verbs:*

try	steal	meet	look	write	make	be knocked
wash	~~play~~	eat	splash	go	drive	take

Example: Do you fancy ....*playing*........ tennis this afternoon?

1 Could you please stop .... so much noise?
2 I don't enjoy .... letters.
3 Does your job involve .... a lot of people?
4 I considered .... the job but in the end I decided against it.
5 If you use the shower, try and avoid .... water on the floor.
6 Jack gave up .... to find a job in Britain and decided to emigrate.
7 Have you finished .... your hair yet?
8 The phone rang while Ann was having her dinner. She didn't answer it; she just carried on ....
9 He admitted .... the car but denied .... it dangerously.
10 Why do you keep on .... at me like that?
11 They had to postpone .... away because their son was ill.
12 If you walk into the road without looking, you risk .... down by a car.

53.2 *This time you have to read a sentence and write a second sentence with the same meaning. Begin your sentence in the way shown.*
Examples: Do you have to travel in your job?   Does your job involve *travelling* .... ?
He is now sorry that he didn't study harder when he was at college.
He now regrets *not studying harder when he was at college.* ....

1 I don't want to go out this evening.   I don't fancy ....
2 Are you sorry you didn't take the job? Do you regret .... ?
3 Why don't you go away tomorrow instead of today?
   Why don't you put off .... until .... ?
4 It's not a good idea to travel during the rush-hour.
   It's better to avoid ....
5 Could you turn the radio down, please?
   Would you mind .... ?
6 The driver of the car said it was true that he didn't have a licence.
   The driver of the car admitted ....
7 Tom said 'Let's have fish for dinner'.
   Tom suggested ....

53.3 *Now make your own sentences. Complete each sentence using -ing.*
Example: I really enjoy *going for long walks in the country.* ....

1 At weekends I enjoy ....
2 This evening I fancy ....
3 I often regret ....
4 Learning English involves ....
5 I think people should stop ....

UNIT 54   Verb + infinitive

a)

agree	offer	decide	appear	forget
refuse	attempt	plan	seem	learn (how)
promise	manage	arrange	pretend	dare
threaten	fail	hope	afford	tend

If these verbs are followed by another verb, the structure is usually *verb* + **to** + *infinitive*:
- As it was late, we **decided to take** a taxi home.
- I like George but I think he **tends to talk** too much.
- How old were you when you **learnt to drive**? (*or* 'learnt how to drive')
- They **agreed to lend** me some money when I told them the position I was in.

Note these examples with the *negative* **not to ...**:
- We **decided not to go** out because of the weather.
- He **pretended not to see** me as he passed me in the street.

With other important verbs you cannot use the infinitive. For example **think** and **suggest**:
- Are you **thinking of buying** a car? (*not* 'thinking to buy')
- Tom **suggested going** to the cinema. (*not* 'suggested to go')

b) There is a *continuous* infinitive (**to be doing**) and a *perfect* infinitive (**to have done**). We use these especially after **seem, appear** and **pretend**:
- I **pretended to be reading**. (= I pretended that I was reading)
- You **seem to have lost** weight. (= it seems that you have lost weight)

c) After **dare** you can use the infinitive with or without **to**:
- I wouldn't **dare to ask** him.   *or*   I wouldn't **dare ask** him.

But after **daren't** you must use the infinitive without **to**:
- I **daren't tell** him what happened. (*not* 'daren't to tell')

d) After the following verbs you can use a question word (**what/where/how** etc.) + **to** + infinitive:

ask   decide   know   remember   forget   explain   understand

We **asked**	how	to get	to the station.
Have you **decided**	where	to go	for your holidays?
Tom **explained** (to me)	how	to change	the wheel of the car.
I don't **know**	whether	to go	to the party or not.

Also: **show/tell/ask** someone **what/how/where** to do something:
- Can someone **show me how to change** the film in this camera?
- Ask Jack. He'll **tell you what to do**.

For verbs + infinitive see also Units 55–7.

108

UNIT 54　Exercises

54.1　*In this exercise you have to complete each sentence with a suitable verb.*
Example: Don't forget ....*to post*........ the letter I gave you.

1　Tom refused .... me any money.
2　Jill has decided not .... a car.
3　The thief got into the house because I forgot .... the window.
4　There was a lot of traffic but we managed .... to the airport in time.
5　I've arranged .... tennis tomorrow afternoon.
6　One day I'd like to learn .... an aeroplane.
7　I shouted to him. He pretended not .... me but I'm sure he did.
8　Why hasn't Sue arrived yet? She promised not .... late.
9　Our neighbour threatened .... the police if we didn't stop the noise.
10　Ann offered .... after our children while we were out.
11　The teacher was very strict. Nobody dared .... during his lessons.

54.2　*This time you have to make sentences with* **seem** *and* **appear**.
Examples: Is he waiting for someone?　He appears *to be waiting for someone.*
　　　　　Has she lost weight?　　　She seems *to have lost weight*

1　Is Tom worried about something?　He seems ....
2　Does Ann like Jack?　　　　　　She appears ....
3　Is that man looking for something?　He appears ....
4　Has that car broken down?　　　It seems ....
5　Have they gone out?　　　　　　They appear ....

54.3　*Now you have to use the structure in section d. Complete each sentence using* **what** *or* **how** *with one of the following verbs:*
do　　say　　~~get~~　　use　　ride　　cook
Example: Do you know ....*how to get*........ to John's house?

1　Have you decided *what*................................ for dinner this evening?
2　Can you show me .... the washing machine?
3　Do you know .... if there's a fire in the building?
4　You'll never forget .... a bicycle once you have learned.
5　I was really astonished. I didn't know ....

54.4　*Now make your own sentences. Complete each sentence with* **to** + *infinitive.*
Example: This evening I have arranged *to go to the theatre*

1　Not many people can afford ....
2　I would like to learn ....
3　One day I hope ....
4　I wouldn't dare ....
5　Sometimes I tend ....

UNIT 55   Verb + object + infinitive

a)

want   ask   expect   help   mean (= intend)   **would like**   **would prefer**

There are two possible structures after these verbs:

verb + **to** + *infinitive*	*verb* + *object* + **to** + *infinitive*
I **asked to see** the manager.	I **asked Tom to help** me.
We **expected to be** late.	We **expected him to be** late.
He **would like to come.**	He **would like me to come.**

After **help** you can use the infinitive with or without **to**:
- Can somebody **help me (to) move** this table?

Be especially careful with **want**. Do not say 'want that ...':
- Everyone **wanted him to win** the race. (*not* 'wanted that he won')
- Do you **want me to come** early? (*not* 'want that I come')

b)

tell	remind	force	enable	persuade
order	warn	invite	teach (how)	get (= persuade)

These verbs have the structure *verb* + *object* + **to** + *infinitive*:
- **Remind me to phone** Ann tomorrow.   – Who **taught you (how) to drive?**
- He **warned me not to touch** anything.   – I **got Jack to repair** my car.

Here is an example in the *passive*:
- I **was warned not to touch** anything.

You cannot use **suggest** with this structure (see also Unit 35c):
- Tom **suggested that I bought** a car. (*not* 'Tom suggested me to buy')

c)

advise   recommend   encourage   allow   permit

There are two possible structures after these verbs. Compare:

verb + **-ing** (without an object)	*verb* + *object* + **to** + *infinitive*
He doesn't **allow smoking** in his house.	He doesn't **allow anyone to smoke** in his house.
I wouldn't **recommend staying** at that hotel.	I wouldn't **recommend you to stay** at that hotel.

d) Make and let

These verbs have the structure *verb* + *infinitive* (without **to**):
- Hot weather **makes me feel** uncomfortable. (= causes me to feel)
- I only did it because they **made me do it.** (= forced me to do it)
- She wouldn't **let me read** the letter. (= allow me to read)

Remember that **make** and **let** have the infinitive without **to**:
- They **made me do it.** (*not* 'they made me to do it')
- Tom **let me drive** his car yesterday. (*not* 'Tom let me to drive')

But in the *passive* **make** has the infinitive with **to**:
- I only did it because I **was made to do it.**

UNIT 55   Exercises

55.1 *Read each sentence and write a second sentence from the words given.*
Example: Jill didn't have any money.
    she / want / Ann / lend her some   *She wanted Ann to lend her some.*

1 Tom's parents were disappointed when he decided to leave home.
    they / want / Tom / stay with them   ....
2 Please don't tell anyone that I'm leaving my job.
    I / not / want / anyone / know   ....
3 There's a football match next Saturday between England and Scotland.
    you / want / Scotland / win?   ....
4 Unfortunately someone had told Sue that I was going to visit her.
    I / want / it / be a surprise   ....

55.2 *Now you have to read a sentence and then write a second sentence with the same meaning.*
Each time begin in the way shown.
Examples: 'Don't touch anything', the man said to me.
    The man told *me not to touch anything.*
    My father said I could use his car.   My father allowed *me to use his car.*

1 'Don't forget to post the letter', Jack said to me.
    Jack reminded   ....
2 She told me that it would be best if I told the police about the accident.
    She advised   ....
3 I told you that you shouldn't tell him anything.
    I warned   ....
4 I was surprised that it rained.   I didn't expect   ....
5 'Would you like to have dinner with me?' Tom said to Ann.
    Tom invited   ....
6 At first I didn't want to play tennis but John persuaded me.
    John persuaded   ....
7 The sudden noise caused me to jump.   The sudden noise made   ....
8 If you've got a car, you are able to travel around more easily.
    Having a car enables   ....
9 She wouldn't allow me to read the letter.   She wouldn't let   ....

55.3 *Now put the verb in the right form: -ing, to + infinitive, or infinitive without to.*
Example: Mr Thomas doesn't allow ......*smoking*...... (smoke) in his office.

1 Mr Thomas doesn't let anyone .... (smoke) in his office.
2 I don't know Jack but I'd like .... (meet) him.
3 Where would you recommend me .... (go) for my holidays?
4 I don't recommend .... (eat) in that restaurant. The food's awful.
5 The film was very sad. It made me .... (cry).
6 Jack's parents have always encouraged him .... (study) hard.
7 We were kept at the police station for an hour and then allowed .... (go).

111

UNIT 56   Infinitive or -ing? (1) – like, would like etc.

a)

like	hate	enjoy	can't bear
dislike	love	mind	can't stand

These verbs and expressions are often followed by **-ing**:

- I **enjoy** being alone.
- Why do you **dislike** living here?
- I **don't like** people shouting at me.
- Ann **hates** flying.
- Tom **doesn't mind** working at night.

After **love** and **can't bear**, you can use **-ing** or **to** + *infinitive*:

- I **love** meeting people.   *or*   I **love to meet** people.
- She **can't bear** being alone.   *or*   She **can't bear to be** alone.

b) Like

Often it doesn't matter whether you say 'I like **doing**' or 'I like **to do**'. For example, you can say:

- I **like getting** up early.   *or*   I **like to get** up early.

We usually say 'I like **doing**' when 'like' means 'enjoy':

- Do you **like** cooking? (= do you enjoy it?)
- I don't **like** driving. (= I don't enjoy it.)

When 'like' does not mean 'enjoy', we use 'I like **to do**'. **I like to do something** = I find it is good or right to do something:

- I **like to wash** my hair twice a week. (This doesn't mean that I enjoy it; it means that I think it is a good thing to do.)
- Tom **likes to do** the washing-up immediately after the meal.

c) Would like is followed by **to** + *infinitive*:

- I **would like to be** rich.
- **Would you like to come** to a party?

Notice the difference in meaning between **I like** and **I would like**. **I would like** is a polite way of saying **I want**. Compare:

- I **like** playing tennis. (= I enjoy it in general)
- I **would like to play** tennis today. (= I want to play)

See also Unit 31d.

We also use **to** + *infinitive* after **would love/hate/prefer**:

- **Would** you **prefer to have** dinner now or later?
- I'd **love to be able** to travel round the world.

d) You can also say 'I would like **to have done** something' (= I regret that I didn't or couldn't do something):

- It's a pity we didn't visit Tom. I **would like to have seen** him again.
- We'd **like to have gone** on holiday but we didn't have enough money.

The same structure is possible after **would love/hate/prefer**:

- Poor old Tom! I **would hate to have been** in his position.
- I'd **love to have gone** to the party but it was impossible.

UNIT 56 Exercises

56.1 *Answer these questions using the verbs given.*
Examples: Why do you never fly? (hate)   I hate flying.
Why does Tom go to the cinema so often? (like)   He likes going to the cinema.

1 Why do you always wear a hat? (like)   I ....
2 Why does Ann watch television so often? (enjoy)   She ....
3 Why do you never go to the cinema? (not/like) ....
4 Why does Jack take so many photographs? (like) ....
5 Why don't you work in the evenings? (hate) ....

56.2 *This time put the verb into the correct form, **-ing** or **to** + infinitive.*
Examples: I enjoy ....being.......... (be) alone.
Would you like ....to come........ (come) to a party?

1 Do you mind .... (travel) such a long way to work every day?
2 Ann loves .... (cook) but she hates .... (wash) up.
3 I can't stand people .... (tell) me what to do when I'm driving.
4 I don't like that house. I would hate .... (live) there.
5 Do you like .... (drive)?
6 When I have to catch a train, I'm always worried about missing it. So I like
   .... (get) to the station in plenty of time.
7 I very much enjoy .... (listen) to classical music.
8 I would love .... (come) to your wedding but it just isn't possible.
9 Sometime I'd like .... (learn) to play the guitar.

56.3 *Now you have to make your own sentences. Say whether you like or don't like the things in
brackets (...). Choose one of these verbs for each of your sentences:*
(don't) like   love   hate   enjoy   don't mind   can't stand
Example: (reading)   I like reading very much.

1 (playing cards)   I ....
2 (learning languages) ....
3 (visiting museums) ....
4 (lying on the beach in the sun) ....
5 (shopping) ....

56.4 *Now you have to write sentences like those in section d.*
Example: It's a pity I couldn't go to the wedding. (like)
       I would like to have gone to the wedding.

1 It's a pity I didn't meet Ann. (love)   I would love ....
2 I'm glad I didn't lose my watch. (hate)   I ....
3 I'm glad I wasn't alone. (not/like) ....
4 It's a pity I couldn't travel by train. (prefer) ....
5 It's a pity I didn't see the film. (like) ....

113

UNIT 57
Infinitive or -ing? (2) – begin, start, intend, continue, remember, try

a)

begin	start	intend	continue

These verbs can usually be followed by **-ing** or **to** + *infinitive*. So you can say:
- The baby **began crying.**   *or*   The baby **began to cry.**
- It has **started raining.**   *or*   It has **started to rain.**
- John **intends buying** a house.   *or*   John **intends to buy** a house.
- He **continued working** after his illness.   *or*   He **continued to work** after his illness.

b) **Remember to do** and **remember doing**
You **remember to do** something *before* you do it. **Remember to do something** is the opposite of 'forget to do something':
- I **remembered to lock** the door before I left but I forgot to shut the windows. (= I remembered to lock the door and then I locked it)
- Please **remember to post** the letter. (= don't forget to post it)

You **remember doing** something *after* you do it. **I remember doing something** = I did something and now I remember it:
- I clearly **remember locking** the door before I left. (= I locked it and now I clearly remember this)
- He could **remember driving** along the road just before the accident happened but he couldn't remember the accident itself.

c) **Try to do** and **try doing**
Try to do = attempt to do, make an effort to do:
- I was very tired. I **tried to keep** my eyes open but I couldn't.
- Please **try to be** quiet when you come home. Everyone will be asleep.

Try doing
Try also means 'do something as an experiment or test':
- **Try** some of this juice – perhaps you'll like it. (= drink some of it to see if you like it)
- We **tried** every hotel in the town but they were all full. (= we went to every hotel to see if they had a room)
If **try** (with this meaning) is followed by a verb, we say **try -ing**:
- 'I can't find anywhere to live.' 'Why don't you **try putting** an advertisement in the newspaper?' (= do this to see if it helps you to find a place to live)
- I've got a terrible headache. I **tried taking** an aspirin but it didn't help. (= I took an aspirin to see if it would stop my headache)

UNIT 57   Exercises

57.1 *Here is some information about Tom when he was a child.*

1 He was in hospital when he was four.
2 He went to Paris when he was eight.
3 He fell into the river.
4 He cried on his first day at school.
5 He said he wanted to be a doctor.
6 He was bitten by a dog.

He can still remember 1, 2 and 4. But he can't remember 3, 5 and 6. Make sentences beginning **He can remember ...** *or* **He can't remember ...** .

1 *He can remember being in hospital.*
2 ....
3 ....
4 ....
5 ....
6 ....

57.2 *Your friend has some problems and you have to be helpful. For each problem write a question with* **try.**

Example: I can't find anywhere to live. (put an advertisement in the newspaper)
Have you tried putting an advertisement in the newspaper?

1 My electric shaver is not working. (change the batteries)
Have you tried ....
2 I can't contact Fred. He's not at home. (phone him at work)
Have you ....
3 I'm having difficulty sleeping at night. (take sleeping tablets)
Have ....
4 The television picture isn't very good. (move the aerial)
....

57.3 *In this exercise you have to put the verb into the correct form,* **-ing** *or* **to** + *infinitive.* *(Sometimes either form is possible.)*

Examples: Please remember ....*to post*............... (post) this letter.
John intends ...*to buy (or buying)* (buy) a house.

1 A: You lent me some money a few months ago.
    B: Did I? That's strange. I don't remember .... (lend) you any money.
2 We tried .... (put) the fire out but we were unsuccessful. We had to call the fire-brigade.
3 When you see Tom, remember .... (give) him my regards, won't you?
4 What do you intend .... (do) about this problem?
5 Someone must have taken my bag. I clearly remember .... (leave) it by the window and now it has gone.
6 When she saw what had happened, she began .... (laugh) loudly.
7 Sue needed some money. She tried .... (ask) Gerry but he couldn't help her.
8 He tried .... (reach) the shelf but he wasn't tall enough.
9 'Did you remember .... (phone) Ann?'   'Oh no, I completely forgot.'
10 I asked them to be quiet but they continued .... (make) a lot of noise.

UNIT 58   Infinitive or -ing? (3) – be afraid, need, help

a) **Be afraid to do** and **be afraid of -ing**
I am afraid to do something = I don't want to do something because it is dangerous or the result could be unpleasant:
  - The streets in this city are not safe at night. Many people are **afraid to go** out alone. (= they don't want to go out alone because it is dangerous)
  - She was **afraid to tell** her parents that she had broken the neighbour's window. (= she didn't want to tell her parents because she knew they would be angry)

I am afraid of something happening = there is a possibility that something bad will happen:
  - We walked along the path very carefully because it was icy and we were **afraid of falling**. (*not* 'afraid to fall')
  - I don't like dogs. I'm always **afraid of being** bitten. (*not* 'afraid to be bitten')

So, you are afraid **to do** something because you are afraid **of something happening** as a result. Compare:
  - The boys were afraid **to play** football in the garden because they were afraid **of breaking** a window.
  - I was afraid **to stay** in the sun because I was afraid **of getting** burnt.

b) **Need to do** and **need -ing**
I need to do something = it is necessary for me to do something:
  - I **need to take** more exercise.
  - He **needs to work** harder.
  - I don't **need to come** to the meeting, do I?

Need -ing = need to be done (so the meaning is *passive*):
  - The batteries in this radio **need changing**. (= need to be changed)
  - This jacket is rather dirty. It **needs cleaning**. (= needs to be cleaned)
  - Do you think the grass **needs cutting**? (= needs to be cut)

c) **Help**
Help is followed by the infinitive with or without **to**:
  - Everybody **helped** (**to**) **clean** up after the party.
  - Can somebody **help** me (**to**) **move** this table?
But there is also an expression '**can't help doing** something'. **I can't help doing something** = I can't stop myself from doing something:
  - I tried to be serious but I **couldn't help laughing**.
  - I'm sorry I broke the glass. Someone pushed me and I **couldn't help dropping** it.
  - He is stupid but it's not his fault. He **can't help being** stupid.

116

UNIT 58   Exercises

58.1 *In this exercise you have to make sentences with* **afraid**. *Read each situation and then use the words in brackets to write your sentence.*
Examples: The streets are unsafe at night.
(I / afraid / go out / alone)   *I'm afraid to go out alone.*
We walked very carefully along the icy path.
(we / afraid / fall)   *We were afraid of falling.*

1 I don't usually carry my passport with me.
   (I / afraid / lose / it)
2 The sea was very rough.
   (we / afraid / go / swimming) ....
3 We rushed to the station.
   (we / afraid / miss / our train) ....
4 I didn't tell Tom that I thought he had behaved foolishly.
   (I / afraid / hurt / his feelings) ....
5 In the middle of the film there was a particularly horrifying scene.
   (we / afraid / look) ....
6 The glasses were very full, so Ann carried them very carefully.
   (she / afraid / spill / the drinks) ....
7 I didn't like the look of the food on my plate.
   a) (I / afraid / eat / it) ....
   b) (I / afraid / make / myself ill) ....

58.2 *Now you have to make sentences with* **need -ing**. *Use the verb in brackets.*
Example: This coat is rather dirty. (clean)   *It needs cleaning.*

1 This room hasn't been painted for years. (paint)   It ....
2 Your hair is too long. (cut)   It ....
3 Those shoes are rather dirty. (polish)   They ....
4 This plant hasn't been watered for some time. (water) ....
5 Those screws are loose. (tighten) ....
6 Your jeans are too long. (take up) ....

58.3 *Put the verb into the correct form,* **-ing** *or* **to** + *infinitive.*
Examples: If you want to pass your exams, you need ......*to study*...... (study) more.
        I'm sorry I broke the glass. I couldn't help ......*dropping*........ (drop) it.

1 Does this job need .... (do) now or can I leave it until later?
2 I've got an extra bed, so when you come to stay, you won't need .... (bring) your sleeping bag.
3 Tom helped his mother .... (get) the dinner ready.
4 When he told me that everybody had made fun of him, I couldn't help .... (feel) sorry for him.
5 Those shirts need .... (iron) but you don't need .... (do) it now.
6 He looks so funny. When I see him, I can't help .... (smile).
7 The fine weather helped .... (make) it a very enjoyable holiday.

UNIT 59 Preposition + -ing

a) If a verb comes after a preposition (**in/at/with/about** etc.), the verb ends in **-ing**. Study these examples:

Are you interested	**in**	working	for us?
I'm not very good	**at**	learning	languages.
I'm fed up	**with**	studying.	
The children are excited	**about**	going	on holiday.
What are the advantages	**of**	having	a car?
This knife is only	**for**	cutting	bread.
John went to work	**in spite of**	feeling	ill. (See Unit 109.)
I bought a new bicycle	**instead of**	going	away on holiday.

b) You can use **-ing** with **before** and **after**:
   - **Before going** out I phoned Ann.
     You can also say: '**Before I went** out I ...'
   - What did you do **after leaving** school?
     You can also say: '... **after you left** school?'

c) You can use **by -ing** to say *how* something happened:
   - They got into the house **by breaking** a kitchen window and climbing in.
   - You can improve your English **by doing** a lot of reading.

d) You can use **-ing** after **without**:
   - Tom left **without finishing** his dinner.
   - She ran five miles **without stopping**.
   - He climbed through the window **without** anybody seeing him.
     (*or* '... **without** being seen.')
   - She needs to work **without** people disturbing her. (*or* '... **without** being disturbed.')
   - It's nice to go on holiday **without** having to worry about money.

e) **To** is often a part of the *infinitive*. For example:
   - They decided **to go** out.
   - I want **to play** tennis.

But **to** is also a *preposition*. For example:
   - Tom went **to** London.
   - He gave the book **to** Ann.
   - I prefer cities **to** the countryside.
   - I'm looking forward **to** the week-end.

If a preposition is followed by a verb, the verb ends in **-ing** (see section a). So, if **to** is a preposition and it is followed by a verb, you must say **to -ing**. For example:
   - I prefer cycling **to driving** (*not* 'to drive')
   - I'm looking forward **to seeing** Ann again. (*not* 'to see')

For **be/get used to -ing** see Unit 62.

UNIT 59   Exercises

59.1 *In this exercise you have to read a sentence and then write a second sentence with the same meaning. Each time begin in the way shown.*
Example: I phoned Ann and then I went out.   After *phoning Ann I went out.*

1 Tom went to bed but first he had a hot drink.
   Before ....
2 The plane took off and soon afterwards it crashed.
   Soon after ....
3 We didn't eat at home. We went to a restaurant instead.
   Instead of ....
4 You put people's lives in danger if you drive dangerously.
   You put people's lives in danger by ....
5 He hurt his leg but he managed to win the race.
   In spite of ....
6 Bill is a very good cook.   Bill is very good at ....
7 I don't intend to lend her any money.   I have no intention of ....
8 George took more exercise and so lost weight.
   By ....
9 He was angry with me because I was late.   He was angry with me for ....
10 Tom thinks that doing nothing is better than working.
   Tom prefers doing nothing to ....

59.2 *Now read each situation and then write a sentence with* **without -ing**.
Examples: She ran five miles. She didn't stop.   *She ran five miles without stopping.*
He left the room. Nobody saw him.   *He left the room without anyone seeing him.*

1 He translated the article. He didn't use a dictionary.
   He translated the article without ....
2 Look right and left before you cross the road.
   Don't cross ....
3 She got married. Nobody knew about it.
   She ....

59.3 *This time read each situation and write a sentence with* **look forward to**.
Examples: You are going on holiday next week. How do you feel about this?
I'm looking forward to going on holiday.
Sue is doing an examination next week. She's not very happy about it. How does she feel about it?   *She is not looking forward to doing the examination.*

1 A good friend is coming to visit you soon, so you will see him/her again. How do you feel about this? I'm ....
2 You are going to the dentist. You don't like visits to the dentist. How do you feel about it?
   ....
3 Carol is a schoolgirl. She hates school but she is leaving school next summer.
   How does she feel about this? She ....

UNIT 60   Verb + preposition + -ing

a) Many verbs have the structure *verb (V) + preposition (P) + object*. For example, **talk about**:
  – We **talked about the problem.** (**the problem** is the *object*)
If the object is another verb, it ends in **-ing**:
  – We talked about **going** to America. (*V + P + -ing*)
Here are some more verbs which have the structure *V + P + -ing*:

succeed in	Has Tom succeeded	**in**	**finding** a job yet?
feel like*	I don't feel	**like**	**going** out tonight.
think about/of	Are you thinking	**of/about**	**buying** a house?
dream of	I've always dreamed	**of**	**being** rich.
approve/disapprove of	She doesn't approve	**of**	**gambling**.
look forward to	I'm looking forward	**to**	**meeting** her.
insist on	He insisted	**on**	**buying** me a drink.
decide against	We decided	**against**	**moving** to London.
apologise for	He apologised	**for**	**keeping** me waiting.

* **I feel like doing** = I'd like to do, I'm in the mood to do.

We say 'apologise **to** someone **for** something':
  – He apologised **to me** for keeping me waiting. (*not* 'he apologised me')
With some of these verbs you can also use the structure *verb + preposition + someone + -ing*. For example:
  – We are all looking forward to **Peter** coming home.
  – She doesn't approve of **her son** staying out late at night.
  – They insisted on **me** (*or* **my**) staying with them. (See also Unit 35c.)

b) These verbs have the structure *verb + object + preposition + -ing*:

accuse	They accused	me	of	telling lies.
suspect	Did they suspect	the man	of	being a spy?
congratulate	I congratulated	Ann	on	passing the exam.
prevent	What prevented	him	from	coming to the wedding?
stop	We stopped	everyone	from*	leaving the building.
thank	I thanked	her	for	being so helpful.
forgive	Please forgive	me	for	not writing to you.
warn	They warned	us	against	buying the car.

* After **stop** you can leave out **from**. So you can say:
  – We stopped everyone **leaving** (*or* **from leaving**) the building.

Some of these verbs are often used in the passive:
  – I was **accused of** telling lies.
  – Was the man **suspected of** being a spy?
  – We were **warned against** buying it.

120

UNIT 60 Exercises

60.1 *In this exercise you have to write the correct preposition and to put the verb into the correct form. Use the verb in brackets at the end of each sentence.*
Example: Jack insisted ....*on going*..... out by himself.   (go)

1 After a long time we eventually succeeded .... a flat.   (find)
2 I've been thinking .... for a new job.   (look)
3 His parents didn't approve .... him .... out so late.   (stay)
4 I wonder what prevented him .... to the party.   (come)
5 I'm getting hungry. I'm looking forward .... dinner.   (have)
6 I don't feel .... today.   (study)
7 Forgive me .... you but I must ask you a question.   (interrupt)
8 The arrested man was suspected .... into a house.   (break)
9 Have you ever thought .... married?   (get)
10 I've always dreamed .... on a small island in the Pacific.   (live)
11 The cold water didn't stop her .... a swim.   (have)
12 Have you ever been accused .... a crime?   (commit)
13 She apologised .... so rude to me.   (be)
14 We have decided .... a new car.   (buy)

60.2 *Now you have to change direct speech into reported speech. Begin each of your sentences in the way shown.*
Example: 'It was nice of you to help me. Thanks very much.'   (George said to you)
George thanked *me for helping him.*................................

1 'I'll drive you to the station. I insist.'   (Tom said to Ann)
Tom insisted ....
2 'I hear you passed your examinations. Congratulations!'   (Jim said to you)
Jim congratulated ....
3 'It was nice of you to visit me. Thank you.'   (Mrs Dent said to Sue)
Mrs Dent thanked ....
4 'Don't stay at the hotel near the airport.'   (I said to Jack)
I warned ....
5 'I'm sorry I didn't phone you earlier.'   (Margaret said to you)
Margaret apologised .... not ....
6 'You didn't pay attention to what I said.'   (The teacher said to the boy)
The teacher accused ....

60.3 *Now you can write some sentences about yourself. Use -ing.*
Example: Today I don't feel like *going out.*................................

1 This evening I feel like ....
2 I'm looking forward to ....
3 I'm thinking of ....
4 I would never dream of ....

UNIT 61   Expressions + -ing

When these expressions are followed by a verb, the verb ends in **-ing**:

It's no use / It's no good ...
- **It's no use worrying** about it. There's nothing you can do.
- **It's no good trying** to persuade me. You won't succeed.

There's no point in ...
- **There's no point in buying** a car if you don't want to drive it.
- **There was no point in waiting,** so we went.

It's (not) worth ...
- My house is only a short walk from here. **It's not worth taking** a taxi.
- It was so late when we got home, **it wasn't worth going** to bed.

You can say: 'a book is **worth reading** / a film is **worth seeing**' etc.:
- Do you think **this book is worth reading?**
- You should go and see the film. **It's** really **worth seeing.**

(Have) difficulty ...
- I had **difficulty finding** a place to live. (*not* 'to find')
- Did you have any **difficulty getting** a visa?
- People often have great **difficulty reading** my writing.

Remember that we say 'difficulty' (*not* 'difficulties'):
- I'm sure you'll have no **difficulty** passing the examination.

You can also say '(have) difficulty **in** -ing':
- He's shy. He has difficulty **in** talking to people he doesn't know well.

A waste of money/time ...
- It's **a waste of time reading** that book. It's rubbish.
- It's **a waste of money buying** things you don't need.

Spend/waste (time) ...
- I **spent hours trying** to repair the clock.
- I **waste a lot of time day-dreaming.**

Go -ing

We use **go -ing** for a number of activities (especially sports):

go shopping   go swimming   go skiing   go fishing
go climbing   go sailing   go riding   go sightseeing

- How often do you **go swimming?**
- I'm **going skiing** next year.
- I have to **go shopping** this morning.
- I've never **been sailing.**

For 'I've **been** / I've **gone**' see Unit 13d.

UNIT 61 Exercises

61.1 *In this exercise you have to join two sentences to make one sentence.*
Examples: Don't worry about it. It's no use.   *It's no use worrying about it.*
Don't get a taxi. It's not worth it.   *It's not worth getting a taxi.*

1 Don't try to escape. It's no use.   It's no use ....
2 Don't smoke. It's a waste of money.   It's a waste ....
3 Don't ask Tom to help you. It's no good.   It's no good ....
4 Don't hurry. It's not worth it.   It's not worth ....
5 Don't study if you're feeling tired. There's no point.
   There's no point ....
6 Don't read newspapers. It's a waste of time.   It's a ....
7 Don't get angry. It's not worth it.   It's not ....
8 Don't work if you don't need the money. There's no point.
   There's no ....

61.2 *Now you have to make sentences with* **worth**.
Examples: I'd read this book if I were you.   This book *is worth reading.*
I wouldn't read this book if I were you.   This book *isn't worth reading.*

1 I'd visit the museum if I were you.   The museum ....
2 I wouldn't repair those shoes if I were you.   Those shoes ....
3 I wouldn't keep these old clothes if I were you.   These old clothes ....
4 I'd consider the plan if I were you.   The plan ....

61.3 *Read these sentences and each time write a new sentence using* **difficulty**.
Example: I found a place to live but it was difficult.
   I had difficulty finding a place to live. ....

1 Tom finds it difficult to meet people.   Tom has ....
2 He found a job. This wasn't difficult.   He had no ....
3 It won't be difficult to get a ticket for the concert.
   You won't have any ....
4 I find it difficult to understand him when he speaks quickly.
   I have ....

61.4 *Complete these sentences with one of the following expressions. Put the verb into the correct form.*
go skiing   go shopping   go swimming   go ~~sailing~~   go riding

1 Barry lives by the sea and he's got a boat, so he often *goes sailing* .
2 There's plenty of snow in the mountains so we'll be able to ....
3 It was a very hot day, so we .... in the river.
4 Margaret likes horses. She often ....
5 The shops are shut now. It's too late to ....

123

UNIT 62   Be/get used to something (I'm used to ...)

a) Study this example situation:

 Jane is American but she has lived in Britain for three years. When she first drove a car in Britain, she found it very difficult because she had to drive on the left instead of on the right. Driving on the left was strange and difficult for her because:

She **wasn't used to it.**
She **wasn't used to driving** on the left.

But after a lot of practice, driving on the left became less strange:
  – She **got used to driving** on the left.
Now after three years, driving on the left is no problem for her:
  – She **is used to driving** on the left.
I'm used to something = it is not new or strange for me:
  – Frank lives alone. He doesn't mind this because he has lived alone for 15 years. So he **is used to it.** He **is used to living** alone.
  – My new shoes felt a bit strange at first because I **wasn't used to them.**
  – Our new flat is on a very busy street. I expect we'll **get used to the noise** but at the moment we find it very disturbing.
  – Fred has a new job. He has to get up much earlier – at 6.30. He finds this difficult at present because he **isn't used to getting** up so early.

b) Notice that we say 'She **is used to driving** on the left.' (*not* 'she is used to drive'). **To** in be/get **used to** is a *preposition*, not a part of the infinitive (see also Unit 59e). So we say:
  – Frank is used **to living** alone. (*not* 'is used to live')
  – Jane had to get used **to driving** on the left. (*not* 'get used to drive')

c) Do not confuse **I am used to doing** (be/get used to) with **I used to do.** They are different in structure and in meaning.
I am used to (doing) something = something isn't strange for me:
  – I am used **to the weather** in this country.
  – I am used **to driving** on the left because I've lived in Britain a long time.
I used to do something means only that I did something regularly in the *past* (see Unit 25). You can't use this structure for the *present*. The structure is 'I **used to do**' (*not* 'I **am** used to do'):
  – These days I usually stay in bed until late. But when I had a job, **I used to get** up early.

62.1 *Read these situations and write three sentences with* **used to** *as in the example.*
Example: Jane is American. She came to Britain and found driving on the left difficult.
  a) At first she *wasn't used to driving on the left.*
  b) But soon she *got used to driving on the left.*
  c) Now she has no problems. She *is used to driving on the left.*

1 Juan came to England from Spain. In Spain he always had dinner late in the evening. But in England dinner was at 6 o'clock. Juan found this strange at first.
  a) At first he wasn't ....
  b) But after some time he got ....
  c) Now he finds it quite normal. He ....
2 Diana is a nurse. She started working nights two years ago. At first she found it strange and didn't like it.
  a) At first she ....
  b) But after a while ....
  c) Now she doesn't mind it at all.

62.2 *Now read these situations and write a sentence with* **be/get used to**.
Example: Frank lives alone. He doesn't mind this. He has always lived alone.
  (he / used / live / alone) *He is used to living alone.*

1 Ron sleeps on the floor. He doesn't mind this. He has always slept on the floor.
  (he / used / sleep / on the floor) He ....
2 Sue moved from a big house to a much smaller one. What did she have to get used to?
  (she had / used / live / in a smaller house) She had ....
3 Jack once went to the Middle East. It was too hot for him.
  (he / not / used / the heat) ....
4 Bill doesn't have any money. He doesn't find this unusual because he has never had any money. (he / used / have / no money) ....
5 Tom is going to live in your country. What will he have to get used to? (*Write your own answer!*) He'll have to ....

62.3 *Now you have to put the verb into the correct form,* -ing *or infinitive* (**I am used to doing** *or* **I used to do**). *If necessary, study Unit 25 first.*
Examples: Jane had to get used to ......*driving*...... on the left. (drive)
  Bill used to ......*be*...... very fit. Now he's in terrible condition. (be)

1 When I was a child, I used to .... swimming every day. (go)
2 It took me a long time to get used to .... glasses. (wear)
3 There used to .... a cinema on this corner but it was knocked down. (be)
4 I'm the boss. I'm not used to .... told what to do. (be)
5 You'll have to get used to .... less if you want to lose weight. (eat)
6 I used to .... Ann but now she gets on my nerves. (like)
7 Ron got tired very quickly. He wasn't used to .... so fast. (run)
8 Tom used to .... a lot of coffee when he was a student. (drink)

UNIT 63
Infinitive of purpose – 'I went out **to post** a letter.'
So that – 'I hurried **so that** I wouldn't be late.'

a) We use **to** + *infinitive* to talk about the purpose of doing something (= why someone does something):
- I went out **to post** a letter. (= because I wanted to post a letter)
- She telephoned me **to invite** me to a party.
- We shouted **to warn** everyone of the danger.

We also use **to** + *infinitive* to talk about the purpose of something, or why someone has/wants/needs something:
- This wall is **to keep** people out of the garden.
- The minister has two bodyguards **to protect** him.
- I need a bottle-opener **to open** this bottle.

You can also use **in order to** + *infinitive*:
- We shouted **in order to warn** everyone of the danger.

Do *not* use **for** in these sentences:
- I'm going to Spain **to learn** Spanish. (*not* 'for learning / for to learn')

b) We also use **to** + *infinitive* to say what can be done or must be done with something:
- It's usually difficult to find **a place to park** in the city centre. (= a place where you can park)
- Have you got a lot of **work to do** this evening? (= work that you must do)
- Would you like **something to eat**?
- There were no **chairs to sit on**, so we all had to sit on the floor.
- She is a bit lonely. She's got **nobody to talk to**.

We also say **time/money/energy to do something**:
- They gave me some **money to buy** some food. (*not* 'for buying')
- Did you have **time to answer** all the questions in the examination?

c) Sometimes you have to use **so that** (*not* **to** + *infinitive*) to talk about the purpose of doing something. We use **so that**:
i)   when the purpose is *negative* (**so that ... won't/wouldn't ...**):
- I hurried **so that I wouldn't** be late. (= because I didn't want to be late)
- Leave early **so that you won't** (or **don't**) miss the bus.
ii)   with **can** and **could** (**so that ... can/could ...**):
- He's learning English **so that** he **can** study in the United States.
- We moved to London **so that** we **could** visit our friends more often.
iii) when one person does something so that *another* person does something else:
- I gave him my address **so that he** could contact me.
- **He** wore glasses and a false beard **so that nobody** would recognise him.

UNIT 63   Exercises

63.1 *Use the words in brackets to answer these questions.*
Example: Why did you go out? (buy some bread)   I went out to buy some bread.

1 Why do you have to go to the bank? (change some money)
   I have to go ....
2 Why did she knock on your door? (wake me up)   She ....
3 Why are you saving money? (go to Canada)   I ....
4 Why is Ron going into hospital? (have an operation)
   ....
5 Why are you wearing two pullovers? (keep warm)   ....
6 Why did you go to the police station? (report that my car had been stolen)
   ....

63.2 *Now you have to complete these sentences with a suitable verb.*
Examples: The minister has a bodyguard .....to protect.... him.
           There were no chairs ....to sit....... on, so we all had to sit on the floor.

1 We are having a party .... Ann's birthday.
2 I didn't have enough time .... the newspaper today.
3 We've got no furniture – not even a bed .... in.
4 I think I need some new clothes ....
5 Tom didn't have enough energy .... the mountain.
6 There will be a meeting next week .... the problem.
7 I need a box .... these books in.
8 It's a pity we haven't got any pictures .... on the wall.
9 I wish I had enough money .... a new car.

63.3 *In this exercise you have to write sentences with so that.*
Examples: I hurried. I didn't want to be late.   I hurried so that I wouldn't be late.
           I'll give you my number. I want you to be able to phone me.
           I'll give you my number so that you can (or will be able to) phone me.

1 We wore warm clothes. We didn't want to get cold.
   We wore ....
2 I spoke very slowly. I wanted the man to understand what I said.
   I ....
3 I whispered. I didn't want anyone to hear our conversation.
   .... no-one ....
4 Please arrive early. We want to be able to start the meeting on time.
   Please arrive ....
5 She locked the door. She didn't want to be disturbed.
   ....
6 I slowed down. I wanted the car behind to be able to overtake.
   ....

UNIT 64   Prefer and would rather

a) **Prefer to do** and **prefer doing**
You can use 'prefer **to do**' or 'prefer **doing**' to say what you prefer in general. 'Prefer **to do**' is more usual:
   – I don't like cities. **I prefer to live** (*or* **I prefer living**) in the country.
Study the difference in structure:

> I prefer (**doing**) something **to** (**doing**)   something else
> *but*: I prefer **to do**   something **rather than** (**do**) something else

   – I **prefer** that coat **to** the coat you were wearing yesterday.
   – Tom **prefers driving to travelling** by train.
   but: Tom **prefers to drive rather than travel** by train.
   – I **prefer to live** in the country **rather than** (**live**) in a city.

b) **Would prefer (to do)**
Use '**would** prefer to do' to say what someone wants to do in a particular situation (not in general):
   – '**Would** you **prefer** tea or coffee?'   'Coffee, please.'
   – 'Shall we go by train?'   'Well, **I'd prefer to go** by car.' (*not* 'going')
Note the structure:

> **I'd prefer to do** something **rather than** (**do**) something else

   – I'd **prefer to stay** at home tonight **rather than go** to the cinema.

c) **Would rather (do)** = would prefer to do. After **would rather** we use the infinitive without **to**.
Compare:

> Shall we go by train? { Well, **I'd prefer to go** by car.
>   { Well, **I'd rather go** by car. (*not* 'to go')

   – '**Would** you **rather have** tea or coffee?'   'Coffee, please.'
   – I'm tired. **I'd rather not go** out this evening, if you don't mind.
   – 'Do you want to go out this evening?'   '**I'd rather not.**'
Note the structure:

> **I'd rather do** something **than** (**do**) something else

   – I'd **rather stay** at home **than go** to the cinema.

d) **Would rather someone did something**
When you want someone else to do something, you can say **I'd rather you did ...** / **I'd rather he did ...** etc. We use the *past* in this structure but the meaning is present or future, not past.
Compare:

> I'd rather **cook** the dinner now.
> I'd rather **you cooked** the dinner now. (*not* 'I'd rather you cook')

   – 'Shall I stay here?'   'Well, **I'd rather you came** with us.'
   – **I'd rather you didn't tell** anyone what I said.
   – 'Do you mind if I smoke?'   '**I'd rather you didn't.**'

UNIT 64   Exercises

64.1 *Make sentences using* **'I prefer** *(something)* **to** *(something else)'.*
Example: (driving / travelling by train)   *I prefer driving to travelling by train.*

1 (Paris / London)   I prefer Paris ....
2 (phoning people / writing letters)   I prefer ....
3 (going to the cinema / watching films on television)
   I ....

Now rewrite sentences 2 and 3 using the structure **'I prefer to do** *(something)* ...'.*
Example: *I prefer to drive rather than travel by train.*

4 (2) I prefer to phone ....
5 (3) I ....

64.2 *Answer these questions using* **I'd prefer ...** *or* **I'd rather ....** *Use the words in brackets for your*
answers.
Examples: Shall we walk? (prefer / go by car)   *I'd prefer to go by car.*
            Shall we eat now? (rather / eat a bit later)   *I'd rather eat a bit later.*

1 Shall we play tennis? (prefer / go for a swim)   ....
2 Shall we watch television? (rather / read a book)   ....
3 Shall we leave now? (rather / wait for a few minutes)   ....
4 Shall we go to a restaurant? (prefer / eat at home)   ....
5 Shall we decide now? (rather / think about it for a while)   ....

Now you have to make sentences using **I'd prefer ... rather than ...** *or* **I'd rather ... than ...**
(see sections b and c).
Examples: (walk / go by car)   I'd rather *walk than go by car.*
            (stay at home / go to the cinema)   I'd prefer *to stay at home rather than*
            go to the cinema.

6   (go for a swim / play tennis)   I'd rather ....
7   (read a book / watch television)   I'd prefer ....
8   (wait for a few minutes / leave now)   I'd prefer ....
9   (eat at home / go to a restaurant)   I'd rather ....
10 (think about it for a while / decide now)   I'd prefer ....

64.3 *Now you have to use* **'I'd rather you** *(did something)'. You are talking to a friend. You say*
you'll do something but really you want your friend to do it.
Example: I'll cook the dinner if you really want me to but *I'd rather you cooked it.*

1 I'll phone Tom if you really want me to but I'd rather ....
2 I'll do the washing-up if you really want me to but ....
3 I'll go to the bank if you really want me to but ....
4 I'll tell Ann what happened if you really want me to but ....

UNIT 65 Had better do something
It's time someone did something

a) Had better do something

The meaning of **had better** (**I'd better**) is similar to **should**. 'I'd better do something' = I should do something or it is advisable for me to do something; if I don't do this, something bad might happen:

           – I have to meet Tom in ten minutes. **I'd better go** now or I'll be late.
           – 'Shall I take an umbrella?' 'Yes, you**'d better**. It might rain.'
           – We've almost run out of petrol. We**'d better stop** at the next petrol station to fill up.

The negative form is **had better not** ('**d better not**):

           – You don't look very well. You**'d better not go** to work today.
           – 'Are you going out tonight?' 'I**'d better not**. I've got a lot of work to do.'

The form is always '**had** better' (usually **'d better** in spoken English). We say **had** but the meaning is present or future, not past:

           – I**'d better go** to the bank **this afternoon**.

Remember that **had better** is followed by the infinitive without **to**:

           – It might rain. We**'d better take** an umbrella. (*not* 'better to take')

b) It's time ...

You can say '**it's time** (for someone) **to do** something':

           – It's time **to go** home.
           – It's time **for us to go** home.

There is another structure: **It's time someone did something**:

           – It's nearly midnight. **It's time we went** home.

We use the *past* (**went**) after **It's time someone ...**, but the meaning is present or future, not past:

           – Why are you still in bed? **It's time you got** up. (*not* 'time you get up')

We use the structure **It's time someone did something** especially when we are complaining or criticising or when we think someone should have already done something:

           – **It's time the children were** in bed. It's long after their bedtime.
           – You've been wearing the same clothes for ages. **Isn't it time you bought** some new ones?
           – I think **it's time the government did** something about pollution.

We also say $\begin{Bmatrix} \text{'It's \textbf{high} time} \\ \text{'It's \textbf{about} time} \end{Bmatrix}$ someone **did** something'.

This makes the complaint or criticism stronger:

           – You're very selfish. **It's high time you realised** that you're not the most important person in the world.
           – **It's about time Jack did** some work for his examinations.

UNIT 65   Exercises

65.1 *Read each situation and write a sentence with* **had better.**
Examples: You're going out for a walk with Tom. You think you should take an umbrella
because it might rain. What do you say to Tom?   *We'd better take an umbrella.*
Tom doesn't look very well. You don't think he should go to work today. What
do you say to Tom?   *You'd better not go to work today.*

1   Ann suddenly begins to feel ill. You think she should sit down. What do you say to
her? ....

2   You and Tom are going to the theatre. You've just missed the bus. You think you should
take a taxi. What do you say to Tom?   We ....

3   Ann wants to play the piano late at night. You know that she'll wake up the people next
door. What do you say to Ann? ....

4   You and Ann are going to a restaurant for a meal. You think you should reserve a table
because the restaurant might be crowded. What do you say to Ann?
....

5   Tom has just cut himself. You think he should put a plaster on the cut. What do you say
to him? ....

6   You are going to take your car on holiday. You think you should have it serviced before
you go. What do you say (to yourself)? ....

7   You are by a river. It's a very warm day and your friend suggests going for a swim.
You don't think you should do this because the river looks very dirty. What do you say?
....

65.2 *Now you have to write sentences with* **It's time someone did something.**
Examples: You think the children should be in bed. It's already 11 o'clock.
It's time the children were in bed. (or went to bed.)
You think something should be done about the traffic problem in the city
centre.   *It's (about) time something was done about the traffic problem in the city centre.*

1   You think you should have a holiday because you haven't had one for a very long
time. It's time I ....

2   You think Tom should write to his parents. He hasn't written to them for ages.
It's time ....

3   This room should be redecorated. It looks awful.
It's ....

4   You're waiting for Ann. She is late. She should be here by now.
....

5   You're sitting in a train waiting for it to leave. It's already five minutes late.
....

6   You feel very strongly that governments should stop spending money on arms and should
concentrate on raising the standard of living.
....

7   You think you should start getting the dinner ready. It's nearly dinner-time now.
....

8   You haven't been to the dentist for nearly a year. You should go every six months.
....

UNIT 66   See someone do and see someone doing

a) Study this example situation:
Tom got into his car and drove away. You saw this. You can say:
   – I **saw** Tom **get** into his car and **drive** away.
In this structure we use the *infinitive* (**get, drive** etc.):

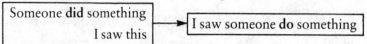

Someone **did** something	
I saw this	→	I saw someone **do** something

Remember that we use the infinitive without **to**:
   – I saw her **go** out. (*not* 'to go out')
But after a *passive* ('he **was seen**' etc.) we use **to** + infinitive:
   – She was seen **to go** out.

b) Now study this example situation:
Yesterday you saw Ann. She was waiting for a bus. You can say:
   – I **saw** Ann **waiting** for a bus.
In this structure we use **-ing** (**waiting**):

Someone **was doing** something	
I saw this	→	I saw someone **doing** something

c) Now study the difference in meaning between the two structures:

'I saw him **do** something' = he did something (*past simple*) and I saw this. I saw the complete action from beginning to end:
   – He **fell** to the ground. I saw this. → I **saw** him **fall** to the ground.
   – The accident **happened**. We saw this. → We **saw** the accident **happen**.

'I saw him **doing** something' = he was doing something (*past continuous*) and I saw this. I saw him when he was in the middle of doing something. This does not mean that I saw the complete action:
   – He **was walking** along the street. I saw this when I drove past in my car.
   → I **saw** him **walking** along the street.

The difference is not always important. Sometimes you can use either form:
   – I've never seen Tom **dance**.   *or*   I've never seen Tom **dancing**.

d) We use these structures especially with **see** and **hear**, and also with **watch, listen to, feel** and **notice**:

– I didn't **hear** you **come** in.
– She suddenly **felt** someone **touch** her on the shoulder.
– Did you **notice** anyone **go** out?

– I could **hear** it **raining**.
– The missing boys **were** last **seen playing** near the river.
– **Listen to** the birds **singing**!

After **smell** and **find** you can use the **-ing** structure only:
   – Can you **smell** something **burning**?
   – She **found** him **reading** her letters.

UNIT 66 Exercises

66.1 *Answer these questions beginning in the way shown.*
Examples: 'Does Tom ever dance?' 'I've never seen *him dance. (or dancing)* ,
'How do you know I came in late?' 'I heard *you come in late.* ,

1 'Does Ann ever smoke?' 'I've never seen .... ,
2 'How do you know the man took the money?' 'I saw .... ,
3 'Did Jack lock the door?' 'Yes, I heard .... ,
4 'Did the bell ring?' 'I'm not sure. I didn't hear .... ,
5 'Does Tom ever swear (= *use bad language*)?' 'I've never heard .... ,
6 'How do you know Ann can play the piano?' 'I've heard .... ,
7 'Did Bill kick the dog?' 'Yes, I saw .... ,
8 'Did the boy fall into the water?' 'I didn't see .... ,

66.2 *In each of these situations you and a friend saw, heard or smelt something. This is what you said at the time:*

> 1 Look! There's Ann! She's waiting for a bus.
> 2 Look! There's Sue! She's playing tennis.
> 3 Look! There's Tom! He's having a meal in that restaurant.
> 4 Listen! That's Bill. He's playing the guitar.
> 5 I can smell something! The dinner's burning!
> 6 Look! There's Dave! He's talking to Charles.

Later you tell someone what you saw, heard or smelt.

1 *We saw Ann waiting for a bus.*
2 We saw ....
3 .... in a restaurant.
4 ....
5 ....
6 ....

66.3 *Complete these sentences. Use one of the following verbs in the correct form.*
run   explode   ~~burn~~   slam   cry   ~~happen~~   sit   collide   open
tell   crawl   climb

1 Can you smell something *burning* ?
2 I saw the accident *happen* .
3 We listened to the old man .... his story from beginning to end.
4 Listen! Can you hear a child .... ?
5 Did anybody see the two cars .... ?
6 We watched the two men .... across the garden, ... a window and .... through it into the house.
7 Everybody heard the bomb .... It was a tremendous noise.
8 Oh! I can feel something .... up my leg! It must be an insect.
9 I heard someone .... the door in the middle of the night. It woke me up.
10 We couldn't find Tom at first. In the end we found him .... in the garden.

133

UNIT 67   -ing clauses – 'Feeling tired, I went to bed early.'

a) A *clause* is a part of a sentence. Some sentences have two clauses:
- **Feeling tired**, I went to bed early.

In this sentence, 'I went to bed early' is the *main clause*.
Feeling tired is the -ing *clause*.

b) When two things happen at the same time, you can use **-ing** for one of the verbs. The main clause usually comes first:
- She was sitting in an armchair **reading** a book. (= she was sitting and she was reading)
- I ran out of the house **shouting**. (= I was shouting when I ran out of the house)

We also use **-ing** when one action happens during another. Use **-ing** for the longer action. The longer action is the second part of the sentence.
- Jim hurt his arm **playing** tennis. (= while he was playing)
- I cut myself **shaving**. (= while I was shaving)

You can also use **-ing** after **while** or **when**:
- Jim hurt his arm **while playing** tennis. (= while he was playing)
- Be careful **when crossing** the road. (= when you are crossing)

c) When one action happens before another action, you can use **having (done)** for the first action:
- **Having found** a hotel, they looked for somewhere to have dinner.
- **Having finished** our work, we went home.

You could also say **After -ing**:
- **After finishing** our work, we went home.

If the second action happens immediately after the first, you can use the simple **-ing** form (**doing** instead of **having done**):
- **Taking** a key out of his pocket, he opened the door.

These structures are used mainly in written English.

d) You can also use an **-ing** clause to explain something or to say why someone did something. The **-ing** clause usually comes first:
- **Feeling** tired, I went to bed early. (=because I felt tired)
- **Being** unemployed, he hasn't got much money. (= because he is unemployed)
- **Not having** a car, she finds it difficult to get around. (= because she doesn't have a car)
- **Having** already **seen** the film twice, I didn't want to go to the cinema. (= because I had already seen it twice)

These structures are used more in written than in spoken English.

UNIT 67   Exercises

67.1 *From each pair of sentences make one sentence using an* **-ing** *clause.*
  Example: She was sitting in an armchair. She was reading a book.
  She was sitting in an armchair reading a book.

  1 Jill was lying on the bed. She was crying.   Jill was ....
  2 I got home. I was feeling very tired.   I got ....
  3 The old man was walking along the street. He was talking to himself.
    The old man ....

  In these sentences one thing happens during another.
  Example: Jim was playing tennis. He hurt his arm.   *Jim hurt his arm playing tennis.*

  4 Ann was watching television. She fell asleep.   Ann ....
  5 The man slipped. He was getting off the bus.   The man ....
  6 The boy was crossing the road. He was knocked over.
    The boy ....
  7 The fireman was overcome by smoke. He was trying to put out the fire.
    The fireman ....

67.2 *This time make sentences beginning* **Having** ...
  Example: We finished our work. We went home.   *Having finished our work, we went home.*

  1 We bought our tickets. Then we went into the theatre.
    ....

  2 They had dinner. Then they continued on their journey.
    ....

  3 Sue did all her shopping. Then she went for a cup of coffee.
    ....

67.3 *Now make sentences beginning* **-ing** *or* **Not -ing** *(as in section d).*
  Example: I felt tired. So I went to bed early.   *Feeling tired, I went to bed early.*

  1 I thought they might be hungry. So I offered them something to eat.
    Thinking ....
  2 She is a foreigner. So she needs a visa to stay in this country.
    ....
  3 I didn't know his address. So I couldn't contact him.
    Not ....
  4 The man wasn't able to understand English. So he didn't know what I said.
    ....
  5 He has travelled a lot. So he knows a lot about other countries.
    Having ....
  6 We had spent nearly all our money. So we couldn't afford to stay in a hotel.
    ....

135

UNIT 68   Chance and opportunity

a) Chance of -ing

We say: 'someone **has** a (good) **chance of doing** something' (passing an examination, winning a match etc.):

- Do you think I **have a chance of passing** the examination?
- We **have a** very good **chance of winning** the match.

You can also say **any/no/little/much chance**:

- I don't think I have **much chance of finding** a job.
- He has **no chance of passing** the examination.

You can also say '**stand** a chance of doing something':

- He **doesn't stand** a chance of passing the examination.

You can also say '**What are the chances of** something (happening)?':

- **What are the chances of success?**
- **What are my chances of passing** the examination?

You can also say '**there is a chance of** something **happening**' or '**there is a chance that** something **will happen**':

- **Is there any chance of** you **lending** me some money until tomorrow?
- **There is a chance that I'll be** late home this evening.

b) Chance to do something

We use 'chance **to do** something' when **chance** = time or opportunity to do something. ('Chance **of -ing**' is less usual with this meaning.)

- 'Have you read the book I lent you?'   'No, I haven't had **a chance to look** at it yet.' (= I haven't had time / an opportunity to look at it)
- We didn't have **much chance to talk** to each other when we last met. (= we didn't have much time/opportunity to talk)
- These days I don't get **much chance to watch** television. I'm too busy.

c) Opportunity

We normally say '**opportunity to do** something' (**opportunity of -ing** is also possible):

- I have **the opportunity to study** in the United States for a year. Do you think I should go? (= the chance to study)
- After the lecture there will be **an opportunity to ask** questions.

You can also say **any/no/little/much/plenty of/more opportunity**:

- Do you have **much opportunity to speak** English? (= much chance to speak)
- We live near the mountains, so we have **plenty of opportunity to go** skiing.

Do *not* say 'possibility to do something':

- I had the **opportunity** to study in Canada. (*not* 'possibility to study')

UNIT 68 Exercises

68.1 *Complete these sentences using* **chance of -ing** *or* **chance to ....** *Each time use the verb in brackets.*
Examples: Do you think I have a ...*chance of passing*... the examination? (pass)
These days I don't get much ...*chance to watch*..... television. . (watch)

1 I'd like to go to the concert but I've got no .... tickets now.
They'll have sold out. (get)
2 He was badly injured in the crash but the doctors at the hospital say that he has a very
good .... completely. (recover)
3 'Have you written that letter to Jack?' 'No, I didn't have a .... it
today. There was so much else to do.' (do)
4 There isn't much .... a cheap apartment in the city centre. (find)
5 We're always very busy at work. We don't get much .... to each
other. (talk)
6 A lot of people have applied for this job. If I apply, I don't think I stand a very good
.... it. (get)
7 I'm afraid I didn't have the .... you while I was in London. I was only
there for three days and there wasn't enough time. (visit)
8 If you work hard at your job, you have a good .... (be promoted)
9 I don't think there is much .... the rain .... The
sky is very grey. (stop)

68.2 *Now you have to write sentences using* **much opportunity to do something.**
Example: 'Do you speak English very often?'
'No, *I don't have much opportunity to speak English* .... ,

1 'Do you see many foreign films?' 'No, I don't have much .... ,
2 'Do you go fishing very often?' 'No, I don't .... ,
3 'Do you travel much?' 'No, ... ,
4 'Do you use your English much?' 'No, ... ,
5 'Do you go to the theatre very often?' 'No, ... ,

---

68.3 *Now use your own ideas to complete these sentences.*
Examples: I'd like to have the opportunity *to go to the United States.* ....
I don't think there is much chance of my *going to England in the near future.*

1 I'd like to have the opportunity ....
2 I don't think there is much chance of my ....
3 People today have much more opportunity ....
4 These days I don't get much chance ....
5 Where I live there is plenty of opportunity ....
6 But there isn't much opportunity ....
7 I think I have a good chance ....
8 I've never had the opportunity ....

137

UNIT 69 — Uncountable nouns (**gold, music, advice** etc.)

Nouns can be *countable* or *uncountable*. For *countable* nouns see Unit 70.

a) *Uncountable* nouns are, for example:

   gold   music   blood   excitement

Uncountable nouns are things we cannot count. They have no plural. You cannot say 'musics', 'bloods' or 'excitements'.

b) Before uncountable nouns you can say **the/some/any/much/this/his** etc.:

   the music   **some** gold   **much** excitement   **his** blood

But you cannot use **a/an** before an uncountable noun. So you cannot say 'a music', 'an excitement' or 'a blood'.

You can also use uncountable nouns alone, with no article (see Unit 74):

   – This ring is made of **gold.**   – **Blood** is red.

c) Many nouns can be used as countable or as uncountable nouns. Usually there is a difference in meaning. For example:

paper	I bought **a paper.** (= a newspaper – *countable*)
	I bought **some paper.** (= material for writing on – *uncountable*)
hair	There's **a hair** in my soup! (= one single hair – *countable*)
	She has beautiful **hair.** (= hair on her head – *uncountable*)
experience	We had **many** interesting **experiences** during our holiday. (= things that happened to us – *countable*)
	You need **experience** for this job. (= knowledge of something because you have done it before – *uncountable*)

d) Some nouns are usually uncountable in English but often countable in other languages. Here are the most important of these:

accommodation	behaviour	furniture	news	scenery	trouble
advice	bread	information	permission	traffic	weather
baggage	chaos	luggage	progress	travel	work

These nouns are *uncountable*, so (i) you cannot use **a/an** before them; and (ii) they cannot be plural:

   – I'm looking for **accommodation.** (*not* 'an accommodation')
   – I'm going to buy **some bread.** (*or* 'a loaf of bread'; *but not* 'a bread')
   – Tom gave me **some** good **advice.** (*not* 'some good advices')
   – Where are you going to put all your **furniture?** (*not* 'furnitures')

Remember that **news** is not plural:

   – The news **is** very depressing today. (*not* 'The news are ...')

Do not use **travel** to mean **journey/trip:**

   – We had **a** good **journey.** (*not* 'a good travel')

Note these pairs of countable (C) and uncountable (UNC) nouns:

   – I'm looking for **a job.** (C)   *but*   I'm looking for **work.** (UNC)
   – What **a** lovely **view!** (C)   *but*   What lovely **scenery!** (UNC)

UNIT 69   Exercises

69.1 *Which of the underlined parts of these sentences is right?*
Example: Sue was very helpful. She gave me some good advice / ~~advices~~.   ('advice' is right)

1 Margaret has got very long black hair / hairs.
2 We had a very good weather / very good weather when we were on holiday.
3 Sorry I'm late. I had trouble / troubles with the car this morning.
4 I want something to read. I'm going to buy a / some paper.
5 I want to write some letters. I need a / some writing paper.
6 It's very difficult to find a work / job at the moment.
7 Bad news don't / doesn't make people happy.
8 Our travel / journey from London to Istanbul by train was very interesting.
9 The flat is empty. We haven't got any furnitures / furniture yet.
10 When the fire alarm rang, there was a complete chaos / complete chaos.
11 I had to buy a / some bread because I wanted to make some sandwiches.
12 After spending most of his life travelling round the world, he is now writing a book
    about his experience / experiences.

69.2 *Now you have to complete these sentences using these words:*
**progress   advice   ~~accommodation~~   hair   work   experience
information   paper   permission**
Example: We haven't got anywhere to live. We're looking for ~~(some) accommodation.~~

1 I don't think Ann will get the job. She hasn't got ....
2 They'll tell you all you want to know. They'll give you plenty of ....
3 You'll easily recognise Alan. He's got green ....
4 Carla's English has improved. She has made ....
5 I want to write down your address. Have you got ....?
6 If you want to leave early, you have to ask for ....
7 George is unemployed at the moment. He is looking for ....
8 I didn't know what to do. So I asked Jack for ....

69.3 *In this exercise you have to write what you would say in these situations. Each time begin
in the way shown and use one of the words in section d of this unit.*
Example: Your friends have just arrived at the station. You can't see any suitcases or bags.
    You say: Have you got *any luggage* ....?

1 You go into the tourist office. You want to know about places to see in the town. You
    say: I'd like ....
2 The weather is beautiful. You say: What ....!
3 You are a pupil at school. You want your teacher to advise you about which examinations
    to take. You say: Can you give me ....?
4 You want to watch the news on television but you don't know what time it is on. You ask
    your friend: What time ....?
5 You are standing at the top of a mountain. You can see a very long way. It is beautiful.
    You say: What ....!

139

UNIT 70   Countable nouns with **a/an** and **some**

Nouns can be *countable* or *uncountable*. For *uncountable* nouns see Unit 69.

a)   Countable nouns are, for example:
   dog   **umbrella**   **job**   **suggestion**   **girl**
Countable nouns are things we can count. We can make them plural:
   two dogs   **six** jobs   **some** girls   **many** suggestions

b)   Before singular countable nouns you can use **a/an**:
   – That's **a** good suggestion.
   – Do you need **an** umbrella?
You cannot use singular countable nouns alone (without **a/the/my** etc.):
   – I'm looking for **a** job. (*not* 'I'm looking for job')
   – Be careful of **the** dog. (*not* 'Be careful of dog')
   – I've got **a** headache.
   – Would you like **a** cigarette?
For **a/an** and **the** see Unit 71.

c)   We often use **a/an** + noun when we say what something/someone is, or what something/someone is like:
   – A dog is **an animal**.   – Tom is **a** very nice **person**.
   – This is **a** really beautiful **house**.   – Jack has got **a** big **nose**.
   – What **a** lovely **dress**!
Remember to use **a/an** for jobs:
   – Tom's father is **a doctor**. (*not* 'Tom's father is doctor')
   – I wouldn't like to be **an English teacher**.
In sentences like these, we use plural countable nouns alone (*not* with *some*):
   – Tom's parents are **very nice people**.   – What **awful shoes**!
   (*not* 'some very nice people')   – Dogs are **animals**.
   – Ann has got **blue eyes**.   – Are most of your friends **students**?

d)   We also use **some** with plural countable nouns. **Some** = **a number of** / **a few of** (but we don't know or say exactly how many):
   – I've seen **some** good **films** recently. (*not* 'I've seen good films')
   – **Some friends** of mine are coming to stay at the week-end.
Do not use **some** when you are talking about things in general:
   – I love **bananas**. (*not* 'some bananas')
Sometimes you can use **some** or leave it out:
   – There are (**some**) eggs in the fridge if you're hungry.
For **some** and **any** see Unit 84.

e)   You have to use **some** when you mean *some but not all* / *not many* etc.
   – **Some children** learn very quickly. (but not all children)
   – **Some policemen** in Britain carry guns but most of them don't.

For plural countable nouns see also Unit 74.

UNIT 70   Exercises

70.1 *What are these things? Try and find out if you don't know.*
Example: an ant? <u>It's an insect.</u>   ants? bees? <u>They are insects.</u>

    1 a cauliflower?   It's ....   5 Earth? Mars? Venus? Jupiter?   They ....
    2 a pigeon?   It ....
    3 a dandelion?   ....   6 the Rhine? the Nile? the Mississippi? ....
    4 a skyscraper?   ....

And who were these people?
Example: Beethoven? <u>He was a composer.</u> Beethoven? Bach? <u>They were composers.</u>

    7 Pele?   He was ....   11 Kennedy? Johnson? Nixon?   They ....
    8 Shakespeare?   He ....
    9 Einstein?   ....   12 Elvis Presley? John Lennon?   ....
   10 Marilyn Monroe?

70.2 *Now you have to read about someone's job and then write what his or her job is.*
Example: Ron flies aeroplanes. <u>He's a pilot.</u>

    1 Vera types letters etc. in an office.   She is ....
    2 Tim arranges people's holidays for them.   He ....
    3 Stella looks after patients in hospital.   She ....
    4 Mary teaches mathematics.   ....
    5 Martha directs films.   ....
    6 John translates what people are saying from one language into another so that they can
       understand each other.   ....

70.3 *Now you have to put in* **a/an** *or* **some** *or leave a space (without a word).*
Examples: I've seen .....<u>some</u>..... good films recently.   Have you got ....<u>a</u>....... headache?
         Are most of your friends ....—............ students?

    1 Have you got .... camera?
    2 Would you like to be .... actor?
    3 Bill's got .... big feet.
    4 Do you collect .... stamps?
    5 Tom always gives Ann ....
       flowers on her birthday.
    6 Those are .... really nice
       trousers. Where did you get them?
    7 What .... beautiful garden!
    8 What .... lovely children!
    9 .... birds, for example the
       penguin, cannot fly.
   10 Jack has got .... very long legs,
       so he's .... fast runner.
   11 You need .... visa to visit ....
       foreign countries, but not all of them.
   12 I'm going shopping. I'm going to get
       .... new clothes.
   13 Jane is .... teacher. Her parents
       were .... teachers too.
   14 When we reached the city centre,
       .... shops were still open but
       most of them were already closed.
   15 Do you enjoy going to ....
       concerts?
   16 When I was .... child, I used to
       be very shy.

UNIT 71   A/an and the

a) Study this example:
For lunch I had $\boxed{a}$ sandwich and $\boxed{an}$ apple. $\boxed{\text{The}}$ sandwich wasn't very nice.

> The speaker says 'a sandwich / **an** apple' because this is the first time he talks about them.

> The speaker says '**the** sandwich' because the listener now knows which sandwich he means – the sandwich he had for lunch.

Here are some more examples:
- There was **a** man talking to **a** woman outside my house. **The** man looked English but I think **the** woman was foreign.
- When we were on holiday, we stayed at **a** hotel. In the evenings, sometimes we had dinner at **the** hotel and sometimes in **a** restaurant.
- I saw **a** film last night. **The** film was about **a** soldier and **a** beautiful girl. **The** soldier was in love with **the** girl but **the** girl was in love with **a** teacher. So **the** soldier shot **the** teacher and married **the** girl.

b) We use **a/an** when the listener doesn't know which thing we mean. We use **the** when it is clear which thing we mean:
- Tom sat down on **a** chair. (we don't know which chair)
  Tom sat down on **the** chair **nearest the door**. (we know which chair)
- Ann is looking for **a** job. (not a particular job)
  Did Ann get **the** job **she applied for**? (a particular job)
- Have you got **a** car? (not a particular car)
  I cleaned **the** car yesterday. (a particular car, my car)

c) We use **the** when it is clear in the situation which thing or person we mean. For example, in a room we talk about '**the** light / **the** floor / **the** ceiling / **the** door / **the** carpet' etc. Study these examples:
- Can you turn off **the** light, please? (= the light in this room)
- Where is **the** toilet, please? (= the toilet in this building/house)
- **The** postman was late this morning. (= our usual postman)
- I took a taxi to **the** station. (= the station of that town)
- We got to **the** airport just in time for our flight.

Also: **the** police / **the** fire-brigade / **the** army.
We also say **the bank, the post office:**
- I must go to **the** bank to change some money and then I'm going to **the** post office to buy some stamps. (The speaker is usually thinking of a particular bank or post office.)

We also say **the doctor, the dentist:**
- John isn't very well. He has gone to **the** doctor. (= his doctor)

For **the** see also Units 72–7.

142

UNIT 71　Exercises

71.1　*In this exercise you have to put in* **a/an** *or* **the**.
　　　Example: There was ....*a*......... man and ....*a*......... woman in the room. ....*The*..... man
　　　　　was English but ....*the*...... woman looked foreign. She was wearing ....*a*........
　　　　　fur coat.

　1　This morning I bought .... newspaper and .... magazine. ....
　　　newspaper is in my bag but I don't know where .... magazine is.
　2　My parents have .... cat and .... dog. .... dog never bites ....
　　　cat but .... cat often scratches .... dog.
　3　I saw .... accident this morning . ... car crashed into .... wall.
　　　.................. driver of .... car was not hurt but .... car was quite badly damaged.
　4　When you turn into Lipson Road, you will see three houses: .... red one, ...
　　　blue one and .... white one. I live in .... white one.
　5　We live in .... old house in .... middle of the village. There is ....
　　　beautiful garden behind .... house. .... roof of .... house is in very
　　　bad condition.

71.2　*Here again you have to put in* **a/an** *or* **the**.
　　　Examples: I'm looking for ....*a*........ job.　　Did Ann get ....*the*...... job she applied for?

　　1　Would you like .... apple?
　　2　Could you close .... door, please?
　　3　We live in .... small flat near .... centre of the city.
　　4　Have you finished with .... book I lent you last week?
　　5　We went out for .... meal last night. .... restaurant we went to was
　　　　excellent.
　　6　Did .... police find .... person who stole your bicycle?
　　7　This is a nice house. Has it got .... garden?
　　8　It was warm and sunny, so we decided to sit in .... garden.
　　9　This morning I had .... boiled egg and toast for breakfast.
　10　.................. President of the United States is elected every four years.
　11　As I was walking along the street, I saw .... £10 note on .... pavement.
　12　I went into the shop and asked to speak to .... manager.
　13　'Have you got .... car?'　'No, I've never had .... car in my life.'
　14　There's no need to buy any milk. .... milkman brings it every morning.

71.3　*Now you have to complete these sentences using* **the** + *noun*.
　　　Example: It was getting dark in the room, so I turned on ..*the light.*..................................

　1　There were no chairs so we all had to sit on ....
　2　As soon as I saw the fire, I called ....
　3　We didn't have any stamps, so we had to go to ....
　4　I had a toothache, so I made an appointment with ....
　5　Ann had to catch a train, so I took her to ....
　6　When we found that someone had broken into our house, we called ....
　7　Bill wasn't feeling well, so he went to ....
　8　We didn't have any money, so we had to go to ....
　9　The plane was delayed, so we had to wait at .... for three hours.

143

UNIT 72   The (1)

For the difference between **the** and **a/an** see Unit 71.

a)   We say **the ...** when there is only one of something:
  — What is **the** longest river in the world? (There is only one longest river in the world.)
  — We went to **the** most expensive restaurant in town.
  — **The** only television programme he watches is the news.
  — Paris is **the** capital of France.
  — Everybody left at **the** end of the meeting.
  — **The** earth goes round **the** sun. (Also: 'the moon / the world / the universe'.)

b)   We say: **the sea   the sky   the ground   the countryside / the country**
  — Would you rather live in a town or in **the country**?
  — Don't sit on **the ground**! It's wet.
  — We looked up at all the stars in **the sky**.
We say **go to sea / be at sea** (without **the**) when the meaning is **go/be on a voyage**:
  — Ken is a seaman. He spends most of his life **at sea**.
  but: I would love to live near **the** sea. (*not* 'near sea')
We say **space** (*not* 'the space') when we mean space in the universe:
  — There are millions of stars **in space**. (*not* 'in the space')
  but: He tried to park his car but **the** space wasn't big enough.

c)   **Cinema   theatre   radio   television**
We say **the cinema / the theatre**:
  — We went to **the cinema** last night.
  — Do you often go to **the theatre**?
Note that when we say '**the cinema / the theatre**', we do not necessarily mean one particular cinema or theatre.
We usually say **the radio**:
  — We often listen to **the radio**.   — I heard the news on **the radio**.
But we usually say **television** (without **the**):
  — We often watch **television**.
  — I watched the news on **television**.
  but: Can you turn off **the** television, please? (= the television set)

d)   *Meals:* We do not normally use **the** with the names of meals:
  — What time is **lunch**?
  — We had **dinner** in a restaurant.
  — What did you have for **breakfast**?
  — Ann invited me to (*or* for) **dinner**.
But we say **a meal**:
  — We had **a meal** in a restaurant.
We also say **a** when there is an adjective before **lunch/breakfast** etc.
  — Thank you. That was **a** very **nice** lunch. (*not* 'that was very nice lunch')

For more information about **the** see Units 71, 73–7.

144

UNIT 72   Exercises

72.1   *Answer these questions in the way shown.*
Example: 'Was it a good film?'   'Yes, it was ....the best film........ I've ever seen.'

1   'Is it a big hotel?'   'Yes, it is .... in the city.'
2   'Is he a rich man?'   'Yes, he is .... I've ever met.'
3   'Was it a bad accident?'   'Yes, it was .... I've ever seen.'
4   'Is it a cheap restaurant?'   'Well, it is .... you will find.'
5   'It's hot today, isn't it?'   'Yes, it is .... day of the year.'

72.2   *In this exercise you have to put in* **a/an** *or* **the**. *Sometimes you don't need either word – you leave it blank. (If necessary see Unit 71 for* **a/an** *and* **the**.)
Examples: We went to ....the..... most expensive restaurant in town.
Do you want to watch ....—........ television this evening?
Last night we went out for ....a........ meal in ....a........ restaurant.

1   I wrote my name at .... top of the page.
2   .... moon goes round .... earth every 27 days.
3   The Soviet Union was .... first country to send a man into .... space.
4   Did you see the film on .... television or at .... cinema?
5   After .... lunch, we went for a walk by .... sea.
6   I'm not very hungry. I had .... big breakfast.
7   John was .... only person I talked to at the party.
8   Tim lives in .... small village in .... country.
9   Peru is .... country in South America. .... capital is Lima.
10   I never listen to .... radio. In fact I haven't got .... radio.
11   It was .... beautiful day. .... sun shone brightly in .... sky.
12   I've invited Tom to .... dinner next Wednesday.
13   What is .... highest mountain in .... world?
14   We don't go to .... theatre very much these days. In fact, in .... town where we live there isn't .... theatre.
15   It was a long voyage. We were at .... sea for four weeks.
16   I prefer swimming in .... sea to swimming in pools.
17   Can you turn .... television down, please? It's a bit loud.

72.3   *Here are some things Tom did yesterday. Write a sentence for each.*

Morning: 8.00 breakfast   8.30–9.00 radio   9.30 walk/country
Afternoon: 1.00 lunch   2.30 cinema
Evening: 6.30 dinner   8.00–10.00 television

1   At 8 o'clock he had breakfast. ....
2   From 8.30 until 9.00 he listened ....
3   At 9.30 he went for a walk in ....
4   At 1.00 he ....
5   At 2.30 ....
6   At 6.30 ....
7   From ....

UNIT 73   The (2)

a) Study these sentences:
- **The rose** is my favourite flower.
- **The giraffe** is the tallest of all animals.

In these examples **the ...** doesn't mean one particular thing. **The rose** = roses in general, **the giraffe** = giraffes in general. We use **the** + *a singular countable noun* in this way to talk about a type of plant, animal etc. Note that you can also use a plural noun without **the**:
- **Roses** are my favourite flowers. (*but not* 'The roses ...' – see Unit 74)

We also use **the** + *a singular countable noun* when we talk about a type of machine, an invention etc. For example:
- When was **the telephone** invented?
- **The bicycle** is an excellent means of transport.

We also use **the** for musical instruments:
- Can you play **the guitar**? (*not* 'Can you play guitar?')
- **The piano** is my favourite instrument.

b) The + *adjective*

We use **the** with some adjectives (without a noun). The meaning is always plural. For example, **the rich** = rich people in general:
- Do you think **the rich** should pay more taxes?

We use **the** especially with these adjectives:

the rich	the old	the blind	the sick	the disabled	the injured
the poor	the young	the deaf	the dead	the unemployed	

- That man over there is collecting money for **the blind**.
- Why doesn't the government do more to help **the unemployed**?

These expressions are always plural. You cannot say 'a blind' or 'an unemployed'. You have to say '**a** blind **man**', '**an** unemployed **woman**' etc.

c) The + *nationality words*

You can use **the** with some nationality adjectives when you mean 'the people of that country'. For example:
- **The French** are famous for their food. (= the French people)
- Why do **the English** think they are so wonderful? (= the English people)

You can use **the** in this way with these nationality words:

the British	the Welsh	the Spanish	the Dutch
the English	the Irish	the French	the Swiss

Also with nationality words ending in -ese (**the Japanese** / **the Chinese** etc.)
With other nationalities you have to use a plural noun ending in -s:
 (the) Russians   (the) Italians   (the) Arabs   (the) Scots   (the) Turks

For **the** see also Units 71, 72 and 74–7.

UNIT 73   Exercises

73.1 *Answer these questions about yourself and your favourite things. Use a dictionary if you don't know the English words you need.*
Example: What is your favourite flower?   the rose ....

1   What is your favourite tree?   ....
2   Which bird do you like most?   ....
3   What is your favourite car?   ....
4   What is your favourite musical instrument?   ....

73.2 *Now you have to make sentences from the words in brackets.*
Example: (Mary / play / piano very well)   Mary plays the piano very well. ....

1   (Jack / play / guitar very badly)   Jack plays ....
2   (Jill / play / violin in an orchestra)   ....
3   (I'd like / learn / play / piano)   ....
4   (you / play / guitar?)   ....

73.3 *This time you have to complete these sentences about animals. Choose one of the words in brackets. Use a dictionary if you don't know these words.*
Example: The giraffe .... is the tallest of all animals.   (elephant/lion/giraffe)

1   .... is the fastest of all animals.   (tiger/cheetah/elephant)
2   .... is a mammal but it lives in the sea.   (octopus/elephant/whale)
3   .... is the largest living bird.   (eagle/sparrow/ostrich)

73.4 *Complete these sentences using* **the** *with these adjectives:*
rich   sick   blind   poor   injured   unemployed   dead
Example: Braille is a system of reading and writing by touch for the blind ....

1   Many people were killed in the plane crash. The bodies of .... were taken
    away. .... were taken to hospital.
2   Every English child knows the story of Robin Hood. It is said that he robbed
    .... and gave the money to ....
3   Those people with jobs have enough money but life is not so easy for ....
4   Agnes has been a nurse all her life. She has spent her life caring for ....

73.5 *What do you call the people of these countries?*
Examples: England? the English ....   Russia? the Russians ....

1   Britain? ....
2   Ireland? ....
3   Wales? ....
4   Scotland? ....
5   Spain? ....
6   France? ....
7   Japan? ....
8   Germany? ....
9   China? ....
10 Switzerland? ....
11 America (the US) ? ....
12 the Netherlands? ....
13 and your country? ....

UNIT 74   Plural and uncountable nouns with and without **the** (flowers / the flowers,   music / the music)

a) We don't use **the** before a noun when we mean something *in general*:
  - I love **flowers**. (*not* 'the flowers')
    (**flowers** = flowers *in general*, not a particular group of flowers)
  - I'm afraid of **dogs**.
  - **Doctors** are paid more than **teachers**.
  - **Crime** is a problem in most big cities. (*not* 'the crime')
  - **Life** has changed a lot since I was a boy. (*not* 'the life')
  - I prefer **classical music** to **pop music**. (*not* 'the classical/pop music')
  - Do you like **English food / French cheese / Swiss chocolate?** (*not* 'the ...')
  - My favourite subject at school was **history/physics/English**.
  - I like **football/athletics/skiing/chess**.
  - Do you collect **stamps**?

We say **most people / most dogs** etc. (*not* 'the most ...'):
  - **Most people** like George. (*not* 'the most people' – see also Unit 82)

b) We say **the ...** when we mean *something in particular*:
  - I like your garden. **The flowers** are beautiful. (*not* 'Flowers are ...')
    (**the flowers** = the flowers in your garden, not flowers in general)
  - **Children** learn a lot from playing. (= children in general)
  - *but:* We took **the children** to the zoo. (= a particular group of children, perhaps the speaker's own children)
  - **Salt** is used to flavour food.
  - *but:* Can you pass **the salt**, please? (= the salt on the table)
  - I often listen to **music**.
  - *but:* The film wasn't very good but I liked **the music**. (= the music in the film)
  - All **cars** have wheels.
  - *but:* All **the students** in the class like their teacher.
  - Are **English people** friendly? (= English people in general)
  - *but:* Are **the English people you know** friendly? (= only the English people you know, not English people in general)

c) The difference between 'something in general' and 'something in particular' is not always very clear. Study these sentences:
  - I like working with **people**. (= people in general)
  - I like working with **people who are lively**. (not all people, but **people who are lively** is still a general idea)
  - *but:* I like **the people I work with**. (= a particular group of people)
  - Do you like **coffee**? (= coffee in general)
  - Do you like **strong black coffee**? (not all coffee, but **strong black coffee** is still a general idea)
  - *but:* Did you like **the coffee we had with our meal last night**? (= particular coffee)

UNIT 74   Exercises

74.1 *In this exercise you have to write whether you like or dislike something. Begin your*
sentences with: I like ... / I don't like ... / I love ... / I hate ... / I don't mind ... / I'm (not)
interested in ... / I have no opinion about ...
Example: (very hot weather)   *I don't like very hot weather*

    1 (football)   ....
    2 (small children)   ....
    3 (cats)   ....
    4 (modern art)   ....
    5 (horror films)   ....

74.2 *What do you think about these things? Write a sentence about each one. Begin with:*
In my opinion ... / I think ... / I don't think ... / I don't agree with ... / I'm against ... / I'm in
favour of ...
Example: (divorce)   *I think divorce is sometimes necessary.*

    1 (terrorism)   ....
    2 (smoking)   ....
    3 (examinations)   ....
    4 (capital punishment)   ....
    5 (nuclear power)   ....

74.3 *In this exercise you have to choose the correct form, with or without* **the**.
    Examples: I'm afraid of <u>dogs</u> / ~~the dogs~~   Can you pass ~~salt~~ / <u>the salt</u>, please?

    1 <u>Apples</u> / The apples are good for you.
    2 Look at <u>apples</u> / the apples on that tree! They're very large.
    3 <u>Women</u> / The women are often better teachers than <u>men</u> / the men.
    4 In Britain <u>coffee</u> / the coffee is more expensive than <u>tea</u> / the tea.
    5 We had a very nice meal in that restaurant. <u>Cheese</u> / The cheese was especially good.
    6 <u>Most people</u> / The most people still believe that <u>marriage</u> / the marriage and <u>family life</u>
       / the family life are the basis of our society.
    7 They got married but <u>marriage</u> / the marriage wasn't successful.
    8 I know someone who wrote a book about <u>life</u> / the life of Gandhi.
    9 <u>Life</u> / The life would be very difficult without <u>electricity</u> / the electricity.
    10 <u>Skiing</u> / the skiing is my favourite sport but I also like <u>swimming</u> / the swimming.
    11 <u>Second World War</u> / The Second World War ended in 1945.
    12 Do you know <u>people</u> / the people who live next door?
    13 Are you interested in <u>art</u> / the art or <u>architecture</u> / the architecture?
    14 <u>All books</u> / All the books on the top shelf belong to me.
    15 Don't stay in that hotel. <u>Beds</u> / The beds are very uncomfortable.
    16 Two of the biggest problems facing our society are <u>crime</u> / the crime and <u>unemployment</u>
       / the unemployment.
    17 I hate <u>violence</u> / the violence.

UNIT 75   Hospital / the hospital,   school / the school etc.

a)   Study this example situation with **hospital**:

Jack had an accident a few days ago.
He had to go **to hospital**.
He is still **in hospital** now.
Jill went **to the hospital** to visit him.
She is **at the hospital** now.

Someone goes **to hospital** or is **in hospital** if he is ill or injured. We are not necessarily thinking of a particular hospital; we are thinking of the idea of hospital.

But Jill is not ill or injured. She is not 'in hospital'. She went there as a visitor. We say 'Jill went to **the** hospital / Jill is at **the** hospital' because we mean a particular hospital, the one where Jack is.

b)   Prison   school   university   college   church
We say a criminal goes **to prison** (*not* 'to the prison'); a child goes **to school**; a student goes **to university/college**. We do not use **the** when we are thinking of the idea of these places and what they are used for:
  – After I leave **school**, I want to go to **university**. (as a pupil/student)
  – Why aren't the children at **school** today? (as pupils)
  – Mrs Kelly goes to **church** every Sunday. (for a religious service)
  – Ken's brother is in **prison** for robbery. (he is a prisoner)
We say 'be **in** prison', but usually 'be **at** school/university/college'. '**In** church' and '**at** church' are both possible.

Now study these sentences with **the**:
  – Mr Kelly went to **the school** to meet his daughter's teacher. (He didn't go there as a pupil.)
  – Excuse me, where is **the university**, please? (a particular building)
  – The workmen went to **the church** to repair the roof. (They didn't go to a religious service.)
  – Ken went to **the prison** to visit his brother. (He went as a visitor, not as a prisoner; he went to the prison where his brother was.)

c)   bed   work   home
We say: 'go **to bed** / be **in bed**' etc. (*not* 'the bed'):
  – It's time to go **to bed** now.   – Is Tom still **in bed**?
'Go **to work** / be **at work** / start **work** / finish **work**' etc. (*not* 'the work'):
  – Why isn't Ann **at work** today?   – What time do you finish **work**?
'Go **home** / come **home** / be **at home** / stay **at home**' etc. (*not* 'the home'):
  – Come on! Let's go **home**.   – Will you be **at home** tomorrow?
There is *no* preposition with **go/come/get/arrive home**. (*not* 'to home')

UNIT 75   Exercises

75.1 *Complete these sentences using the words in this unit.*
Example: Two people were injured in the accident and were taken   *to hospital.*

1 I was very tired and it was very late, so I went ....
2 Fred robbed a bank but was caught by the police. He was sent ....
3 Tom doesn't often go out in the evenings. He usually stays ....
4 Jill isn't a religious person. She never goes ....
5 In Britain, children from the age of five have to go ....
6 Children sometimes get into trouble if they are late for ....
7 There is a lot of traffic in the morning when everybody is going ....
8 Mrs Grimes has just had an operation. She is still ....
9 When David leaves school, he wants to study economics ....
10 Bill never gets up before 9 o'clock. It's 8.30 now, so he is still ....

75.2 *Write short answers to these questions.*
Example: If you wanted to meet your children's teachers, where would you go?
   To the school. ....

1 A friend of yours is in hospital. Where would you go to visit him? ....
2 A friend of yours is in prison. Where would you go to visit him? ....
3 A friend of yours is at church. If you wanted to meet him immediately after the service, where would you go? ....

75.3 *This time you have to choose the correct form, with or without* **the**.
Example: Ken's brother is in prison / the prison for robbery. ('prison' is correct)

1 Some children hate school / the school.
2 What time do your children finish school / the school?
3 After leaving school / the school, Nora worked as a cleaner in hospital / at the hospital.
4 My brother is very ill in hospital / the hospital.
5 All over the world, people are in prison / the prison because of their political beliefs.
6 The other day the fire-brigade had to go to prison / the prison to put out a fire.
7 On the way to London we passed through a small village with an old church. We stopped to visit church / the church. It was a beautiful building.
8 John's mother is a regular churchgoer. She goes to church / the church every Sunday. John himself doesn't go to church / the church.
9 Every term parents are invited to school / the school to meet the teachers.
10 After work / the work, Ann usually goes home / to home.
11 Tom left university / the university without doing his examinations.
12 When Ann was ill, we all went to hospital / the hospital to visit her.
13 I like to read in bed / the bed before going to sleep.
14 What time do you have to start work / the work tomorrow morning?
15 How many people go to university / the university in your country?

UNIT 76   Geographical names with and without **the**

a) *Continents:*   We do not say **the** with the names of continents:
Africa (*not* 'the Africa')   Asia   Europe   South America

b) *Countries and states:*   We do not usually say **the** with the names of countries and states:
France (*not* 'the France')   Japan   West Germany   Nigeria   Texas
But we say **the** with names which include words like 'republic', 'union', 'kingdom', 'states':
the German Federal **Republic**   the Soviet **Union**   the United **States** (of
(usually called 'West Germany')   the United **Kingdom**   America)
the **Republic** of Ireland   the United Arab **Emirates**
We also use **the** with *plural* names:
the Netherlands   the Philippines

c) *Cities:*   We do not use **the** with the names of cities/towns/villages:
Cairo (*not* 'the Cairo')   New York   Glasgow   Madrid
Exception: **The** Hague (in the Netherlands)

d) *Islands:*   Island groups usually have *plural* names with **the**:
the Bahamas   the Canaries / the Canary Islands   the British Isles
Individual islands usually have singular names without **the**:
Corfu   Sicily   Bermuda   Easter Island

e) *Regions:*   We say:
the Middle East   the Far East
the north of England   the south of Spain   the west of Canada
(*but:* **northern** England / **southern** Spain / **western** Canada – without **the**)

f) *Mountains:*   Mountain ranges usually have *plural* names with **the**:
the Rocky Mountains / the Rockies   the Andes   the Alps
But individual mountains usually have names without **the**:
(Mount) Everest   Ben Nevis (in Scotland)   (Mount) Etna

g) *Lakes:*   Lakes usually have names without **the**:
Lake Superior   Lake Constance

h) Names of *oceans/seas/rivers/canals* have **the**:
the Atlantic (Ocean)   the Indian Ocean
the Mediterranean (Sea)   the Red Sea   the (English) Channel
the Nile   the Amazon   the Thames   the Rhine
the Suez Canal   the Panama Canal
Note: On maps **the** is not usually included in the name.

UNIT 76   Exercises

76.1 *Read these sentences carefully. Some are correct, but some need* **the** *(perhaps more than once). Correct the sentences where necessary.*
Examples: Everest was first climbed in 1953.   RIGHT
Milan is in north of Italy.   WRONG – the north of Italy

1 Last year we visited Canada and United States. ....
2 Africa is much larger than Europe. ....
3 South of England is warmer than north. ....
4 We went to Spain for our holidays and swam in Mediterranean. ....
5 Tom has visited most countries in western Europe. ....
6 A friend of mine used to work as a reporter in Middle East. ....
7 Next year we are going skiing in Swiss Alps. ....
8 Malta has been a republic since 1974. ....
9 Nile is longest river in Africa. ....
10 United Kingdom consists of Great Britain and Northern Ireland. ....

76.2 *Here are some geography questions. You have to choose the right answer. Sometimes you need* **the**, *sometimes not. Try and find out the answers if you don't know them.*
Example: What is the longest river in the world? (Amazon / Rhine / Nile)   the Amazon.

1 Where is Bolivia? (Africa / South America / North America) ....
2 Where is Ethiopia? (Asia / South America / Africa) ....
3 Of which country is Manila the capital? (Indonesia / Philippines / Japan) ....
4 Of which country is Stockholm the capital?
(Norway / Denmark / Sweden) ....
5 Which country lies between Mexico and Canada?
(Venezuela / El Salvador / United States) ....
6 Which is the largest country in the world?
(United States / China / Soviet Union) ....
7 Which is the largest continent? (Africa / South America / Asia) ....
8 What is the name of the mountain range in the west of North America?
(Rocky Mountains / Andes / Alps) ....
9 What is the name of the ocean between America and Asia?
(Atlantic / Pacific / Indian Ocean) ....
10 What is the name of the ocean between Africa and Australia?
(Atlantic / Pacific / Indian Ocean) ....
11 What is the name of the sea between England and France?
(Mediterranean Sea / English Channel/ French Sea) ....
12 What is the name of the sea between Africa and Europe?
(Black Sea / Red Sea / Mediterranean Sea) ....
13 What is the name of the sea between Britain and Norway?
(Norwegian Sea / English Channel / North Sea) ....
14 Which river flows through Vienna, Budapest and Belgrade?
(Rhine / Danube / Volga) ....
15 What joins the Atlantic and Pacific oceans?
(Suez Canal / Panama Canal) ....

UNIT 77   Names of streets, buildings etc. with and without **the**

a) We do not normally use **the** with names of streets/roads/squares etc.:

Regent Street (*not* 'the ...')	Fifth Avenue	Piccadilly Circus
Cromwell Road	Broadway	Red Square

There are some exceptions (for example: '**The** Mall' in London).

b) Many names (for example, of airports or universities) are two words:
   Kennedy Airport   **Cambridge University**
The first word is usually the name of a person ('Kennedy') or a place ('Cambridge'). We do not usually say **the** with names like these:

Victoria Station (*not* 'the ...')	Edinburgh Castle	Hyde Park
Westminster Abbey	Buckingham Palace	London Zoo
Canterbury Cathedral		

But we say '**the** White House', '**the** Royal Palace' because 'white' and 'royal' are not names. This is only a general rule. There are exceptions. See section c for hotels etc. and section e for names with **of**.

c) We usually say **the** before the names of these places:

hotels	**the** Hilton (Hotel), **the** Station Hotel
restaurants/pubs	**the** Bombay Restaurant, **the** Red Lion (pub)
theatres	**the** Palace Theatre, **the** National Theatre
cinemas	**the** ABC, **the** Odeon, **the** Classic
museums/galleries	**the** British Museum, **the** Tate Gallery

Again there are exceptions. See also section d of this unit.

d) Many shops, restaurants, hotels, banks etc. are named after the people who started them. These names end in **s** or **'s**. We do not use **the** with these names:

shops	Selfridges (*not* 'the Selfridges'), Harrods
restaurants	Maxim's, Macdonalds, Luigi's Italian Restaurant
hotels	Claridge's
banks	Barclays Bank, Lloyds Bank

Churches are usually named after saints (**St** = saint):
   St John's Church   St Paul's Cathedral

e) We say **the** before the names of places, buildings etc. with **of**:

the Bank **of** England (*not* 'Bank of England')	**the** Great Wall **of** China
the Houses **of** Parliament	**the** Museum **of** Modern Art
the Tower **of** London	

f) We say **the** with the names of newspapers:
   the *Times*   **the** *Washington Post*   **the** *Evening Standard*

UNIT 77   Exercises

77.1 *Use the map to answer the questions in the way shown. Write the name of the place and the street it is in. On maps we don't normally use* **the**; *in your sentences, use* **the** *if necessary.*

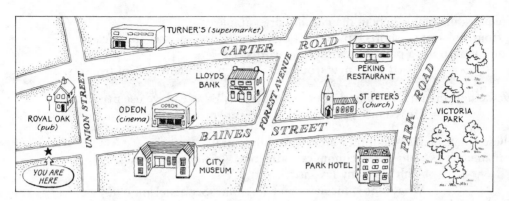

Example: 'Is there a cinema near here?'   'Yes, <u>the Odeon in Baines Street</u>   '

1 'Is there a supermarket near here?'   'Yes, ... in .... '
2 'Is there a hotel near here?'   'Yes, ... in .... '
3 'Is there a bank near here?'   'Yes, ... in .... '
4 'Is there a restaurant near here?'   'Yes, ... in .... '
5 'Is there a church near here?'   'Yes, ... '
6 'Is there a pub near here?'   'Yes, ... '
7 'Is there a museum near here?'   'Yes, ... '
8 'Is there a park near here?'   'Yes, ... at the end of .... '

77.2 *In this exercise you have to choose the correct form, with or without* **the**.
Example: When we were in London, we visited ~~National Gallery~~ / the National Gallery.

1 The British Prime Minister lives in <u>Downing Street / the Downing Street</u>.
2 One of the nicest parks in London is <u>St James's Park / the St James's Park</u>, which is very near <u>Buckingham Palace / the Buckingham Palace</u>.
3 Frank is a student at <u>Liverpool University / the Liverpool University</u>.
4 Mr Jenkins reads *Daily Telegraph* / the *Daily Telegraph* but his wife reads *Times* / the *Times*.
5 If you want to buy some new clothes, the shop I would recommend is <u>Harrison's / the Harrison's</u>.
6 We flew from London to <u>Orly Airport / the Orly Airport</u> in Paris.
7 <u>Tate Gallery / The Tate Gallery</u> is the main modern art museum in London.
8 My local pub is called <u>Prince of Wales / the Prince of Wales</u>.
9 Have you ever visited <u>Tower of London / the Tower of London</u>?
10 'Which hotel are you staying at?'   'At <u>Sheraton / the Sheraton</u>.'
11 Diana and George got married in <u>St Matthew's Church / the St Matthew's Church</u>.
12 You must visit <u>Science Museum / the Science Museum</u> when you are in London.
13 Did you see the film at <u>Classic / the Classic</u> (cinema)?

UNIT 78   Singular or plural?

a) We use some nouns only in the *plural*. For example:

   trousers   jeans   shorts   pyjamas   tights   scissors   glasses/spectacles

   You can also use **a pair of ...** with these words:
   - I need **some** new **trousers.**   *or*   I need **a** new **pair of trousers.**

b) We do not often use the plural of **person** ('persons'). Instead we use **people**:
   - He is **a** nice **person.**   - They are nice **people.**

c) These nouns end in -s but they are not usually plural:

   mathematics   physics   economics   athletics   gymnastics   news
   - **Athletics is** my favourite sport.
   - What time **is the news** on television? (See also Unit 69d.)

   These words end in -s and can be singular *or* plural:

means	a **means** of transport	many **means** of transport
series	a television **series**	two television **series**
species	a **species** of bird	200 **species** of bird

d) Some singular nouns are often used with a plural verb. For example:

   government   staff   team   family   audience   committee

   We often think of these things as a number of people ('they'), not as one thing ('it'). So we often use a plural verb:
   - **The government** (= they) **want** to reduce taxes.
   - **The staff** (= they) **aren't** happy with **their** new working conditions.

   A singular verb ('The government **wants** ...') is also possible.

   Note that we normally use a plural verb with the names of sports teams:
   - **Scotland are** playing France in a football match next week.

   We always use a plural verb with **the police**:
   - The police **have** arrested Tom.
   - **Are** the police well-paid?

e) Sometimes we use a plural noun with a singular verb. We do this when we talk about a sum of money, a period of time, a distance etc.:
   - **Five thousand pounds** (= it) was stolen in the robbery. (*not* 'were stolen')
   - **Three years** (= it) is a long time to be without a job. (*not* 'are')

f) We say 'a holiday of three **weeks**' but 'a three-**week** holiday':
   - I've got **a three-week** holiday in July. (*not* 'a three-weeks holiday')

   Here, **three-week** is used as an adjective before 'holiday'. When we use 'three-weeks' as an adjective, it loses the **s**. So we say:

a ten-**pound** note (*not* 'pounds')	two 14-**year**-old girls
a four-**week** English course	a six-**hour** journey

   You can also say 'I've got three weeks' holiday'. See Unit 79d.

UNIT 78   Exercises

78.1 *In this exercise you have to complete the sentences with words from sections a, b and c. Sometimes you need **a** or **some**.*
Examples: She can't see very well. She needs glasses (or spectacles).
This plant is ....a.... very rare species.

1 Footballers don't wear trousers when they play. They wear ....
2 The bicycle is .... of transport.
3 The bicycle and the car are .... of transport.
4 I want to cut this piece of material. I need ....
5 Ann is going to write .... of articles for her local newspaper.
6 There are a lot of American television .... on British television.
7 While we were out walking, we saw 25 different .... of bird.
8 We need at least four .... to play this game.

78.2 *This time you have to choose the correct form of the verb, singular or plural. Sometimes either a singular or a plural verb is possible.*
Example: Gymnastics is / ~~are~~ my favourite sport. ('is' is correct)

1 The trousers you bought for me doesn't / don't fit me.
2 Physics was / were my best subject at school.
3 Fortunately the news wasn't / weren't as bad as we had expected.
4 The police wants / want to interview Fred about a robbery.
5 Three days isn't / aren't long enough for a good holiday.
6 Where does / do your family live?
7 England has / have lost all their football matches this season.
8 Does / Do the police know about the stolen money?
9 Can I borrow your scissors? Mine isn't / aren't sharp enough.
10 I'm going to take a taxi. Six miles is / are too far for me to walk.

78.3 *In this exercise you have to use the structure in section f.*
Examples: Our holiday lasted three weeks.   It was a three-week holiday.
The girls were 14 years old.   They were 14-year-old girls

1 The woman was 27.   She was a ....
2 The flight lasted three hours.   It was a ....
3 The strike lasted four days.   It was a ....
4 The book has 200 pages.   It is a ....
5 The boys were ten years old.   They were ....
6 The television series has ten parts.   It is ....
7 The bottle holds two litres.   It is ....
8 Each of the tickets cost ten pounds.   They were ....
9 The building has ten storeys (= *floors*).   It is ....
10 This bag of potatoes weighs five kilos.   It is ....
11 We walked for five miles.   It was ....

UNIT 79   ...'s (apostrophe s) and ... of ...

a) We normally use **'s** when the first noun is a person or an animal:
   the **manager's** office (*not* 'the office of the manager')
   Mr Evans's daughter   the **horse's** tail   a **policeman's** hat
   Otherwise (with things) we normally use **... of ...**:
   the door **of the room** (*not* 'the room's door')
   the beginning **of the story** (*not* 'the story's beginning')
   Sometimes you can use **'s** when the first noun is a thing. For example, you can say:
   the book's title *or* **the title of the book**
   But it is safer and more usual to use **... of ...** (but see also section b).

b) You can usually use **'s** when the first noun is an organisation (= a group of people). So you
   can say:
   the government's decision   *or*   the decision **of the government**
   the company's success   *or*   the success **of the company**
   It is also possible to use **'s** with places. So you can say:
   the city's new theatre   **the world's** population
   Britain's system of government   **Italy's** largest city

c) After a singular noun we use **'s**. After a plural noun (which ends in -s) we use only an
   apostrophe ('):
   my **sister's** room (*one* sister)   Mr **Carter's** house
   my **sisters'** room (*more than one* sister)   the **Carters'** house (*Mr and Mrs Carter*)
   If a plural noun does not end in **-s**, we use **'s**:
   a **children's** book
   Note that you can use **'s** after more than one noun:
   Jack and Jill's wedding   **Mr and Mrs Carter's** house
   But we would not use **'s** in a sentence like this:
      – I met the wife **of the man who lent us the money.** ('the man who lent us the
        money' is too long to be followed by **'s**)
   Note that you can use **'s** without a following noun:
      – Tom's flat is much larger than **Ann's.** (= Ann's flat)

d) You can also use **'s** with time words (**tomorrow** etc.):
      – **Tomorrow's** meeting has been cancelled.
      – Have you still got **last Saturday's** newspaper?
   You can also say: **yesterday's ...   today's ...   this evening's ...   next week's ...
   Monday's ...** etc.
   We also use **'s** (or only an apostrophe (') with plurals) with periods of time:
      – I've got **a week's** holiday.
      – I've got **three weeks'** holiday.
      – I need **eight hours'** sleep a night.
      – My house is very near here – only about **five minutes'** walk.
   Compare this structure with '**a three-week** holiday' (Unit 78f).

UNIT 79   Exercises

79.1 *In this exercise you have to join two nouns. Sometimes you have to use an apostrophe ('), with or without **s**. Sometimes you have to use ... of ....*
Examples: the door / the room **the door of the room.**   the mother / Ann **Ann's mother**

  1 the camera / Tom ....
  2 the eyes / the cat ....
  3 the top / the page ....
  4 the daughter / Charles ....
  5 the newspaper / today ....
  6 the toys / the children ....
  7 the name / your wife ....
  8 the name / this street ....

  9 the name / the man I saw you with yesterday ....
10 the new manager / the company ....
11 the result / the football match ....
12 the car / Mike's parents ....
13 the birthday / my father ....
14 the new headmaster / the school ....
15 the garden / our neighbours ....
16 the ground floor / the building ....
17 the children / Don and Mary ....
18 the economic policy / the government ....
19 the husband / the woman talking to Tom ....
20 the house / my aunt and uncle ....

79.2 *Read each sentence and write a new sentence using* **'s** *with the underlined words.*
Example: The meeting <u>tomorrow</u> has been cancelled.   **Tomorrow's meeting has been cancelled.**

  1 The storm <u>last week</u> caused a lot of damage.
    Last ....
  2 The only cinema in <u>the town</u> has been closed down.
    The t............................
  3 Exports from <u>Britain</u> to the United States have fallen recently.
    B............................
  4 There will be a big crowd at the football match <u>this evening</u>.
    There will be a big crowd at this ....
  5 Tourism is the main industry in <u>the region</u>.
    The r............................

79.3 *Now you have to use the information given to complete the sentences.*
Example: If I leave my house at 9 o'clock and drive to London, I arrive at about 12 o'clock.
       So it's about ......**three hours'**...... drive to London from my house.

  1 I'm going on holiday on the 12th. I have to be back at work on the 26th.
    So I've got .... holiday.
  2 I went to sleep at 3 o'clock this morning and woke up an hour later at 4 o'clock.
    So I only had .... sleep.
  3 If I leave my house at 8.50 and walk to work, I get to work at 9 o'clock.
    So it's only .... walk from my house to work.

UNIT 80 'A friend of **mine**', '**my own** house'
On my own / by myself

a) A friend of mine / a friend of Tom's
We say 'a friend **of mine/yours/his/hers/ours/theirs**'. (*not* 'a friend of me/you/him' etc.):
- A friend **of mine** is coming to stay with me next week. (*not* 'a friend of me')
- We went on holiday with some friends **of ours**. (*not* 'some friends of us')
- Tom had an argument with a neighbour **of his**.
- It was a good suggestion **of yours** to go swimming this afternoon.

We also say 'a friend **of Tom's**', 'a friend **of my brother's**' etc.:
- That man over there is a friend **of my brother's**.
- It was a good idea **of Tom's** to go swimming.

b) My own ... / your own ... etc.
You cannot say 'an own ...' ('an own house', 'an own car', etc.)
You must use **my/your/his/her/its/our/their** before **own**:
   my own house   **your own** car   **her own** room

My own ... = something that is only mine, not shared or borrowed:
- Do many people in England have **their own house**? (*not* 'an own house')
- I don't want to share with anyone. I want **my own room**.
- Unfortunately the flat hasn't got **its own entrance**.
- It's **my own fault** that I've got no money. I spend it too quickly.
- Why do you want to borrow my car? Why can't you use **your own** (car)?

You can also use **...own...** to say that you do something yourself instead of somebody else doing it for you. For example:
- Ann always cuts **her own hair**. (= she cuts it herself; she doesn't go to the hairdresser)
- Do you grow **your own vegetables**? (= do you grow them yourself in your garden instead of buying them from shops?)

c) On my own / by myself
On my own and **by myself** both mean **alone**. We say:

on	my/your/his/her/its/our/their **own**
by {	myself/yourself/himself/herself/itself (*singular*)
	ourselves/yourselves/themselves (*plural*)

- I like living **on my own / by myself**.
- Did you go on holiday **on your own / by yourself**?
- Jack was sitting **on his own / by himself** in a corner of the café.
- Learner drivers are not allowed to drive **on their own / by themselves**.

For **myself/yourself** etc. see also Unit 81.

UNIT 80   Exercises

80.1 *Write new sentences using the structure in section a (a **friend of mine** etc.).*
Example: I am writing to <u>one of my friends</u>.   *I'm writing to a friend of mine.*

1 We met <u>one of your relations</u>.   We met a ....
2 Henry borrowed <u>one of my books</u>.   Henry ....
3 Tom invited <u>some of his friends</u> to his flat.   Tom ....
4 We had dinner with <u>one of our neighbours</u>.   ....
5 Ann is in love with <u>one of her colleagues</u>.   ....
6 They went on holiday with <u>two of their friends</u>.   ....

80.2 *Make sentences from the words in brackets. Each time use **my own** / **your own** etc.*
Example: I don't want to share a room. (want / have / room) *I want to have my own room.*

1 I don't watch television with the rest of the family. (have / television / in my bedroom)   I
   have .... in my bedroom.
2 Jack and Bill are fed up with working for other people. (want / start / business)
   They ....
3 Henry is extremely rich. (have / private jet)   He ....
4 The Isle of Man is an island off the coast of Britain. It is not completely independent but
   (have / parliament and laws) it ....

80.3 *Now you have to complete these sentences using **my own** / **your own** etc.*
Examples: Why do you want to borrow my car? Why can't you use *your own car?*
            Ann never goes to the hairdresser. She cuts *her own hair.*

1 Don't blame me. It's not my fault. It's ....
2 He's always smoking my cigarettes. Why doesn't he buy .... ?
3 Why do you want my pen? Can't you use .... ?
4 I don't often buy clothes. I usually make ....
5 Nobody cooks Don's meals for him. He has to cook ....
6 She doesn't buy ready-made cigarettes. She rolls ....

80.4 *Complete these sentences using **on my own** / **by myself** etc.*
Example: Learner drivers are not allowed to drive on *their own.*

1 I'm glad I live with other people. I wouldn't like to live on ....
2 The box was too heavy for me to lift by ....
3 I went over to talk to Tim at the party because he was by ....
4 Very young children should not be allowed to go swimming by ....
5 Hasn't she got any friends? When I see her, she is always on ....
6 I don't like strawberries with cream. I like them on ....
7 Do you like working with other people or do you prefer working by .... ?
8 We had no help decorating the flat. We did it completely on ....

UNIT 81   Reflexive pronouns (**myself / yourself** etc.)

a) The *reflexive pronouns* are:

singular: myself	yourself (*one person*)	himself/herself/itself
plural: ourselves	yourselves (*more than one person*)	themselves

We use a reflexive pronoun when the subject and object are the same:

⌐Tom⌐ cut ⌐himself⌐ while he was shaving. (*not* 'Tom cut him')
  – I don't want you to pay for me. I'll pay for **myself**.
  – **The old lady** sat in a corner talking to **herself**.
  – Don't get angry. Control **yourself**! (*said to one person*)
  – If **you** want more to eat, help **yourselves**. (*said to more than one person*)
  – The party was great. **We** enjoyed **ourselves** very much.
But we do not use 'myself' etc. after **bring/take something with ...**:
  – I went out and **took** an umbrella **with me**. (*not* 'with myself')

b) We do not use 'myself' etc. after **feel/relax/concentrate**:
  – **I feel great** after having a swim. (*not* 'I feel myself great')
  – You must try and **concentrate**.
  – It's good to **relax**.
We do not normally use 'myself' etc. after **wash/dress/shave**:
  – I got up, **shaved, washed** and **dressed**. (*not* 'shaved myself' etc.)
But we say: **I dried myself**.

Note how we use **meet**:
  – What time shall we **meet**? (*not* 'meet ourselves / meet us')

c) Study the difference between **–selves** and **each other**:
  – Tom and Ann stood in front of the mirror and looked at **themselves**.
    (= *Tom and Ann* looked at *Tom and Ann*)
  but: **Tom** looked at **Ann** and **Ann** looked at **Tom**. They looked at **each other**.
You can use **one another** instead of **each other**:
  – How long have you and Bill known **each other** (*or* **one another**)?
  – Sue and Ann don't like **each other** (*or* **one another**).

d) We also use **myself** etc. in another way. For example:
  – 'Who repaired your bicycle for you?' 'Nobody. **I repaired it myself**.'
I repaired it myself =*I* repaired it, not anybody else. We use **myself** here to emphasise **I**. Here are some more examples:
  – I'm not going to do it for you. **You** can do it **yourself**.
  – **Let's** paint the house **ourselves**. It will be much cheaper.
  – **The film itself** wasn't very good but I liked the music.
  – I don't think Tom will get the job. **Tom himself** doesn't think he'll get it. (*or* '**Tom** doesn't think he'll get it **himself**.')

For '**by** myself / **by** yourself' etc. see Unit 80c.

162

UNIT 81   Exercises

81.1 *Complete these sentences using* **myself/yourself** *etc. with these verbs:*

kick   teach   ~~cut~~   lock   look after   hurt   burn   talk to   blame

Example: Tom *cut himself* .... while he was shaving this morning.

1 Be careful! That pan is very hot. Don't ....
2 They couldn't get back into the house. They had .... out.
3 It isn't her fault. She really shouldn't ....
4 What a stupid fool I am! I could .... !
5 The boy was lucky when he fell down the stairs. He didn't ....
6 I'm trying to .... Spanish but I'm not making much progress.
7 He spends most of his time alone, so it's not surprising that he ....
8 Don't worry about us. We can ....

81.2 *Complete these sentences with these verbs. This time, use* **myself** *etc. only where necessary:*

dry   concentrate   feel   enjoy   relax   wash   ~~shave~~   meet

Example: Tom is growing a beard because he doesn't like *shaving.* ....

1 I really .... well today – much better than yesterday.
2 He climbed out of the pool, picked up a towel and ....
3 I tried to study but I just couldn't ....
4 Jack and I first .... at a party five years ago.
5 You're always rushing about. Why don't you .... more?
6 It was a lovely holiday. We really .... very much.
7 I overslept this morning. I didn't have time to .... or have breakfast.

81.3 *In these sentences you have to write* **-selves** *or* **each other***.*
Examples: Tom and Ann stood in front of the mirror and looked at *themselves* ....
How long have Tom and Ann known *each other* ...... ?

1 At Christmas friends often give .... presents.
2 Did the children enjoy .... when they were on holiday?
3 Jack and Jill are very happy together. They love .... very much.
4 They had an argument last week. They are still not speaking to ....
5 Some people are very selfish. They only think of ....
6 Nora and I don't see .... very often these days.

81.4 *Answer these questions using* **myself/yourself** *etc.*
Example: 'Who repaired the bicycle for you?'   'Nobody. I *repaired it myself.* .... '

1 'Who cut your hair for you?'   'Nobody. I cut .... '
2 'Who told you Linda was getting married?'   'Linda .... '
3 'Does Mr Thomas have a secretary to type his letters?'   'No, he .... '
4 'Do you want me to post that letter for you?'   'No, I'll .... '
5 'Can you clean the windows for me?'   'Why don't you .... ?'

UNIT 82 All / all of, no / none of, most / most of etc.

a)

all no/none some any much/many most little/few each half

You can use these words (except **none** and **half**) with a noun:
- **Some people** are very unfriendly.
- Did you put **any salt** in the soup?
- I've got **no money.**
- **All cars** have wheels.
- Hurry! We have very **little time.**
- Study **each sentence** carefully.

Be careful with **most**:
- **Most tourists** do not visit this part of the town. (*not* 'most of tourists', *not* 'the most tourists')
- George is much richer than **most people.**

b) You can also use these words (except **no**) alone, without a noun:
- 'I need some money. Have you got **any**?' 'Yes, but not **much.**'
- 'How many cigarettes have you got?' '**None.**'
- Most people like Tom but **some** don't.

We usually say **each one** instead of **each** alone:
- There were three boxes on the table. **Each one** was a different colour.

For **all** see Unit 87a.

c) You can also use these words (except **no**) with **of** .... So you can say **some of the people, all of these cars, none of my money** etc.

When you use these words with **of**, you need **the/this/that/these/those/my/your/his** etc. You cannot say 'some of people', 'all of cars'. You must say: 'some of **the** people', 'all of **these** cars' etc.:
- **Some of the** people at the party were very friendly.
- **Most of my** friends live in London.
- **None of this** money is mine.
- **Each of the** rooms in the hotel has its own bathroom.
- I haven't read **many of these** books.

With **all** and **half** we usually leave out **of**:
all my friends (= all of my friends)
half the money (= half of the money) (*not* 'the half')

d) After **all of / none of** etc. you can also use **it/us/you/them**:
- 'How many of these people do you know?' '**None of them.**'
- Do **any of you** want to come to a party tonight?
- 'Do you like this music?' '**Some of it. Not all of it.**'

You must say 'all **of**' and 'half **of**' before **it/us/you/them**:
all of us (*not* 'all us')   **half of them** (*not* 'half them')

For **no** and **none** see Unit 85b.
For more information about the words in this unit see Units 83–7.

UNIT 82   Exercises

82.1 Read each situation and then make a sentence from the words in brackets.
Example: I need someone who can speak Spanish. (any / your friends / speak Spanish?)
Do any of your friends speak Spanish?

1 We went out and it started to rain. We all got wet because (none / us / have / an umbrella)
none ....
2 When they got married, they kept it a complete secret. (they / not / tell / any / their friends)
They ....
3 I don't want all this cake. (you / want / some / it?) Do ....
4 This is a very old town. (many / the buildings / over 800 years old)
....
5 Jim won a lot of money last year. (he / spend / half / it on a new car)
....
6 A lot of people were interested in the job. (the manager / interview / each / the people who applied) ....
7 Not many people live in the north of the country. (most / the population / live / the south)
....
8 The club is mainly for younger people. (few / the members / over 25)
....
9 When the post arrived, she looked through it hopefully but (none / the letters / for her)
....

82.2 Complete these sentences with **most** or **most of**.
Example: *Most* .... tourists do not visit this part of the town.

1 I spend .... my spare time gardening.
2 The public transport system is bad but .... people have a car.
3 .... days I get up early.
4 We had a lazy holiday. .... the time we lay on the beach.
5 The church is very old. .... it was built in the 12th century.
6 I expect .... you are very tired after your long journey.

82.3 Answer these questions using the word(s) in brackets.
Example: Do you like this music? (some)   *Some of it*...............

1 Did you watch the film? (most)   ....
2 Did you take these photographs? (some)   ....
3 Have you read these books? (a few)   ....
4 Are those people English? (most)   ....
5 How much of this luggage is yours? (all)   ....
6 How many of these people do you know? (not many)   ....
7 Does this furniture belong to you? (some)   ....
8 Have you spent all the money I gave you? (not all)   ....
9 How much of this money is yours? (half)   ....

UNIT 83   Both / both of,   neither / neither of, either / either of

a)   We use **both**, **neither** and **either** when we are talking about two things. You can use these words with a noun:
- **Both restaurants** are very good. (*not* 'the both restaurants')
- **Neither restaurant** is expensive.
- We can go to **either restaurant**. I don't mind. (**either** = one or the other, it doesn't matter which one)
- I didn't like **either restaurant**. (not the one or the other)

b)   You can also use **both/neither/either** with **of** .... When you use these words with **of**, you always need **the/these/those/my/your/his** etc. You cannot say 'both of restaurants'. You have to say 'both of **the** restaurants', 'both of **these** restaurants' etc.:
- **Both of these** restaurants are very good.
- **Neither of the** restaurants we went to was (*or* were) expensive.
- We can go to **either of those** restaurants. I don't mind.

With **both** you can leave out **of**. So you can say:
   both my parents   *or*   **both of my parents**

c)   After **both of / neither of / either of** you can also use **us/you/them**:
- Can **either of you** speak Spanish?
- I wanted Tom and Ann to come but **neither of them** wanted to.

You must say 'both **of**' before **us/you/them**:
- **Both of us** were very tired. (*not* 'Both us ...')

d)   After **neither of** ... you can use a singular or a plural verb:
- Neither of the children **wants** (*or* **want**) to go to bed.
- Neither of us **is** (*or* **are**) married.

e)   You can say **both ... and ...**, **neither ... nor ...** and **either ... or ...**. Study these examples:
- **Both** Tom **and** Ann were late.
- They were **both** tired **and** hungry.
- **Neither** Tom **nor** Ann came to the party.
- He said he would contact me but he **neither** wrote **nor** phoned.
- I'm not sure where he is from. He's **either** Spanish **or** Italian.
- **Either** you apologise **or** I'll never speak to you again.

f)   You can also use **both/neither/either** alone:
- 'Is he British or American?'   '**Neither**. He's Australian'.
- 'Do you want tea or coffee?'   '**Either**. I don't mind.'
- I couldn't decide which one to choose. I liked **both**.

For **I don't either** and **neither do I** see Unit 51c.

UNIT 83   Both / both of,   neither / neither of, either / either of

a) We use **both, neither** and **either** when we are talking about two things. You can use these words with a noun:
  - **Both restaurants** are very good. (*not* 'the both restaurants')
  - **Neither restaurant** is expensive.
  - We can go to **either restaurant**. I don't mind. (**either** = one or the other, it doesn't matter which one)
  - I didn't like **either restaurant**. (not the one or the other)

b) You can also use **both/neither/either** with **of** .... When you use these words with **of**, you always need **the/these/those/my/your/his** etc. You cannot say 'both of restaurants'. You have to say 'both of **the** restaurants', 'both of **these** restaurants' etc.:
  - **Both of these** restaurants are very good.
  - **Neither of the** restaurants we went to was (*or* were) expensive.
  - We can go to **either of those** restaurants. I don't mind.

With **both** you can leave out **of**. So you can say:
  both my parents   *or*   both **of** my parents

c) After **both of / neither of / either of** you can also use **us/you/them**:
  - Can **either of you** speak Spanish?
  - I wanted Tom and Ann to come but **neither of them** wanted to.

You must say 'both **of**' before **us/you/them**:
  - **Both of us** were very tired. (*not* 'Both us ...')

d) After **neither of ...** you can use a singular or a plural verb:
  - Neither of the children **wants** (*or* **want**) to go to bed.
  - Neither of us **is** (*or* **are**) married.

e) You can say **both ... and ..., neither ... nor ...** and **either ... or ....** Study these examples:
  - **Both** Tom **and** Ann were late.
  - They were **both** tired **and** hungry.
  - **Neither** Tom **nor** Ann came to the party.
  - He said he would contact me but he **neither** wrote **nor** phoned.
  - I'm not sure where he is from. He's **either** Spanish **or** Italian.
  - **Either** you apologise **or** I'll never speak to you again.

f) You can also use **both/neither/either** alone:
  - 'Is he British or American?' '**Neither.** He's Australian'.
  - 'Do you want tea or coffee?' '**Either.** I don't mind.'
  - I couldn't decide which one to choose. I liked **both**.

For **I don't either** and **neither do I** see Unit 51c.

UNIT 82   Exercises

82.1 *Read each situation and then make a sentence from the words in brackets.*
Example: I need someone who can speak Spanish. (any / your friends / speak Spanish?)
    Do any of your friends speak Spanish?

1   We went out and it started to rain. We all got wet because (none / us / have / an umbrella)
    none ....

2   When they got married, they kept it a complete secret. (they / not / tell / any / their friends)
    They ....

3   I don't want all this cake. (you / want / some / it?) Do ....

4   This is a very old town. (many / the buildings / over 800 years old)
    ....

5   Jim won a lot of money last year. (he / spend / half / it on a new car)
    ....

6   A lot of people were interested in the job. (the manager / interview / each / the people who
    applied) ....

7   Not many people live in the north of the country. (most / the population / live / the south)
    ....

8   The club is mainly for younger people. (few / the members / over 25)
    ....

9   When the post arrived, she looked through it hopefully but (none / the letters / for her)
    ....

82.2 *Complete these sentences with* **most** *or* **most of**.
Example: <u>Most</u> .... tourists do not visit this part of the town.

1   I spend .... my spare time gardening.
2   The public transport system is bad but .... people have a car.
3   .... days I get up early.
4   We had a lazy holiday. .... the time we lay on the beach.
5   The church is very old. .... it was built in the 12th century.
6   I expect .... you are very tired after your long journey.

82.3 *Answer these questions using the word(s) in brackets.*
Example: Do you like this music? (some)   <u>Some of it</u>.............

1   Did you watch the film? (most)   ....
2   Did you take these photographs? (some)   ....
3   Have you read these books? (a few)   ....
4   Are those people English? (most)   ....
5   How much of this luggage is yours? (all)   ....
6   How many of these people do you know? (not many)   ....
7   Does this furniture belong to you? (some)   ....
8   Have you spent all the money I gave you? (not all)   ....
9   How much of this money is yours? (half)   ....

UNIT 83 Exercises

83.1 *Complete these sentences with* **both/neither/either**. *Sometimes you need* of.
Examples: There are two windows in my room. It was very warm so I had both of............
them open.
'Do you want tea or coffee?' 'Either................ . I really don't mind.'

1 After the accident .... cars stopped. .... drivers got out and
   started shouting at each other. .... them were very aggressive.
2 It wasn't a very good football match. .... team played well.
3 A: Which of the two films did you prefer? The first one or the second one?
   B: Actually I didn't like .... them.
4 There are two ways to the city centre. You can go along the footpath by the river or you
   can go along the main road. You can go .... way.
5 .... these pullovers are very nice. I don't know which one to buy.
6 .... my parents is English. My father is Polish and my mother is Italian.
7 'Do you mind which sandwich I take?' 'No, take ....'
8 'Is today the 18th or the 19th?' '................................ . It's the 20th.'
9 Tom and I hadn't eaten for a long time, so .... us were very hungry.
10 When the boat started to sink, we were really frightened because .... us
   could swim.
11 A: Did you go to Scotland or Ireland for your holidays?
   B: We went to .... A week in Scotland and a week in Ireland.

83.2 *This time you have to make sentences with* **both ... and ...**, **neither ... nor ...** *and* **either ... or ...**
Examples: Tom was late. So was Ann. Both Tom and Ann were late.
He didn't write. He didn't telephone. He neither wrote nor telephoned.

1 The hotel wasn't clean. And it wasn't comfortable.
   The hotel was neither ....
2 It was a very boring film. It was very long too.
   The film was ....
3 Is that man's name Richard? Or is it Robert? It's one of the two.
   That man's name ....
4 I haven't got the time to go on holiday. And I haven't got the money.
   I've got ....
5 We can leave today or we can leave tomorrow – whichever you prefer.
   We ....
6 He gave up his job because he needed a change. Also because the pay was low.
   He gave up his job both ....
7 George doesn't smoke. And he doesn't drink.
   ....
8 The front of the house needs painting. The back needs painting too.
   ....

UNIT 84   Some and any
Some/any + -one/-body/-thing/-where

a) In general we use **some** in positive sentences and **any** in negative sentences (but see also sections b and d):

 - Ann has bought **some** new shoes.
 - I've got **something** in my eye.
 - They haven't got **any** children.
 - He's lazy. He **never** does **any** work.

We use **any** in the following sentences because the meaning is negative:

 - He left home **without any money.** (He didn't have any money.)
 - She **refused to say anything.** (She didn't say anything.)

b) We often use **any/anyone/anything** etc. after **if**:

 - **If any** letters arrive for me, can you send them to this address?
 - **If anyone** has any questions, I'll be pleased to answer them.
 - **If** you need **anything**, just ask.
 - Buy some pears **if** you see **any**.

The following sentences are without **if**, but they have the idea of **if**:

 - **Anyone** who wants to do the examination must give me their names before Friday. (= if there is anyone who ...)
 - I'll send on **any letters** that arrive for you. (= if there are any)

c) In questions we usually use **any** (not 'some'):

 - Have you got **any** money?   – Has **anybody** seen Tom?

But we often use **some** in questions when we expect the answer 'yes':

 - What's wrong with your eye? Have you got **something** in it? (= I think you have got something in your eye and I expect you to say 'yes')

We use **some** in questions especially when we offer or ask for things:

 - Would you like **some** tea?   – Can I have **some** of those apples?

d) **Any** also has another meaning. **Any/anyone/anybody/anything/anywhere** can mean **it doesn't matter which/who/what/where**:

 - You can catch **any of these buses.** They all go to the centre. (= it doesn't matter which of these buses)
 - Come and see me **any time** you want. (= it doesn't matter when)
 - You can have **anything you want** for your birthday present.
 - We left the door unlocked. **Anybody** could have come in.
 - I'd rather go **anywhere** than stay at home during my holiday.
 - 'Sing a song.' 'Which song shall I sing?' '**Any song.** I don't mind.'

e) **Someone/somebody/anyone/anybody** are singular words:

 - Someone **wants** to see you.
 - **Is** anybody there?

But we often use **they/them/their** after these words:

 - If **anyone wants** to leave early, **they** can. (= he or she can)
 - **Somebody has** spilt **their** (= his or her) coffee on the carpet.

For **some of / any of** see Unit 82. For **not ... any** see Unit 85.

168

UNIT 84   Some and any
Some/any + -one/-body/-thing/-where

a) In general we use **some** in positive sentences and **any** in negative sentences (but see also sections b and d):

    — Ann has bought **some** new shoes.   — They haven't got **any** children.

    — I've got **something** in my eye.   — He's lazy. He **never** does **any** work.

We use **any** in the following sentences because the meaning is negative:

    — He left home **without any money**. (He didn't have any money.)

    — She **refused to say anything**. (She didn't say anything.)

b) We often use **any/anyone/anything** etc. after **if**:

    — **If any** letters arrive for me, can you send them to this address?

    — **If anyone** has any questions, I'll be pleased to answer them.

    — **If** you need **anything**, just ask.

    — Buy some pears **if** you see **any**.

The following sentences are without **if**, but they have the idea of **if**:

    — **Anyone** who wants to do the examination must give me their names before Friday. (= if there is anyone who ...)

    — I'll send on **any letters** that arrive for you. (= if there are any)

c) In questions we usually use **any** (not 'some'):

    — Have you got **any** money?   — Has **anybody** seen Tom?

But we often use **some** in questions when we expect the answer 'yes':

    — What's wrong with your eye? Have you got **something** in it? (= I think you have got something in your eye and I expect you to say 'yes')

We use **some** in questions especially when we offer or ask for things:

    — Would you like **some** tea?   — Can I have **some** of those apples?

d) Any also has another meaning. **Any/anyone/anybody/anything/anywhere** can mean **it doesn't matter which/who/what/where**:

    — You can catch **any of these buses**. They all go to the centre. (= it doesn't matter which of these buses)

    — Come and see me **any time** you want. (= it doesn't matter when)

    — You can have **anything you want** for your birthday present.

    — We left the door unlocked. **Anybody** could have come in.

    — I'd rather go **anywhere** than stay at home during my holiday.

    — 'Sing a song.' 'Which song shall I sing?' '**Any song**. I don't mind.'

e) **Someone/somebody/anyone/anybody** are singular words:

    — Someone **wants** to see you.

    — **Is** anybody there?

But we often use **they/them/their** after these words:

    — If **anyone wants** to leave early, **they** can. (= he or she can)

    — **Somebody has** spilt **their** (= his or her) coffee on the carpet.

For **some of / any of** see Unit 82. For **not ... any** see Unit 85.

UNIT 83 Exercises

83.1 *Complete these sentences with* **both/neither/either**. *Sometimes you need* **of**.
Examples: There are two windows in my room. It was very warm so I had both of
them open.
'Do you want tea or coffee?' 'Either . I really don't mind.'

1 After the accident .... cars stopped. .... drivers got out and
   started shouting at each other. .... them were very aggressive.
2 It wasn't a very good football match. .... team played well.
3 A: Which of the two films did you prefer? The first one or the second one?
   B: Actually I didn't like .... them.
4 There are two ways to the city centre. You can go along the footpath by the river or you
   can go along the main road. You can go .... way.
5 .... these pullovers are very nice. I don't know which one to buy.
6 .... my parents is English. My father is Polish and my mother is Italian.
7 'Do you mind which sandwich I take?' 'No, take ....'
8 'Is today the 18th or the 19th?' '.................................. . It's the 20th.'
9 Tom and I hadn't eaten for a long time, so .... us were very hungry.
10 When the boat started to sink, we were really frightened because .... us
   could swim.
11 A: Did you go to Scotland or Ireland for your holidays?
   B: We went to .... A week in Scotland and a week in Ireland.

83.2 *This time you have to make sentences with* **both ... and ...**, **neither ... nor ...** *and* **either ... or ...**
Examples: Tom was late. So was Ann. Both Tom and Ann were late.
He didn't write. He didn't telephone. He neither wrote nor telephoned.

1 The hotel wasn't clean. And it wasn't comfortable.
   The hotel was neither ....
2 It was a very boring film. It was very long too.
   The film was ....
3 Is that man's name Richard? Or is it Robert? It's one of the two.
   That man's name ....
4 I haven't got the time to go on holiday. And I haven't got the money.
   I've got ....
5 We can leave today or we can leave tomorrow – whichever you prefer.
   We ....
6 He gave up his job because he needed a change. Also because the pay was low.
   He gave up his job both ....
7 George doesn't smoke. And he doesn't drink.
   ....
8 The front of the house needs painting. The back needs painting too.
   ....

UNIT 84   Exercises

84.1 *Complete these sentences with* **some/any/someone/anyone/somebody/anybody/
something/anything/somewhere/anywhere.**
Examples: Ann has bought ....*some*.......... new shoes.
The boy refused to tell us .....*anything:*.......

1 Does .... mind if I smoke?
2 Would you like .... to eat?
3 Do you live .... near Jim?
4 The prisoners refused to eat ....
5 There's .... at the door. Can you go and see who it is?
6 We slept in the park because we didn't have .... to stay. We didn't know
.... we could stay with and we didn't have .... money for a hotel.
7 Can I have .... milk in my coffee, please?
8 Sue is very secretive. She never tells .... (*two words*).
9 Why are you looking under the bed? Have you lost .... ?
10 You can cash these travellers cheques at .... bank.
11 I haven't read .... of these books but Tom has read .... of them.
12 He left the house without saying .... to ....
13 Would you like .... more coffee?
14 The film is really great. You can ask .... who has seen it.
15 This is a No Parking area. .... who parks their car here will have to pay a fine.
16 Can you give me .... information about places to see in the town?
17 With this special tourist bus ticket you can go .... you like on
.... bus you like.

84.2 *In this exercise you have to write sentences with* **if.**
Example: Perhaps someone will need help. If so, they can ask me.
If *anyone needs help, they can ask me.*..

1 Perhaps someone will ring the doorbell. If so, don't let them in.
If .... , don't let them in.
2 Perhaps someone will ask you some questions. If so, don't tell them anything.
If ....
3 Perhaps someone saw the accident. If so, they should contact the police.
If ....

84.3 *Complete these sentences. Use* **any/anyone/anybody/anything/anywhere.**
Example: I don't mind what you tell him.   *You can tell him anything you like*................

1 I don't mind what you wear to the party.   You can wear ....
2 I don't mind where you sit.   You can ....
3 It doesn't matter which day you come.   You ....
4 I don't mind who you talk to.   You ....
5 It doesn't matter which flight you travel on.   You ....
6 I don't mind who you marry.
7 It doesn't matter what time you phone. ....

UNIT 85   No/none/any
No/any + -one/-body/-thing/-where

a) **No   none   no-one   nobody   nothing   nowhere**
We use these negative words especially at the beginning of a sentence or alone:
- **No-one** (*or* **Nobody**) came to visit me when I was in hospital.
- **No** system of government is perfect.
- 'Where are you going?'   '**Nowhere.** I'm staying here.'
- **None** of these books are mine.
- 'What did you do?'   '**Nothing.**'

You can also use these words in the middle or at the end of a sentence. But don't use 'not' with these words. They are already negative:
- I saw **nothing.** (*not* 'I didn't see nothing.')

In the middle or at the end of a sentence, we more often use: **not ... any/anyone/anybody/ anything/anywhere**:
- I did**n't** see **anything.** (= I saw nothing.)
- We have**n't** got **any** money. (= We've got no money.)
- The station is**n't anywhere** near here. (= ... is nowhere near here)
- She did**n't** tell **anyone** about her plans. (= She told no-one)

Where there is another negative word, you don't need 'not':
- **Nobody** tells me **anything.** (= people don't tell me anything)

b) **No** and **none**
We use **no** with a noun. **No** = **not a** or **not any**:
- We had to walk because there was **no bus.** (= there wasn't a bus)
- I can't talk to you now. I have **no time.** (= I haven't any time)
- There were **no shops** open. (= there weren't any shops)

We use **none** alone (without a noun):
- 'How much money have you got?'   '**None.**'

Or we use **none of**:
  none of these shops   none of my money   none of it/us/you/them
After **none of** + a *plural* word ('none of **the girls** / none of **them**' etc.), you can use a singular or a plural verb. A plural verb is more usual:
- None of the **people** I met **were** English.

c) After **no-one/nobody** we often say **they/them/their**:
- **Nobody** phoned, did **they**? (= did he or she)
- **No-one** in the class did **their** homework. (= his or her homework)

d) You can use **any/no** with *comparatives* (**any better / no bigger** etc.):
- Do you feel **any better** today? (= Do you feel better at all? – *said to someone who felt ill yesterday*)
- We've waited long enough. I'm **not** waiting **any longer.** (= not even a minute longer)
- I expected your house to be very big but it's **no bigger** than mine. (= not even a little bigger)

For **any** see also Unit 84.

UNIT 85   Exercises

85.1 *Answer these questions with* **none (of)/no-one/nobody/nothing/nowhere.**
Example: What did you do? .Nothing...

   1 Where are you going? ....
   2 How many children has he got? ....
   3 What did you tell them? ....

   4 Who were you talking to? ....
   5 How much of this money is
      yours? ....

Now write answers to these questions with **any/anyone/anybody/anything/anywhere.**
Example: 'What did you do?' ' I didn't do anything...,

   6 'Where are you going?' 'I ....,
   7 'How many children have they got?' 'They ....,
   8 'Who did you dance with?' 'I ....,
   9 'What did they give you?' ' ....,

85.2 *Complete these sentences with* **no/none/no-one/nobody/nothing/nowhere/any/anyone/
anybody/anything/anywhere.**
Examples: There were ......no........ shops open.   I don't want anything to eat.

   1 The bus was completely empty. There wasn't .... on it.
   2 'Where did you go for your holidays?' '............................. . I stayed at home.'
   3 I couldn't make an omelette because I had .... eggs.
   4 I didn't say .... Not a word.
   5 The accident looked serious but fortunately .... was injured.
   6 The town was still the same when I returned years later. .... had changed.
   7 We took a few photographs but .... of them were very good.
   8 I can't find my watch .... I've looked all over the house.
   9 'What did you have for breakfast?' '............................. . I don't usually have
      .... for breakfast.'
  10 We cancelled the party because .... of the people we invited could come.
  11 .... intelligent person could do such a stupid thing.
  12 There was complete silence in the room. .... said ....
  13 'How many cinemas are there in this town?' '............................. . The last one closed six
      months ago.'
  14 The four of us wanted to go to a restaurant but we couldn't because .... of
      us had .... money.

85.3 *Now you have to make sentences with* **any/no** + *a comparative.*
Example: I hear you weren't feeling well yesterday. Do you feel any better...............today?

   1 I'm going as fast as I can. I can't go ....
   2 What makes you think Harry is old? He is .... than you.
   3 I'm sorry I've come a bit late but I couldn't come ....
   4 This restaurant is a bit expensive. Is the other one ....?
   5 I must stop for a rest. I can't walk ....

UNIT 86 Much, many, little, few, a lot, plenty

a) Much many few little
We use **much** and **little** with uncountable nouns:
   much time   **much** luck   **little** energy   **little** money
We use **many** and **few** with plural nouns:
   many friends   **many** people   **few** cars   **few** countries

b) A lot (of) lots (of) plenty (of)
We use **a lot of** / **lots of** / **plenty of** with uncountable and plural nouns:

   a lot of luck   **lots of** time   **plenty of** money
   a lot of people   **lots of** books   **plenty of** ideas

Plenty = more than enough:
   – 'Have some more to eat.'   'No, thank you. I've had **plenty**.'
   – There's no need to hurry. We've got **plenty of time**.

c) We use **much** and **many** mainly in negative sentences and questions:
   – We did**n't** spend **much** money.
   – Have you got **many** friends?
In positive sentences it is usually better to use **a lot (of)**. **Much** is especially unusual in positive sentences:
   – We spent **a lot of** money. (*not* 'we spent much money')
   – There has been **a lot of** rain recently. (*not* 'much rain')
But we use **too much** and **so much** in positive sentences:
   – I can't drink this tea. There's **too much** sugar in it.

d) Little / a little   few / a few
Little and **few** (without a) are negative ideas
   – Hurry up! We've got **little** time. (= not much, not enough time)
   – He's not popular. He has **few** friends. (= not many, not enough friends)
We also use **very little** and **very few**:
   – We've got **very little** time.
   – He has **very few** friends.
'A little' and 'a few' are more positive ideas. **A little** / **a few** = some, a small amount or a small number:
   – Let's go and have a drink. We've got **a little** time before the train leaves.
     (= some time, enough time to have a drink)
   – 'Have you got any money?'   'Yes, **a little**. Do you want to borrow some?'
     (a little = not much but enough for you to borrow some)
   – I enjoy my life here. I have **a few** friends and we meet quite often.
     (a few friends = not many but enough to have a good time)
   – 'When did you last see Tom?'   '**A few** days ago.' (= some days ago)
But 'only a little' and 'only a few' have a negative meaning:
   – Hurry up! We've **only** got **a little** time.
   – The village was very small. There were **only a few** houses.

UNIT 86   Exercises

86.1 *Complete these sentences with* **much, many** *and* **a lot** (of). *Sometimes there are two possibilities.*
Examples: There weren't ....*many*........ people at the party I had seen before.
   It cost me ...:.....*a lot of*..... money to furnish this house.

1 We'll have to hurry. We haven't got .... time.
2 Tom drinks .... milk – one litre a day.
3 She is a very quiet person. She doesn't say ....
4 I put .... salt in the soup. Perhaps too ....
5 .... people do not like flying.
6 The man was badly injured in the accident. He lost .... blood.
7 It's not a very lively town. There isn't .... to do.
8 This car is expensive to run. It uses .... petrol.
9 Don't disturb me. I've got .... work to do.
10 He's got so .... money, he doesn't know what to do with it.
11 He always puts .... salt on his food.
12 We didn't take .... photographs when we were on holiday.

86.2 *Now you have to make sentences with* **plenty** (of). *Use the word in brackets.*
Example: We needn't hurry. (time) We've *got plenty of time*...........................

1 He's got no financial problems. (money)   He's got ....
2 We don't need to go to a petrol station. (petrol)   We ....
3 Come and sit at our table. (room)   There is ....
4 We can make omelettes for lunch. (eggs)   We ....
5 We'll easily find somewhere to stay. (hotels)   There ....
6 I can't believe you're still hungry. (to eat)   You've had ....
7 Why are you sitting there doing nothing? (things to do)   You ....

86.3 *Complete these sentences with* **little / a little / few / a few**.
Examples: Hurry! We've got ....*little*........... time.
   I last saw Tom .....*a few*.... days ago.

1 We didn't have any money but Tom had ....
2 He doesn't speak much English. Only .... words.
3 Nora's father died .... years ago.
4 'Would you like some more cake?' 'Yes, please, but only ....'
5 This town isn't very well-known and there isn't much to see, so ....
   tourists come here.
6 I don't think Jill would be a good teacher. She's got .... patience with
   children.
7 This is not the first time the car has broken down. It has happened ....
   times before.
8 The cinema was almost empty. There were very .... people there.
9 There is a shortage of water because there has been very .... rain recently.

173

UNIT 87 All, every and whole

a) **All   everyone   everybody   everything**
We do not normally use **all** to mean **everyone/everybody**:
- **Everybody** enjoyed the party. (*not* 'All enjoyed ...')
- Ann knows **everyone** in her street. (*not* '... all in her street')

Sometimes you can use **all** to mean **everything**, but it is usually better to say **everything**:
- He thinks he knows **everything**. (*not* 'knows all')
- It was an awful holiday. **Everything** went wrong. (*not* 'all went wrong')

But you can use **all** in the expression **all about**:
- They told us **all about** their holiday.

We also use **all** to mean **the only thing(s)**:
- **All** I've eaten today is a sandwich. (= the only thing I've eaten)

b) We use a *singular* verb after **every/everyone/everybody/everything**:
- **Every seat** in the theatre **was** taken.
- **Everybody looks** tired today.
- **Everything** he said **was** true.

But we often use **they/them/their** after **everyone/everybody**:
- Has **everyone** got **their** tickets? (= his or her ticket)
- **Everybody** said **they** would come. (= he or she would come)

c) **All** and **whole**
We use **whole** mainly with singular nouns:
- Have you read **the whole book**? (= all the book, not just a part of it)
- He was very quiet. He didn't say a word **the whole evening**.
- She has spent **her whole life** in India.

We say **the/my/her** etc. before **whole**. Compare:
  the whole book / all **the** book   **her** whole life / all **her** life

You can also say 'a whole ...':
- Jack ate **a whole chocolate cake** last night. (= a complete cake)

We do not normally use **whole** with uncountable nouns:
  all the money (*not* 'the whole money')

d) **Every/all/whole** with time words
We use **every** to say how often something happens. So we say **every day / every week / every Monday / every ten minutes / every three weeks** etc.:
- We go out **every Friday night**.
- The buses run **every ten minutes**.
- Ann goes to see her mother **every three weeks**.

All day / the whole day = the complete day:
- We spent **all day / the whole day** on the beach.
- I've been trying to find you **all morning / the whole morning**.

Note that we say **all day / all week** etc. (*not* 'all the day / all the week')

For **all** see also Units 82 and 106.

174

UNIT 87 Exercises

87.1 *Complete these sentences with* **all**, **everything** *or* **everyone/everybody**.
Examples: Ann knows ......*everyone*....... in her street.
All .... I've eaten today is a sandwich.

1 Tom is very popular. .... likes him.
2 .... was very kind to us. They did .... they could to help us.
3 Jill doesn't do any of the housework. Her husband does ....
4 Margaret told me .... about her new job. It sounds quite interesting.
5 Can .... write their names on a piece of paper, please?
6 I can't lend you any money. .... I've got is a pound and I need that.
7 I can't stand him. He disagrees with .... I say.
8 I didn't spend much money in the shops. .... I bought was a pair of gloves.
9 Why are you always thinking about money? Money isn't ....
10 He didn't say where he was going. .... he said was that he was going away.
11 .... has got their faults. Nobody is perfect.

87.2 *Now you have to make sentences with* **the whole**.
Example: He read the book from beginning to end. He read the whole book....................

1 He opened a box of chocolates. When he finished eating, there were no chocolates left in the box. He ate ....
2 The police came to our house. They were looking for something. They searched everywhere, every room. They searched ....
3 She worked from early in the morning until late in the evening.
   ....
4 Everyone in Tim and Carol's family plays tennis. Tim and Carol play, and so do all their children. The .... tennis.
5 Jack and Jill went on holiday to the seaside for a week. It rained from the beginning of the week to the end. It ....
6 It was a terrible fire. Nothing was left of the building afterwards.
   .... destroyed in the fire.
7 Everyone in the team played well. ....

Now make sentences for 3 and 5 again. This time use **all** *instead of* **whole**.

8 (3) She ....
9 (5) ....

87.3 *Now you have to say how often something happens. Use* **every** *with these periods of time:*
four years   ten minutes   four hours   six months   ~~five minutes~~
Example: There's a good bus service to the centre. The buses run *every five minutes.*.........

1 Tom is ill in bed. He has some medicine. He has to take it ....
2 The Olympic Games take place ....
3 Everyone should have a check-up with the dentist ....
4 We live near a busy airport. A plane flies over the house ....

UNIT 88 Relative clauses (1) – clauses with **who/that/which**

a) Study this example:

The man ⟨who lives next door⟩ is very friendly.
└ *relative clause* ┘

A *clause* is a part of a sentence. A *relative clause* tells us which person or thing (or what kind of person or thing) the speaker means:

- The man **who lives next door** ... (**who lives next door** tells us which man)
- People **who live in London** ... (**who live in London** tells us what kind of people)

We use **who** in a relative clause when we are talking about *people*. We use **who** instead of **he/she/they**:

the man – ⟨he⟩ lives next door – is very friendly

→ The man ⟨who⟩ **lives next door** is very friendly.

we know a lot of people – ⟨they⟩ live in London

→ We know a lot of people ⟨who⟩ **live in London**.

- An architect is someone **who designs buildings**.
- What was the name of the man **who lent you the money?**
- The girl **who was injured in the accident** is now in hospital.
- Anyone **who wants to do the examination** must enter before next Friday.

It is also possible to use **that** instead of **who**:

- The man **that** lives next door is very friendly.

But sometimes you must use **who** for people – see Unit 91.

b) When we are talking about *things*, we use **that** (not **who**) in a relative clause. We use **that** instead of **it/they**:

where are the eggs? – ⟨they⟩ were in the fridge
Where are the eggs ⟨that⟩ **were in the fridge?**

- I don't like stories **that have unhappy endings**.
- Gerry works for a company **that makes typewriters**.
- Everything **that happened** was my fault.
- The window **that was broken** has now been repaired.

You can also use **which** for things (but not for people):

- Where are the eggs **which** were in the fridge?

That is more usual than **which** in the sentences in this unit. But sometimes you must use **which** – see Unit 91.

c) Remember that we use **who/that/which** instead of **he/she/they/it**:

- Do you know the man **who** lives next door? (*not* '... who *he* lives ...')

Now study the next unit for more information about relative clauses.

88.1 *In this exercise you have to explain what some words mean. Choose the right meaning from the list and then write a sentence with* **who**. *Use a dictionary if necessary.*

he/she steals from a shop	he/she breaks into a house and steals things
he/she doesn't eat meat	he/she doesn't drink alcohol
~~he/she designs buildings~~	he/she buys something from a shop

1 (an architect)   *An architect is someone who designs buildings.*
2 (a burglar)   A burglar is someone ....
3 (a vegetarian)   A vegetarian ....
4 (a customer)   ....
5 (a shoplifter)   ....
6 (a teetotaller)   ....

88.2 *Now you have to read two sentences and then write one sentence with the same meaning. Use a relative clause in your sentence.*
Example: A girl was injured in the accident. She is now in hospital.
     The girl *who was injured in the accident is now in hospital.*

1 A man answered the phone. He told me you were out.
   The man ....
2 A waitress served us. She was very impolite and impatient.
   The ....
3 Some boys were arrested. They have now been released.
   The boys ....

88.3 *The sentences in this exercise are not complete. Choose the most suitable ending from the list and make it into a relative clause.*

he invented the telephone	~~it makes typewriters~~
she runs away from home	it gives you the meanings of words
they are never on time	it won the race
they stole my car	it can support life
they used to hang on that wall	it was found last week

1 Gerry works for a company *that (or which) makes typewriters.*
2 The book is about a girl ....
3 What was the name of the horse .... ?
4 The police have caught the men ....
5 Alexander Bell was the man ....
6 Where are the pictures .... ?
7 The police are still trying to identify the body ....
8 A dictionary is a book ....
9 I don't like people ....
10 It seems that Earth is the only planet ....

UNIT 89   Relative clauses (2) – clauses with or without who/that

a) Look again at these examples from Unit 88:
- The man **who lives next door** is very friendly. (*or* 'that' lives')
- Where are the eggs **that were in the fridge**? (*or* 'which' were')

In these sentences **who** and **that** are *subjects* of the verbs in the relative clauses: the man lives next door, the eggs were in the fridge. You cannot leave out **who** or **that** in these sentences.

Sometimes **who** and **that** are *objects* of the verbs:

the man – I wanted to see ⎡him⎤ – was away on holiday

→   The man ⎡who⎤ (or **that**) **I wanted to see** was away on holiday.

have you found the keys? – you lost ⎡them⎤

→   Have you found the keys ⎡that⎤ **you lost**?

When **who** or **that** are objects of the verb in the relative clause, you can leave them out:
- **The man I wanted to see** was away on holiday. (*but not* 'The man I wanted to see *him* was away on holiday.')
- Have you found **the keys you lost**? (*but not* 'Have you found the keys you lost *them*?')
- **The dress Ann bought** doesn't fit her very well. (= the dress **that** Ann bought)
- **The girl Gerry is going to marry** is American. (= the girl **who/that** Gerry is going to marry)
- Is there **anything I can do**? (= is there anything **that** I can do?)

b) There are often prepositions (**in/at/with** etc.) in relative clauses. Study the position of the prepositions in these sentences:

do you know the girl? – Tom is talking ⎡to⎤ her

→   Do you know the girl (**who/that**) **Tom is talking** ⎡to⎤ ?

the bed – I slept ⎡in⎤ it last night – wasn't very comfortable

→   The bed (**that**) **I slept** ⎡in⎤ **last night** wasn't very comfortable.

- The man (**who/that**) **I sat next to on the plane** talked all the time.
- Are these the books (**that**) **you have been looking for**?
- The girl (**who/that**) **he fell in love with** left him after a few weeks.

c) You cannot use **what** instead of **that**:
- Everything (**that**) **he said** was true. (*not* 'everything what he said')
- I gave her **all the money (that) I had**. (*not* 'all ... what I had')

What = **the thing(s) that**:
- Did you hear **what I said**? (= the words that I said)
- I won't tell anyone **what happened**. (= the thing that happened)

178

UNIT 89   Exercises

89.1 *The sentences in this exercise are not complete. Complete each one with a relative clause.*
Use the sentences in the box to make your relative clauses.

we met her yesterday	we wanted to visit it	Tom tells them
Tom recommended it	we had it for dinner	~~you lost them~~
Ann is wearing it	the police arrested him	I invited them to the party

1 Have you found the keys ..you lost......................... ?
2 I like the dress ....
3 The museum .... was shut when we got there.
4 Most of the people .... couldn't come.
5 I didn't like that woman ....
6 The fish .... was really delicious.
7 We stayed at a hotel ....
8 The stories .... are usually very funny.
9 The man .... has now been released.

89.2 *This time you have to make a relative clause with a preposition.*

you were with her last night	I am living in it	~~I slept in it~~
they were talking about them	she is married to him	I work with them
we wanted to travel on it	I applied for it	we went to it

1 The bed ......*I slept in*............... was too soft.
2 I didn't get the job ....
3 The man .... has been married twice before.
4 The party .... wasn't very enjoyable.
5 Who was that girl .... ?
6 The flight .... was fully booked.
7 I enjoy my job because I like the people ....
8 I wasn't interested in the things ....
9 The house .... is not in very good condition.

89.3 *Complete these sentences, where necessary, with* **that, who** *or* **what.** *If it is possible to*
write **that** *or leave it out, write* (**that**) *– in brackets.*
Examples: Did you hear ...*what*... I said?   Everything ...*(that)*... he said was true.

1 She gives her children everything .... they want.
2 Tell me .... you want and I'll try to help you.
3 Why do you blame me for everything .... goes wrong?
4 I won't be able to do very much but I'll do the best .... I can.
5 I can't lend you any money. All .... I've got is a pound.
6 Nora is the only person .... understands me.
7 Why do you always disagree with everything .... I say?
8 I don't agree with .... you've just said.
9 This is an awful film. It's the worst .... I've ever seen.

UNIT 90   Relative clauses (3) – **whose, whom** and **where**

a) Whose

We use **whose** in relative clauses instead of **his/her/their**:

> we saw some people – | their | car had broken down
>
> → We saw some people | whose | car had broken down.

We use **whose** mostly for people:

- A widow is a woman **whose husband is dead.** (**her** husband is dead)
- What's the name of the girl **whose car you borrowed?** (you borrowed **her** car)
- The other day I met someone **whose brother I went to school with.** (I went to school with **his** brother)

b) **Whom** is possible instead of **who** (for people) when it is the *object* of the verb in the relative clause (like the sentences in Unit 89):

- The man **whom I wanted to see** was away on holiday. (I wanted to see **him**)

You can also use **whom** with a preposition (**to/from/with whom** etc.):

- The girl **with whom he fell in love** left him after a few weeks. (he fell in love **with her**)

But we do not often use **whom.** In spoken English we normally prefer **who** or **that** (or you can leave them out – see Unit 89):

- The man (**who/that**) **I wanted to see** ...
- The girl (**who/that**) **he fell in love with** ...

For **whom** see also Units 91 and 92.

c) Where

You can use **where** in a relative clause to talk about places:

> the hotel – we stayed | there | – wasn't very clean
>
> → The hotel | where | we stayed wasn't very clean.

- I recently went back to **the town where I was born.** (*or* 'the town (that) I was born in')
- I would like to live in **a country where there is plenty of sunshine.**

d) We use **that** (or we leave it out) when we say **the day / the year / the time** (etc.) **that something happened:**

- Do you still remember **the day (that) we first met?**
- **The last time (that) I saw her,** she looked very well.
- I haven't seen them since **the year (that) they got married.**

e) You can say **the reason why something happens** or **the reason that something happens.** You can also leave out **why** and **that:**

- **The reason (why/that) I'm phoning you** is to invite you to a party.

180

UNIT 90 Exercises

90.1 *You were on holiday with a friend of yours. You met some people who had some bad experiences during their holiday. You met:*

1 some people / their car broke down
2 a man / his wife became ill and was taken to hospital
3 a woman / her husband was arrested by the police
4 a girl / her passport was stolen
5 a couple / their luggage disappeared

You can't remember the names of these people, so you ask your friend. Make sentences with **whose.**

1 What was the name of the people whose car broke down .... ?
2 What was the name of the man .... ?
3 What .... ?
4 .... ?
5 .... ?

90.2 *The sentences in this exercise are not complete. You have to complete them with* **where ....** *Use the sentences in the box to make your relative clauses.*

I can buy postcards there	I was born there
she had bought it there	we spent our holidays there
people are buried there	we can have a really good meal there

1 I recently went back to the town where I was born. ....
2 The dress didn't fit her, so she took it back to the shop ....
3 Do you know a restaurant .... ?
4 Is there a shop near here .... ?
5 The place .... was really beautiful.
6 A cemetery is a place ....

90.3 *Again you have to complete the sentences with a relative clause. Use the sentences in the box to make your relative clauses.*

(her) dog bit me	they haven't got a car (for this reason)
John is staying (there)	I didn't write to you (for this reason)
we first met (on that day)	the Second World War ended (in that year)
(his/her) parents are dead	you telephoned (that evening)

1 Do you remember the day (that) we first met .... ?
2 An orphan is a child ....
3 The reason .... was that I didn't know your address.
4 Unfortunately I wasn't at home the evening ....
5 I protested to the woman ....
6 The reason .... is that they can't afford one.
7 Do you know the name of the hotel .... ?
8 1945 was the year ....

181

UNIT 91 Relative clauses (4) – 'extra information' clauses (1)

a) Look again at these examples from Units 88 and 89:
- The man **who lives next door** is very friendly.
- Gerry works for a company **that makes typewriters**.
- Have you found the keys **(that) you lost**?

In these examples, the relative clauses tell us *which person or thing (or what kind of person or thing)* the speaker means:

'The man **who lives next door**' tells us *which* man.

'a company **that makes typewriters**' tells us *what kind* of company.

'the keys **(that) you lost**' tells us *which* keys.

But not all relative clauses are like this. For example:
- Tom's father, **who is 78**, goes swimming every day.
- The house at the end of the street, **which has been empty for two years**, has just been sold.

In these examples the relative clauses (**who is 78** and **which has been empty for two years**) do *not* tell us which person or thing the speaker means. *We already know* which person or thing is meant: '**Tom's father**' and 'the house **at the end of the street**'. The relative clauses in these sentences give us *extra information* about the person or thing.

b) In these 'extra information' relative clauses you have to use **who** for people and **which** for things. You cannot use **that** and you cannot leave out **who** or **which**.

When you write clauses like this, you have to put *commas* (,) at the beginning and at the end of the clause. Study these examples:
- Yesterday I met John, **who told me he was getting married**.
- Mr Yates, **who has worked for the same company all his life**, is retiring next month.
- She told me her address, **which I wrote down on a piece of paper**.
- The strike at the car factory, **which lasted ten days**, is now over.

Remember that we use **who/which** instead of **he/she/it/they**:
- Last night we went to Ann's party, **which** we enjoyed very much. (*not* 'which we enjoyed *it* very much')

c) You can also use **whose**, **whom** and **where** in 'extra information' relative clauses:
- Martin, **whose mother is Spanish**, speaks both Spanish and English fluently.
- Mr Hogg is going to Canada, **where his son has been living for five years**.
- My sister, **whom** (or **who**) **you once met**, is visiting us next week.

For more information about **whose**, **whom** and **where** see Unit 90.

See also the next unit for 'extra information' relative clauses.

UNIT 91   Exercises

91.1 *In this exercise you have to write these sentences again together with a relative clause. Sometimes the relative clause is in the middle of the sentence, sometimes at the end. Use the sentences in brackets to make your relative clauses.*
Examples: Tom's father goes swimming every day. (Tom's father is 78.)
Tom's father, who is 78, goes swimming every day.
She told me her address. (I wrote her address down on a piece of paper.)
She told me her address, which I wrote down on a piece of paper.

1 She showed me a photograph of her son. (Her son is a policeman.)
She showed me a photograph of her son, ...

2 We decided not to swim in the sea. (The sea looked rather dirty.)
We ....

3 The new stadium will be opened next month. (The stadium holds 90,000 people.)
The ....

4 John is one of my closest friends. (I have known John for eight years.)
....

5 That man over there is an artist. (I don't remember his name.) (*use* **whose**)
....

6 Opposite our house there is a nice park. (There are some beautiful trees in this park.)
(*use* **where**) ....

7 The storm caused a lot of damage. (Nobody had been expecting the storm.)
....

8 The postman was late this morning. (The postman is nearly always on time.)
....

9 We often go to visit our friends in Bristol. (Bristol is only 30 miles away.)
....

10 Mr Edwards has gone into hospital for some tests. (His health hasn't been good recently.) (*use* **whose**) ....

11 Jack looks much nicer without his beard. (His beard made him look much older.)
....

12 I went to see the doctor. (The doctor told me to rest for a few days.)
....

13 Thank you for your letter. (I was very happy to get your letter.)
....

14 A friend of mine helped me to get a job. (His father is the manager of a company.)
(*use* **whose**) ....

15 Next week-end I'm going to Glasgow. (My sister lives in Glasgow.) (*use* **where**)
....

16 The population of London is now falling. (London was once the largest city in the world.) ....

17 I looked up at the moon. (The moon was very bright that evening.)
....

18 We spent a pleasant day by the lake. (We had a picnic by the lake.) (*use* **where**)
....

UNIT 92 Relative clauses (5) – 'extra information' clauses (2)

You should study Unit 91 before you study this unit.

a) *Prepositions* + **whom/which**

In 'extra information' clauses you can use a preposition before **whom** (for people) and **which** (for things). So you can say '**to whom** / **with** whom / **about** which / **for** which' etc.:

- Mr Carter, **to whom** I spoke on the phone last night, is very interested in our plan.
- Fortunately we had a map, **without which** we would have got lost.

But in spoken English we often keep the preposition after the verb in the relative clause. When we do this, we normally use **who** (not 'whom'):

- This is Mr Carter, **who** I was telling you **about**.
- Yesterday we visited the City Museum, **which** I'd never been **to** before.

b) All of / most of etc. + **whom/which**   Study these examples:

> Jack has three brothers. All of them are married. (*2 sentences*)
> → Jack has three brothers, **all of whom** are married. (*1 sentence*)
>
> Ann has a lot of books. She hasn't read most of them. (*2 sentences*)
> → Ann has a lot of books, **most of which** she hasn't read. (*1 sentence*)

You can also say:

none of / many of / much of / (a) few of / some of
any of / half of / each of / both of / neither of   + **whom** (people)
either of / one of / two of etc.   + **which** (things)

- He tried on three jackets, **none of which** fitted him.
- They've got three cars, **two of which** they never use.
- Tom has a lot of friends, **many of whom** he was at school with.
- Two men, **neither of whom** I had seen before, came into my office.

c) Which (*not* 'what')

Study this example:

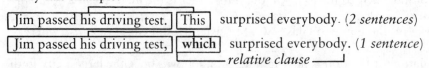

In this example **which** = the fact that he passed his driving test. You can*not* use **what** instead of **which** in sentences like this:

- She couldn't come to the party, **which was a pity**. (*not* ' ... what was a pity')
- The weather was very good, **which we hadn't expected**. (*not* '... what we hadn't expected')

For **what** see Unit 89c.

UNIT 92   Exercises

92.1 *In this exercise you have to write these sentences again, together with a relative clause. Use the sentences in brackets to make your relative clauses.*
Example: Mr Carter is very interested in our plan. (I spoke to him on the phone last night.)
Mr Carter, who I spoke to on the phone last night, is very interested in our plan.
or: *Mr Carter, to whom I spoke on the phone last night, is very interested in our plan.*

1 This is a photograph of our friends. (We went on holiday with them.)
    This is ....
2 The wedding took place last Friday. (Only members of the family were invited to it.)
    The ....
3 I've just bought some books about astronomy. (I'm very interested in astronomy.)
    ....

92.2 *Now you have to make sentences with* **all of / most of** *etc.* + **whom/which.**
Example: Jack has three brothers. All of them are married.
    Jack has three brothers, all of whom are married.

1 They gave us a lot of information. Most of it was useless.
    They gave ....
2 There were a lot of people at the party. I had met only a few of them before.
    ....
3 I have sent him two letters. Neither of them has arrived.
    ....
4 Norman won £20,000. He gave half of it to his parents.
    ....
5 Ten people applied for the job. None of them were suitable.
    ....
6 Tom made a number of suggestions. Most of them were very helpful.
    ....

92.3 *Now you have to complete these sentences with a relative clause. Use the sentences in the box to make your relative clauses.*

this means I can't leave the country	this was very nice of him
this makes it difficult to contact her	this was perfectly true
this makes it difficult to sleep	~~this was a pity~~
I thought this was very rude of them	

1 She couldn't come to the party, *which was a pity.* ....
2 Jill isn't on the phone, ...
3 They said they didn't have any money, ...
4 I haven't got a passport, ...
5 He offered to let me stay in his house, ...
6 They didn't thank us for the meal before they left, ...
7 The part of town where I live is very noisy at night, ...

185

UNIT 93   -ing and -ed clauses ('the girl talking to Tom', 'the man injured in the accident')

a) A *clause* is a part of a sentence. Some clauses begin with **-ing** or **-ed**:
  – Do you know the girl ⌈ talking to Tom ⌉ ? (**-ing** clause)

  – The man ⌈ injured in the accident ⌉ was taken to hospital. (**-ed** clause)

b) We use **-ing** clauses to say what someone (or something) is doing or was doing at a particular time:
  – Do you know the girl **talking to Tom**? (the girl **is talking** to Tom)
  – The policemen **investigating the robbery** are looking for three men. (the policemen **are investigating** the robbery)
  – I was woken up by a bell **ringing**. (the bell **was ringing**)
  – Who was that man **standing outside**? (the man **was standing** outside)
  – Can you hear someone **singing**? (someone **is singing**)
For **see/hear someone doing something** see Unit 66.

When you are talking about *things* (and sometimes people), you can use an **-ing** clause for permanent characteristics (what something does all the time, not just at a particular time):
  – The road **joining the two villages** is very narrow. (the road joins the two villages)
  – I live in a pleasant room **overlooking the garden**. (the room overlooks the garden)

c) **-ed** clauses have a *passive* meaning:
  – The man **injured in the accident** was taken to hospital. (the man **was injured** in the accident)
  – None of the people **invited to the party** can come. (the people **have been invited** to the party)
Injured and **invited** are *past participles*. Many verbs have irregular past participles which do not end in **-ed**. For example: **stolen/made/bought/written** etc.:
  – The money **stolen in the robbery** was never found. (the money **was stolen** in the robbery)
  – Most of the goods **made in this factory** are exported. (the goods **are made** in this factory)
For a full list of irregular verbs see Appendix 2.

d) We often use **-ing** and **-ed** clauses after **there is / there was** etc.:
  – **Is there** anybody **waiting** to see me?
  – **There were** some children **swimming** in the river.
  – When I arrived, **there was** a big red car **parked** outside the house.

For more information about **-ing** clauses see Unit 67.

UNIT 93   Exercises

93.1 *In this exercise you have to re-write the sentences. Each time use the information in brackets to make an **-ing** clause.*
Example: That girl is Australian. (she is talking to Tom)
          The girl talking to Tom is Australian.

1 A plane crashed into the sea yesterday. (it was carrying 28 passengers)
   A plane .... yesterday.
2 When I was walking home, there was a man. (he was following me)
   When ....
3 I was woken up by the baby. (she was crying)
   I ....
4 At the end of the street there is a path. (the path leads to the river)
   At ....
5 Some paintings were stolen from the palace. (they belong to the Queen)
   Some ....

93.2 *This exercise is similar but this time you have to make an **-ed** clause.*
Example: The man was taken to hospital. (he was injured in the accident)
          The man injured in the accident was taken to hospital.

1 The window has now been repaired. (it was broken in last night's storm)
   The window .... repaired.
2 Most of the suggestions were not very practical. (they were made at the meeting)
   ....
3 The paintings haven't been found yet. (they were stolen from the museum)
   ....
4 Did you hear about the boy? (he was knocked down on his way to school this morning)
   Did ....

93.3 *Complete these sentences with the following verbs. Each time you have to put the verb in the correct form:*
blow   call   ~~invite~~   live   offer   post   read   ~~ring~~   sit   study
wait   work

1 I was woken up by a bell *ringing* .
2 None of the people .... *invited* .... to the party can come.
3 Tom has got a brother .... in a bank in London and a sister ....
   economics at university in Glasgow.
4 Somebody .... Jack phoned while you were out.
5 All letters .... today should arrive tomorrow.
6 When I entered the waiting-room there was nobody .... except for a
   young man .... by the window .... a magazine.
7 A few days after the interview, I received a letter .... me the job.
8 There was a tree .... down in the storm last night.
9 Sometimes life must be very unpleasant for people .... near airports.

UNIT 94   Adjectives ending in -ing and -ed (boring/bored etc.)

a) There are many pairs of adjectives ending in **-ing** and **-ed**. For example: **boring** and **bored**.
Study this example situation:

Jane has been doing the same job for a very long time.
Every day she does exactly the same thing again and
again. She doesn't enjoy it any more and would like to
do something different.

Jane's job is **boring**.
Jane is **bored** (with her job).

Someone is **-ed** if something (or someone) is **-ing**. Or, if something is **-ing**, it makes you **-ed**.
So:

– Jane is bored because her job is boring.
– Jane's job is boring, so Jane is bored. (*not* 'Jane is boring')

Now study these examples:

Someone is **interested** because something (or someone) is **interesting**:
– Tom is interested in politics. (*not* 'interesting in politics')
– Tom finds politics interesting.
– Are you interested in buying a car?
– Did you meet anyone interesting at the party?

Someone is **surprised** because something is **surprising**:
– Everyone was surprised that he passed the examination.
– It was quite surprising that he passed the examination.

Someone is **disappointed** because something is **disappointing**:
– I was disappointed with the film. I expected it to be much better.
– The film was disappointing. I expected it to be much better.

Someone is **tired** because something is **tiring**:
– He is always very tired when he gets home from work.
– He has a very tiring job.

b) Other pairs of adjectives ending in **-ing** and **-ed** are:

fascinating	fascinated	horrifying	horrified
exciting	excited	terrifying	terrified
amusing	amused	frightening	frightened
amazing	amazed	depressing	depressed
astonishing	astonished	worrying	worried
shocking	shocked	annoying	annoyed
disgusting	disgusted	exhausting	exhausted
embarrassing	embarrassed	satisfying	satisfied
confusing	confused		

UNIT 94   Exercises

94.1 *In this exercise you have to complete two sentences for each situation. Use an adjective ending in -ing or -ed to complete each sentence.*
Example: The film wasn't as good as we had expected.   (disappoint-)
      a) The film was .disappointing. .
      b) We were .disappointed. with the film.

1 It's been raining all day. I hate this weather.   (depress-)
  a) This weather is ....   b) This weather makes me ....
2 Astronomy is one of Tom's main interests.   (interest-)
  a) Tom is .... in astronomy.
  b) He finds astronomy very ....
3 I turned off the television in the middle of the programme.   (bor-)
  a) The programme was ....   b) I was ....
4 Ann is going to America next month. She has never been there before.   (excit-)
  a) She is really .... about going.
  b) It will be an .... experience for her.
5 Diana teaches young children. It's a hard job.   (exhaust-)
  a) She often finds her job ....
  b) At the end of the day's work she is often ....

94.2 *Choose the right adjective.*
Example: I was ~~disappointing~~/disappointed with the film. I had expected it to be better.

1 We were all horrifying/horrified when we heard about the disaster.
2 It's sometimes embarrassing/embarrassed when you have to ask people for money.
3 Are you interesting/interested in football?
4 I enjoyed the football match. It was quite exciting/excited.
5 It was a really terrifying/terrified experience. Afterwards everybody was very shocking/shocked.
6 I had never expected to be offered the job. I was really amazing/amazed when I was offered it.
7 The kitchen hadn't been cleaned for ages. It was really disgusting/disgusted.
8 Do you easily get embarrassing/embarrassed?

94.3 *Complete these sentences with an adjective ending in -ing or -ed. The first letter(s) of the adjective are given each time.*
Example: Jane finds her job boring................... . She wants to do something different.

1 I seldom visit art galleries. I'm not very in................................. in art.
2 We went for a very long walk. It was very ti................................. .
3 Why do you always look so b................................. ? Is your life really so b................................. ?
4 He's one of the most b................................. people I've ever met. He never stops talking and never says anything in................................. .
5 I was as................................. when I heard they were getting divorced. They had always seemed so happy together.
6 I'm starting a new job next week. I'm quite ex................................. about it.

189

UNIT 95

Adjectives: word order ('a **nice new** house')
Adjectives after verbs ('Do you **feel tired**?')

a) Sometimes we use two or more adjectives together:
- Tom lives in a **nice new** house.
- In the kitchen there was a **beautiful large round wooden** table.

Adjectives like **new/large/round/wooden** are *fact* adjectives. They give us objective information about something (age, size, colour etc.). Adjectives like **nice/beautiful** are *opinion* adjectives. They tell us what someone thinks of something.
Opinion adjectives usually go before *fact* adjectives:

	opinion	fact	
a	**nice**	**sunny**	day
	delicious	**hot**	soup
an	**intelligent**	**young**	man
a	**beautiful**	**large round wooden**	table

b) Sometimes there are two or more *fact* adjectives. Very often (but not always) we put *fact* adjectives in this order:

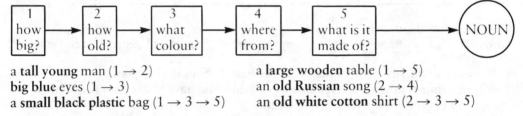

a **tall young** man (1 → 2)   a **large wooden** table (1 → 5)
big blue eyes (1 → 3)   an **old Russian** song (2 → 4)
a **small black plastic** bag (1 → 3 → 5)   an **old white cotton** shirt (2 → 3 → 5)

Adjectives of size and length (**big/small/tall/short/long** etc.) usually go before adjectives of shape and width (**round/fat/thin/slim/wide** etc.):
a **large round** table   a **tall thin** girl   a **long narrow** street

c) We also use adjectives after some verbs, especially **be/get/become**:
Are you **tired**?   **Be careful**!   I'm **getting hungry**.
We also use adjectives after: **feel   smell   taste   sound   seem   look**:
- Do you **feel tired**?
- The dinner **smells good**.
- Tom **sounded angry** when I spoke to him on the phone.
- This tea **tastes** a bit **strange**.
- Your friend **seems** very **nice**.

But after other verbs you must use an *adverb* (see also Units 96 and 97):
- **Drive carefully**! (*not* 'drive careful')
- Susan **plays** the piano very **well**. (*not* 'plays ... very good')
- Tom **shouted** at me **angrily**. (*not* 'shouted ... angry')

Look   We use an adjective after **look** when it means **seem**:
- Tom **looked sad** when I saw him.
But after **look at** we use an adverb:
- Tom **looked at** me **sadly**. (*not* 'looked at me sad')

UNIT 95   Exercises

95.1 *Put the adjectives in brackets in the correct position.*
Example: a beautiful table (wooden round)   *a beautiful round wooden table*

1 an unusual ring (gold) ....
2 an old lady (nice) ....
3 a good-looking man (young) ....
4 a modern house (attractive) ....
5 black gloves (leather) ....
6 an American film (old) ....
7 a large nose (red) ....
8 a sunny day (lovely) ....
9 a hot bath (nice) ....
10 an ugly dress (orange) ....
11 a red car (old / little) ....
12 a metal box (black / small) ....
13 a long face (thin) ....
14 a wide avenue (long) ....
15 a big cat (fat / black) ....
16 a little village (old / lovely) ....
17 long hair (fair / beautiful) ....
18 an old painting (interesting / French) ....

95.2 *Complete each sentence with a verb and an adjective from the box.*

feel	look	~~seemed~~	awful	fine	interesting
smell	sounded	tastes	nice	~~upset~~	wet

1 Ann **seemed upset** ...... this morning. Do you know what was wrong?
2 I can't eat this. I've just tried it and it ....
3 Jim told me about his new job last night. It .... quite
    .... , much better than his old job.
4 I wasn't very well yesterday but I .... today.
5 What beautiful flowers! They .... too.
6 You .... Have you been out in the rain?

95.3 *Choose the right word, adjective or adverb.*
Examples: The dinner smells good/~~well~~.   Drive ~~careful~~/carefully!

1 Please shut the door quiet/quietly.
2 Can you be quiet/quietly, please?
3 This soup tastes nice/nicely.
4 Tom cooks very good/well.
5 Don't go up that ladder. It doesn't look safe/safely.
6 We were relieved that he arrived safe/safely after his long journey.
7 Do you feel nervous/nervously before examinations?
8 Hurry up! You're always so slow/slowly.
9 He looked at me angry/angrily when I interrupted him.

191

UNIT 96 Adjectives and adverbs (1) (**quick/quickly**)

a) Study these examples:
- Our holiday was too short – the time went **quickly**.
- The driver of the car was **seriously** injured in the accident.

Quickly and **seriously** are *adverbs*. Many adverbs are made from an adjective + -ly:

| *adjective:* | quick | serious | careful | quiet | heavy | bad |
| *adverb:* | quickly | seriously | carefully | quietly | heavily | badly |

For spelling rules see Appendix 3. For **hard/fast/well** see Unit 97.

Not all words ending in -ly are adverbs. Some adjectives end in -ly too. For example:
friendly lively elderly lonely silly lovely

b) *Adjective or adverb?*
An adjective tells us more about a *noun*. We use adjectives before nouns and after a few verbs (especially **be**):
- Tom is a **careful driver**.
- **Be quiet**, please!
- We didn't go out because of the **heavy rain**.
- I was disappointed that my exam results **were** so **bad**.

For adjectives after **look/smell/feel** etc. see Unit 95c.

An adverb tells us more about a *verb*. An adverb tells us in what way someone does something or in what way something happens:
- Tom **drove carefully** along the narrow road. (*not* 'drove careful')
- **Speak quietly**, please! (*not* 'speak quiet')
- We didn't go out because it was **raining heavily**. (*not* 'raining heavy')
- I was disappointed that I **did** so **badly** in the exam. (*not* 'did so bad')

Compare: She speaks **perfect English**.   (*adjective + noun*)

She **speaks** English **perfectly**.   (*verb + object + adverb*)

c) We also use adverbs before *adjectives* and *other adverbs*. For example:

reasonably cheap   (*adverb + adjective*)
terribly sorry   (*adverb + adjective*)
incredibly quickly   (*adverb + adverb*)

- It's a **reasonably cheap** restaurant and the food is **extremely good**.
- Oh, I'm **terribly sorry**. I didn't mean to push you.
- Maria learns languages **incredibly quickly**.
- I was **bitterly disappointed** that I didn't get the job.
- The examination was **surprisingly easy**.

You can use an adverb before a *past participle* (**injured/organised** etc.):
- The meeting was very **badly organised**.
- The driver of the car was **seriously injured** in the accident.
- The building was **totally destroyed** in the fire.

192

UNIT 96   Exercises

96.1 *In this exercise you have to decide whether the underlined words are right or wrong.*
Correct those which are wrong.
Examples: The driver of the car was <u>serious</u> injured.   WRONG – seriously
             Be <u>quiet</u>, please! I'm trying to concentrate.   RIGHT

1 I waited <u>nervous</u> in the waiting-room before the interview.   ....
2 Why were you so <u>unfriendly</u> when I saw you yesterday?   ....
3 It rained <u>continuous</u> for three days.   ....
4 Alice and Stan are very <u>happy</u> married.   ....
5 Tom's French is not very <u>good</u> but his German is almost <u>fluent</u>.   ....
6 Eva lived in America for five years, so she speaks very <u>well</u> English.   ....
7 Everybody at the party was very <u>colourful</u> dressed.   ....
8 Ann likes wearing <u>colourful</u> clothes.   ....
9 Sue is <u>terrible</u> upset about losing her job.   ....

96.2 *This time you have to complete the sentences with adverbs. The first letter(s) of each adverb*
are given.
Example: We didn't go out because it was raining h*eavily*.................. .

1 We had to wait for a long time but we didn't complain. We waited pat................................. .
2 I lost the match because I played very ba............................... .
3 I don't think he trusted me. He looked at me so sus............................... .
4 Sorry, I didn't mean to kick you. I didn't do it int............................... .
5 Nobody knew he was coming. He arrived unex............................... .
6 Jill has just got a job in a shop but she won't be staying there long. She is only working
   there tem............................... until she can find another job.
7 My French isn't very good but I can understand per............................... if people speak
   sl............................... and cl............................... .
8 I had little difficulty finding a flat. I found one quite ea............................... .

96.3 *Choose two words (one from each box) to complete each sentence.*

absolutely	~~reasonably~~	badly
completely	seriously	fully
extremely	unusually	slightly

~~cheap~~	enormous	planned
changed	ill	quiet
damaged	insured	sorry

1 I thought the restaurant would be expensive but it was *reasonably cheap*.................. .
2 George's mother is .... in hospital.
3 The fire destroyed our house but luckily we were ....
4 What a big house! It's ....
5 It wasn't a serious accident. The car was only ....
6 A lot of things went wrong during our holiday because it was ....
7 The children are normally very lively but they're .... today.
8 When I returned home after 20 years, everything had ....
9 I'm .... about losing your book. I'll buy you another one.

193

UNIT 97   Adjectives and adverbs (2) (good/well, fast/hard/late, hardly)

a) Good/well   **Good** is an *adjective*. The *adverb* is **well**:
- Your **English** is very **good**.   You **speak** English **well**.
- Susan is a **good pianist**.   She **plays** the piano **well**.

We often use **well** with *past participles* (dressed/known etc.):
   well-dressed (*not* 'good dressed')   **well-known**   **well-educated**

But **well** is also an *adjective* with the meaning 'in good health':
- 'How are you today?'   'I'm very **well**, thanks.' (*not* 'I'm very good')

b) Fast/hard/late   These words are both adjectives and adverbs:

adjective	*adverb*
Jack is a very **fast runner**.	Jack can **run** very **fast**.
Ann is a **hard worker**.	Ann **works hard**. (*not* 'works hardly')
The train **was late**.	I **got up late** this morning.

The adverb **lately** = recently:
- Have you seen Tom **lately**?

c) **Hardly** has a completely different meaning from **hard**:
Hardly = almost not. Study these examples:
- George asked Hilda to marry him. She was surprised because they had only known each other for two days. She said: 'We can't get married now! We **hardly** know each other.' (= we know each other very little; we almost don't know each other)
- Why was Tom so unfriendly at the party last night? He **hardly** spoke to me. (= he spoke to me very little)

We often use **hardly** with **can/could**:
- Your writing is terrible. I **can hardly** read it. (= I can read it but only with a lot of difficulty)
- My leg was hurting me. I **could hardly** walk.

We also use **hardly** with **any/anyone/anything/anywhere**:
- 'How much money have you got?'   '**Hardly any**.' (= almost none, very little)
- I'll have to go shopping. We've got **hardly any** food. (= almost no food, very little food)
- The examination results were very bad. **Hardly anyone** passed. (= almost no-one passed, very few people passed)
- She ate **hardly anything** because she didn't feel hungry. (= she ate almost nothing, she ate very little)

Note that you can say:
- She ate **hardly anything**.   *or*   She **hardly** ate **anything**.
- We've got **hardly any** food.   *or*   We've **hardly** got **any** food.

Hardly ever = almost never:
- I'm nearly always at home in the evenings. I **hardly ever** go out.

UNIT 97   Exercises

97.1 *In this exercise you have to decide whether the underlined words are right or wrong. Correct those which are wrong.*
   Examples: We lost the match because we didn't play very <u>good</u>.   WRONG – well
           Ann has been working very <u>hard</u> recently.   RIGHT

   1 Give my best wishes to your parents. I hope they are <u>well</u>.   ....
   2 The children behaved themselves very <u>good</u>.   ....
   3 I tried <u>hardly</u> to remember his name but I couldn't.   ....
   4 The company's financial situation is not <u>well</u> at present.   ....
   5 Jack has started his own business. Everything is going quite <u>good</u>.   ....
   6 Don't walk so <u>fast</u>! Can't you walk more slowly?   ....
   7 See you soon! Don't work too <u>hard</u>.   ....

97.2 *This time you have to finish these sentences with* **well** + *one of the following words:*
   balanced   ~~**behaved**~~   **dressed**   **informed**   **kept**   **known**

   1 The children were very good. They were .*well-behaved*.. .
   2 Many people have heard of him. He is quite well- ....
   3 Their garden is neat and tidy. It is very ....
   4 You should eat different types of food. Your diet should be ....
   5 Ann knows quite a lot about many things. She is quite ....
   6 His clothes weren't very smart. He wasn't very ....

97.3 *Now you have to make sentences with* **hardly**. *Use the words in brackets.*
   Example: George and I have only met once. (know / each other)   *We hardly know each other.*

   1 I'm very tired this morning. (slept / last night)   I .... night.
   2 You're speaking very quietly. (can / hear)   I can .... you.
   3 I met Keith a few days ago. I hadn't seen him for a long time. He looks very different
      now. (recognised)   I ....
   4 They were really shocked when they heard the news. (could / speak)
      ....

97.4 *Complete these sentences with* **hardly** + **any/anyone/anything/anywhere/ever**.
   Example: I'll have to go shopping. We've got .... *hardly any* .... food.

   1 I listen to the radio a lot but I .... watch television.
   2 The weather was good during our holiday. There was .... rain.
   3 He is not very popular. .... likes him.
   4 It's crowded in here. There's .... to sit down.
   5 We used to be good friends but we .... see each other now.
   6 I hate this town. There's .... to do and .... to go.
   7 I enjoyed driving this morning. There was .... traffic.

UNIT 98   So and such

a) Study these examples:
- I didn't enjoy the book. The story was **so** stupid.
- I didn't enjoy the book. It was **such** a stupid story.

> We use **so** with an adjective *without* a noun: **so stupid**
> We use **such** with an adjective *with* a noun: **such** a stupid **story**

You can also use **so** with an adverb:
- He's difficult to understand because he speaks **so quickly**.

b) **So** and **such** make the meaning of the adjective stronger:
- It's a lovely day, isn't it? It's **so warm**. (= really warm)
- We enjoyed our holiday. We had **such a good time**. (= a really good time)

Compare **so** and **such** in these sentences:
- I like Tom and Ann. They are **so nice**.
- I like Tom and Ann. They are **such** nice **people**. (*not* 'so nice people')

We often say **so ... that ...** and **such ... that ...**:
- I was **so tired that** I went to bed at seven o'clock.
- She worked **so hard that** she made herself ill.
- It was **such lovely weather that** we spent the whole day in the garden.
- {The book was **so good that** I couldn't put it down.
  {It was **such a good book that** I couldn't put it down.

You can leave out **that** in these sentences:
- I was so tired (that) I went to bed at 7 o'clock.

c) In these sentences we use **so** and **such** in a different way:
- I expected the weather to be much cooler. I didn't expect it to be **so warm**. (= as warm as it is)
- I'm tired because I got up at 6 o'clock. I don't usually get up **so early**. (= as early as 6 o'clock)
- Hurry up! Don't walk **so slowly**. (= as slowly as you are walking)
- I was surprised when Jack told me the house was built 100 years ago. {I didn't realise it was **so old**. {I didn't realise it was **such an old house**.   (= as old as it is)

d) We say: **so long** but 'such a long **time**'; **so far** but 'such a long **way**'; **so many, so much** but 'such a lot (of)':
- I haven't seen him for **so long** that I've forgotten what he looks like. (*or* ... for **such a long time** ...)
- I didn't know you lived **so far** from the city centre. (*or* ... **such a long way** from ...)
- Why did you buy **so much** food? (*or* ... **such a lot of** food?)

UNIT 98   Exercises

98.1 *In this exercise you have to put in* **so** *or* **such**.
    Examples: Come on! Don't walk ....*so*.......slowly!
                I've never read .....*such*.....a stupid book.

1 I was surprised that he looked .... well after his recent illness.
2 They've got .... a lot of money, they don't know what to do with it.
3 She is a very attractive girl. She's got .... beautiful eyes.
4 Everything is .... expensive these days, isn't it?
5 Why did you ask them .... stupid questions?
6 It was .... a boring film that I fell asleep in the middle of it.
7 The wind was .... strong, it was difficult to walk.
8 The food at the hotel was very bad. I've never eaten .... awful food.

98.2 *This time you have to make a sentence with* **so** *from two sentences.*
    Example: She worked very hard. She made herself ill.
        She worked so hard (that) she made herself ill.

1 I was very excited about going away. I couldn't sleep.
   I was so ....
2 The water was very dirty. We decided not to go swimming.
   ....
3 She speaks English very well. You would think it was her native language.
   ....

98.3 *In this exercise you have to use* **such** *instead of* **so**.
    Example: The book was so good that I couldn't put it down.
        It was such a good book that I couldn't put it down.

1 The road is so narrow that it is difficult for two cars to pass each other.
   It is ....
2 The weather was so warm that I didn't need a coat.
   It ....
3 His feet are so big that he has difficulty finding shoes to fit him.
   He has got ....
4 There were so many people in the room that we couldn't move.
   There were ....

98.4 *Now you have to complete these sentences.*
    Example: We had a lot of problems.   We hadn't expected to have so .*many problems*.........

1 It's quite a long way from your house to the station.
   I didn't know it was so ....
2 It took us a long time to get home this evening.
   It doesn't usually take us so ....
3 You've got a lot of furniture in this room.
   Why have you got so .... ?

UNIT 99   Enough and too

a) The position of **enough**:

Enough goes *after* adjectives and adverbs:

- He didn't get the job because he wasn't **experienced enough**. (*not* 'enough experienced')
- You won't pass the examination if you don't work **hard enough**.
- She can't get married yet. She's not **old enough**.

Enough goes *before* nouns:

- He didn't get the job because he didn't have **enough experience**. (*not* 'experience enough')
- I'd like to go on holiday but I haven't got **enough money**.
- Some of us had to sit on the floor because there weren't **enough chairs**.

You can also use **enough** alone (without a noun):

- I'll lend you some money if you haven't got **enough**.

b) After **enough** and **too** you can say **for someone/something**:

- I haven't got enough money **for a holiday**.
- He wasn't experienced enough **for the job**.
- This shirt is too big **for me**. I need a smaller size.

But we do not usually say 'enough/too ... for doing something'. We use **to** + *infinitive* after **enough** and **too**. So we say '**enough** money **to do** something', 'old **enough to do** something', '**too** young **to do** something' etc.:

- I haven't got **enough money to go** on holiday. (*not* 'for going')
- He wasn't **experienced enough to do** the job.
- She's only sixteen. She's not **old enough to get** married. (*or* She's **too young to get** married.)
- Let's get a taxi. It's **too far to walk**.
- There weren't **enough chairs** for everyone **to sit down**.
- The weather wasn't **nice enough to go** swimming.
- He spoke **too quickly** for us **to understand**.

c) We say:

- The food was so hot that we couldn't eat **it**.

    and: The food was very hot. We couldn't eat **it**.

or we say: – The food was **too hot to eat**. (without 'it')

Here are some more examples like this:

- That picture is **too heavy to hang** on the wall.
- I had to carry my wallet in my hand. It was **too big to put** in my pocket.
- The water wasn't **clean enough to swim in**.

UNIT 99 Exercises

99.1 *Complete these sentences using* **enough** *with one of the following words:*
big ~~old~~ warm well cups money qualifications room time

1 She can't get married yet. She's not *old enough*............ .
2 Tom would like to buy a car but he hasn't got ....
3 I couldn't make coffee for everybody. There weren't ....
4 Are you .... ? Or shall I switch on the heating?
5 It's only a small car. There isn't .... for all of you.
6 George didn't feel .... to go to work this morning.
7 I didn't finish the examination. I didn't have ....
8 Do you think I've got .... to apply for the job?
9 Try this jacket on and see if it's .... for you.

99.2 *Answer these questions using the words in brackets.*
Example: 'Is she getting married?' (not old enough)
    'No, *she isn't old enough to get married*........................,'

1 'Why can't you talk to me now?' (too busy) 'I'm too .... now.'
2 'Let's go to the cinema.' (too late) 'No, it's .... cinema.'
3 'Why don't we sit in the garden?' (not warm enough)
    'It's not ....,'
4 'Would you like to be a politician?' (too nice)
    'No, I'm ....,'
5 'Are you going on holiday this year?' (not enough money)
    'No, I haven't got ....,'
6 'Shall we take a photograph?' (too dark) 'No, ...,'
7 'Did you hear what he was saying?' (too far away)
    'No, we ....,'
8 'Can he make himself understood (in English)?' (not enough English)
    'No, he doesn't speak ....,'
9 'Does Harry work?' (too lazy) 'No, he's ....,'

99.3 *In this exercise you have to make one sentence (using* **too** *or* **enough***) from the two sentences given.*
Example: We couldn't eat the food. It was too hot. *The food was too hot (for us) to eat.*......

1 I can't drink this coffee. It's too hot. This coffee is ....
2 Nobody could move the piano. It was too heavy.
    The piano ....
3 I can't wear this coat in winter. It's not warm enough.
    This coat ....
4 Don't stand on that chair. It's not strong enough.
    That chair ....
5 Two people can't sleep in this bed. It's not wide enough for two people.
    This bed ....

199

UNIT 100 To + infinitive   after adjectives

a) Compare these two sentences:

> Jim doesn't speak very clearly. $\Big\{$
> A **It is difficult to understand him.**
> B **He is difficult to understand.**
>
> Sentences A and B have the same meaning. But note that we say 'He is difficult **to understand.**' (*not* 'He is difficult to understand *him*.')

You can use the structure in sentence B after **difficult/easy/impossible/hard** and after a few other adjectives:

  - Your writing is almost **impossible to read.** (*not* '... to read it')
  (= It is almost impossible to read your writing.)
  - Do you think this water is **safe to drink?** (*not* '... to drink it')
  - Jill is very **interesting to talk to.** (*not* '... to talk to her')

You can also use this structure with an *adjective + noun*:

  - This is a very **difficult question** to answer. (*not* '... to answer it')
  - Jill is an **interesting person** to talk to.
  - I enjoyed the football match. It was an **exciting game** to watch.

b) We use to + *infinitive* after **the first / the second / the third** etc. and also after **the next** and **the last**:

  - Who was **the first** man **to reach** the South Pole?
  - If I have any more news, you'll be **the first to know.**
  - **The next** train **to arrive** at platform 4 will be the 6.58 to Cardiff.
  - Who was **the last** person **to leave** the building last night?

c) You can use to + *infinitive* after a number of adjectives to say how someone feels about something. For example:

  - I was **sorry to hear** that your father is ill.
  - Was Tom **surprised to see** you when you visited him?
  - I was **delighted to get** your letter last week.

Other adjectives you can use in this way include:

happy	pleased	disappointed	amazed
glad	sad	relieved	astonished

d) Note the structure **(it is) nice of someone to do something.** This structure is possible after a number of adjectives including:

nice	mean	silly	polite	generous
kind	stupid	clever	careless	

  - It was **nice of you to take** me to the station. Thank you very much.
  - It was **careless of Jack to leave** the door unlocked when he went out.
  - It's **stupid of him to give** up his job when he needs the money.
  - It was very **generous of Ann to lend** us the money.

UNIT 100   Exercises

100.1 *Write these sentences in another way, beginning as shown.*
Example: It is difficult to understand him.   He *is difficult to understand.* ....

1 It's quite easy to find our house.   Our house is ....
2 It was very difficult to open the window.   The window ....
3 It's impossible to translate some words.   Some words ....
4 It's not very difficult to make bread.   Bread ....
5 It's not safe to stand on that chair.   That chair ....
6 It's difficult to explain some grammatical rules.
   Some grammatical rules ....
7 It's hard to find a good restaurant in this town.
   A good restaurant ....

100.2 *Use the following words to complete each sentence:*
first man/walk   first/complain   last/arrive   last person/see
~~next train/arrive~~

1 The ...... *next train to arrive* .... at platform 2 will be the 7.45 to Birmingham.
2 When anything goes wrong, Harry is always ....
3 Nobody has seen Keith for days. Who was .... him?
4 Neil Armstrong was .... on the moon.
5 We always have to wait for him. He's always ....

100.3 *Use the following words to complete these sentences:*
~~delighted/get~~   astonished/find   sorry/hear   pleased/see   glad/hear

1 I was really ...... *delighted to get* .... your letter last week.
2 Thank you for your letter. I'm .... that you're keeping well.
3 When I walked into my bedroom, I was .... a complete stranger
   sleeping in my bed.
4 Hello! I'm so glad you could come. I'm really .... you again.
5 I'm .... that your mother is ill. I hope she gets better soon.

100.4 *Make sentences using the words in brackets.*
Example: Jack left the door unlocked when he went out.   (careless)
           It was careless of Jack to leave the door unlocked when he went out. ....

1 Tom offered to help me.   (kind)
   It was .... me.
2 You make the same mistake again and again.   (careless)
   It's ....
3 She went out in the rain without a raincoat.   (stupid)
   It was ....
4 Don and Jenny invited me to stay with them for a few days.   (nice)
   It ....
5 He left without saying thank you.   (not polite)
   It wasn't ....

UNIT 101   Comparison (1) – **cheaper, more expensive** etc.

a) Study these examples:

> Let's go by car. It's **cheaper**.
> Don't go by train. It's **more expensive**.
>
> **Cheaper** and **more expensive** are *comparative* forms.

After comparatives we use **than**:
　　　　　　　　– It's cheaper to go by car **than** to go by train.
For **than** see also Unit 103.

b) We use **-er** for the comparative of short adjectives and adverbs:
　　cheap/cheaper hard/harder large/larger thin/thinner
　　　　　　　　– This jacket is too small. I need a **larger** size.
　　　　　　　　– Ann works **harder** than most of her friends.
We prefer **-er** with some two-syllable adjectives, especially adjectives ending in **-y**. For example:
　　lucky/luckier funny/funnier easy/easier pretty/prettier
　　and also: **quiet/quieter clever/cleverer narrow/narrower simple/simpler**
　　　　　　　　– The examination was **easier** than we expected.
　　　　　　　　– It's too noisy here. Can we go somewhere **quieter**?
For spelling rules see Appendix 3.

c) We use **more ...** (*not* '-er') for other two-syllable adjectives and longer adjectives:
　　more modern more serious more expensive more comfortable
　　　　　　　　– **More expensive** hotels are usually **more comfortable** than cheaper ones.
　　　　　　　　– Her illness was **more serious** than we at first thought.
We also use **more ...** for adverbs which end in **-ly**:
　　more slowly more seriously more quietly more carefully
　　　　　　　　– Could you speak **more slowly**, please?
We also say **more often**:
　　　　　　　　– I don't play tennis much now. I used to play **more often**.
But we say **earlier** (*not* 'more early'):
　　　　　　　　– You're always tired in the mornings. You should go to bed **earlier**.

d) Before the comparative of adjectives and adverbs you can use:
　　a bit a little much a lot far (= a lot)
　　　　　　　　– Let's go by car. It's **much** (*or* **a lot**) **cheaper**.
　　　　　　　　– Don't go by train. It's **much** (*or* **a lot**) **more expensive**.
　　　　　　　　– Ann works **a lot** (*or* **much**) **harder** than most of her friends.
　　　　　　　　– Could you speak **a bit** (*or* **a little**) **more slowly**?
　　　　　　　　– Her illness was **far more serious** than we at first thought.

UNIT 101   Exercises

101.1 *Complete these sentences. Each time use the comparative form of one of the following adjectives or adverbs:*

crowded   early   easily   expensive   interested   ~~large~~   near   often
quiet   thin

1 This jacket is too small. I need a .... *larger* .... size.
2 You look .... Have you lost weight?
3 He's not so keen on his studies. He's .... in having a good time.
4 You'll find your way around the town .... if you have a map.
5 You're making too much noise. Can you be a bit .... ?
6 There were a lot of people on the bus. It was .... than usual.
7 You're late. I expected you to be here ....
8 You hardly ever write to me. Why don't you write a bit .... ?
9 The hotel was surprisingly cheap. I expected it to be much ....
10 It's a pity you live so far away. I wish you lived ....

101.2 *Complete these sentences. Use the comparative of the words in brackets +* **than.**
Example: Her illness was *more serious than* we at first thought.   (serious)

1 Sorry I'm late. It took me .... to get here .... I expected.   (long)
2 My toothache is .... it was yesterday.   (painful)
3 She looks about 20, but in fact she's much .... she looks.   (old)
4 The problem is not so complicated. It's .... you think.   (simple)
5 Your English has improved. You speak a lot .... you did when we last met.   (fluently)
6 Health and happiness are .... money.   (important)
7 We always go camping when we go on holiday. It's much .... staying in a hotel.   (cheap)
8 I like the countryside. It's .... and .... living in a town.   (healthy/peaceful)

101.3 *This exercise is similar but this time you also have to use* **a bit / a little / much / a lot / far.**
Use **than** *where necessary.*
Example: Her illness was *much more serious than* we at first thought.
              (much / serious)

1 It's .... today .... it was yesterday.   (a little / warm)
2 You're driving too fast. Can you drive .... ?   (a bit / slowly)
3 A: Did you enjoy your visit to the museum?
    B: Yes, I found it .... I expected.   (far / interesting)
4 I prefer this armchair. It's .... the other one.
    (much / comfortable)
5 You looked depressed this morning but you look .... now.
    (a bit / happy)
6 This flat is too small for me. I need something ....   (much / big)
7 It's .... to learn a foreign language in the country where it is spoken.
    (a lot / easy)

UNIT 102   Comparison (2)

a) Some adjectives and adverbs have irregular comparative forms:

good/well	better	Let me ask him. I know him **better** than you do.
		The garden looks **better** since you tidied it up.
bad/badly	worse	'Is your headache better?' 'No, it's **worse**.'
		The situation was much **worse** than we expected.
far	further	I'm very tired. I can't walk much **further**.
	(*or* **farther**)	(*or* ... much **farther**.)

Further (but not 'farther') can also mean **more** or **additional**:
     – Let me know immediately if you hear any **further** news. (= any more news)
Note the comparative words **more** and **less**:
     – I smoke **more** than I used to.
     – We've got **less** time than I thought.

b) **Older** and **elder**
The comparative of **old** is **older**:
     – Tom looks **older** than he really is.
We use **elder** when we are talking about members of a family. We say (**my**) **elder brother/sister/ son/daughter**:
     – **My elder brother** is a pilot.
We use **elder** only before a noun:
     – My brother is **older** than me. (*not* 'elder than me')
For **eldest** see Unit 104c.

c) Sometimes you can use two comparatives together. For example: **harder and harder, more and more, more and more difficult**. We use this structure to say that something is changing continuously:
     – It's becoming **harder and harder** to find a job.
     – Your English is improving. It's getting **better and better**.
     – It's becoming **more and more difficult** to find a job.
     – These days **more and more** people are learning English.

d) Note the structure **the** +*comparative* **the better**. For example:
     – 'What time shall we leave?' '**The sooner the better**.' (= it will be best if we leave as soon as possible)
     – 'What size box do you want?' '**The bigger the better**.' (= it will be best if the box is as big as possible)
We also use **the ... the ...** (with two comparatives) to say that one thing depends on another thing:
     – **The warmer** the weather, **the better** I feel.
     – **The earlier** we leave, **the sooner** we will arrive.
     – **The more expensive** the hotel, **the better** the service.
     – **The more** electricity you use, **the higher** your bill will be.
     – **The more** you have, **the more** you want.

UNIT 102   Exercises

102.1 *Complete these sentences using these words:* **better   worse   further   older   elder**
You have to use some of these words more than once. Use **than** *where necessary.*
Example: Let me ask him. I know him ....*better than*.. you do.

1 We complained about the food in our hotel. But instead of improving, it got
   ....
2 Your work isn't very good. I'm sure you can do .... this.
3 Ann's younger sister is still at school. Her .... sister is a nurse.
4 Our team played really badly this afternoon. We played .... we have ever
   played before.
5 You're standing too near the camera. Can you move a bit .... away?
6 'Is Jim younger than Tom?'   'No, he's ....'
7 The damage to our car wasn't so bad. It could have been much ....
8 If you need any .... information, please contact our head office.

102.2 *In this exercise you have to use the structure* **... and ...** *(see section c).*
Examples: It's becoming ......*harder and harder*...... to find a job.   (hard)
          It's becoming ...*more and more difficult*.. to find a job.   (difficult)

1 As I waited for my interview, I became ....   (nervous)
2 That hole in your pullover is getting ....   (big)
3 The suitcase seemed to get .... as I carried it along the road.
   (heavy)
4 As the day went on, the weather got ....   (bad)
5 As the conversation went on, he became ....   (talkative)
6 Travelling is becoming ....   (expensive)
7 Since she has been in Britain, her English has got ....   (good)

102.3 *In this exercise you have to write sentences with* **the ... the ....** *Choose a half-sentence from
box A to go with a half-sentence from box B.*

A ~~the earlier we leave~~	B the faster you'll learn
the longer he waited	the more you have to pay
the more I got to know him	~~the sooner we'll arrive~~
the more you practise your English	the more profit you'll make
the longer the telephone call	the more impatient he became
the more goods you sell	the more I liked him

1 The earlier we leave, *the sooner we'll arrive.*..................................
2 ....
3 ....
4 ....
5 ....
6 ....

205

UNIT 103   Comparison (3) – as ... as / than

a) Study this example situation:

Joe, Henry and Arthur are all millionaires. They are all very rich. Joe has £5 million, Henry has £4 million and Arthur has £2 million. So:

Henry is rich.
He is **richer than** Arthur.
But he **isn't as rich as** Joe. (= Joe is **richer than** he is)

Here are some more examples of **not as ... as:**
- Jack **isn't as old as** he looks. (= he looks **older than** he is)
- The city centre **wasn't as crowded** this morning **as** it usually is. (= it is usually **more crowded**)
- Jim **didn't** do **as well** in his examination **as** he had hoped. (= he had hoped to do **better**)
- 'The weather's better today, isn't it?'   'Yes, it's **not as cold**.' (= yesterday was **colder**)
- I **don't** know **as many** people **as** you do. (= you know **more** people)

You can also say 'not **so** ...as' (instead of 'not **as** ...as'):
- Henry isn't **so** rich as Joe.

b) You can also use **as ... as** (but not 'so ... as') in positive sentences and in questions:
- I'm sorry I'm late. I got here **as fast as** I could.
- There's plenty of food, so eat **as much as** you like.
- Let's walk. It's **just as quick as** taking the bus.
- Can you send me the money **as soon as** possible, please?

We also say **twice as ... as, three times as ... as** etc.
- Petrol is **twice as expensive as** it was a few years ago.
- Their house is about **three times as big as** ours.

c) We say **the same as** (*not* 'the same like'):
- Ann's salary is **the same as** mine. (*or* Ann gets **the same** salary **as** me.)
- Tom is **the same** age **as** George.
- 'What would you like to drink?'   'I'll have **the same as** last time.'

d) After **than** and **as** it is more usual to say **me/him/her/them/us** when there is no verb. Compare these sentences:
- You are taller **than I am**.   *but:* You are taller **than me**.
- They have more money **than we have**.   *but:* They have more money **than us**.
- I can't run as fast **as he can**.   *but:* I can't run as fast **as him**.

UNIT 103   Exercises

103.1 *In this exercise you have to complete the sentences using* **as ... as.**
  Examples: I'm quite tall but you are taller.   I'm not *as tall as you.*
           Ann works reasonably hard but she used to work much harder.
           Ann doesn't *work as hard as she used to.*

1 My salary is high but yours is higher.   My salary isn't ....
2 You know a bit about cars but I know more.   You don't ....
3 I still smoke but I used to smoke a lot more.   I don't ....
4 I still feel quite tired but I felt a lot more tired yesterday.
   I don't ....
5 They've lived here for quite a long time but we've lived here longer.
   They haven't ....
6 I was a bit nervous before the interview but usually I'm a lot more nervous.
   I wasn't ....
7 The weather is still unpleasant today but yesterday it was worse.
   The weather isn't ....

103.2 *Re-write these sentences so that they have the same meaning. Begin as shown.*
  Example: Jack is younger than he looks.   Jack isn't *as old as he looks.*

1 It's warmer today than yesterday. It isn't ....
2 The station was nearer than I thought.   The station wasn't ....
3 I go out less than I used to.   I don't ....
4 The hotel is cheaper than I expected.   The hotel isn't ....
5 There were fewer people at this meeting than at the last one.
   There weren't ....
6 The examination was easier than we expected.
   The examination wasn't ....

103.3 *Complete these sentences using* **just as** *with one of the following words:*
  bad   comfortable   expensive   ~~quick~~   well-qualified

1 Let's walk. It's ....*just as quick as*.......... taking the bus.
2 I'm going to sleep on the floor. It's .... sleeping in that bed.
3 Why did he get the job? I'm .... him.
4 I thought you were nice but you're .... everybody else.
5 You won't find a cheaper restaurant than this. They'll all be ....

103.4 *Now you have to make sentences with* **the same as.**
  Example: (Tom / same age / George)   *Tom is the same age as George.*

1 (your hair / same colour / mine)   Your hair ....
2 (I arrived here / same time / you) ....
3 (you made / same mistake / I made) ....

207

UNIT 104   Superlatives – **the longest, the most enjoyable** etc.

a) Study these examples:

> What is **the longest** river in the world?
> What was **the most enjoyable** holiday you've ever had?
>
> **Longest** and **most enjoyable** are *superlative* forms.

b) We use **-est** or **most ...** to form the superlative of adjectives and adverbs. In general we use **-est** for shorter words and **most ...** for longer words. (The rules are the same as those for the comparative – see Unit 101.) For example:

> long/longest   hot/hottest   easy/easiest   hard/hardest
> *but:* **most** famous   **most** boring   **most** difficult   **most** expensive

For spelling rules see Appendix 3.
  – Yesterday was **the hottest** day of the year.
  – That was **the most boring** film I've ever seen.
  – 'Why did you stay at that hotel?' 'It was **the cheapest** we could find.'
  – She is a really nice person – one of **the nicest** people I know.
Note the irregular superlatives **best** and **worst**:
  – That was a delicious meal. It's one of **the best** I've ever had.
  – Why does he always come to see me at **the worst** possible moment?
Don't forget that we normally use **the** with superlatives: 'the best', 'the most boring' etc.

c) **Oldest** and **eldest**
The superlative of **old** is **oldest**:
  – That house over there is **the oldest** building in the town.
We use **eldest** when we are talking about the members of a family:
  – **My eldest son** is 13 years old.
  – Are you **the eldest** in your family?

d) After superlatives, we use **in** with places (towns, buildings etc.):
  – What's the longest river **in the world**? (*not* 'of the world')
  – We were lucky to have one of the nicest rooms **in the hotel**.
Also: (the best ...) **in the class** / **in the team** / **in the company** etc.
But: the happiest day **of my life**, the hottest day **of the year**.
Note that we often use the *present perfect* (**I have done**) after a superlative (see also Unit 14a):
  – What's the **best** film **you've** ever **seen**?
  – That was the **most delicious** meal **I've had** for a long time.

e) We sometimes use **most** + adjective (without 'the') to mean **very**:
  – The book you lent me was **most interesting**. (= very interesting)
  – Thank you for the money. It was **most generous** of you. (= very generous)

104.1 *Complete the sentences with a superlative and preposition.*
Example: It's a very nice room.   It's ....*the nicest room in*........ the hotel.

1 It's a very cheap restaurant.   It's .... the town.
2 It was a very happy day.   It was .... my life.
3 She's a very intelligent student.   She .... the school.
4 It's a very valuable painting.   It .... the gallery.

In the following sentences use **one of the** *+ superlative.*
Example: It's a very nice room.   It's ...*one of the nicest rooms in*.. the hotel.

5 He's a very rich man.   He's one .... the world.
6 It's a very old castle.   It's .... Britain.
7 He's a very good player.   He .... the team.
8 It was a very bad experience.   It was .... my life.
9 He's a very dangerous criminal.   He .... the country.

104.2 *Read these sentences and then write a new sentence with the same meaning. Use a*
superlative each time and begin each sentence as shown.
Example: I've never seen such a boring film.   It's ...*the most boring film I've ever seen*......

1 I've never heard such a funny story.   That's the .... heard.
2 He's never made such a bad mistake.   It's ....
3 I haven't tasted such good coffee for a long time.
   That's .... time.
4 I've never slept in such an uncomfortable bed.
   This is ....
5 I've never had such a big meal.   It's ....
6 I've never met such a generous person as Ann.
   Ann is ....
7 I've never had such a good friend as you.   You ....
8 I haven't had to make such a difficult decision for years.
   This is .... years.

104.3 *Now here are some questions for you to answer. But first you have to write the questions*
using the words in brackets. Then answer them.

1 (what / large / city / your country?)   What ..*is the largest city in your country?*......
2 (who / famous singer / your country?)   Who .... your country?
3 (what / popular sport / your country?)   What ....
4 (what / expensive thing / you / ever bought?)   ....
5 (what / happy / day / your life?)   What was ....
6 (what / stupid thing / you / ever done?)   ....
7 (who / intelligent person / you know?)   .... you know?
8 (who / beautiful person / you know?)   ....

UNIT 105   Word order (1) – verb + object; place and time

a) *Verb + object*

The *verb* and the *object* of the verb normally go together. We do *not* usually put other words between them:

	verb	*+ object*	
I	**like**	**children**	very much. (*not* 'I like very much children.')
Did you	**see**	**Norman**	yesterday?
Ann often	**plays**	**tennis.**	

Here are some more examples. Notice how each time the verb and the object go together:

- Do you **clean the house** every week-end? (*not* 'Do you clean every week-end the house?')
- Everybody **enjoyed the party** very much. (*not* 'Everybody enjoyed very much the party.')
- Our guide **spoke English** fluently. (*not* '... spoke fluently English.')
- I not only lost all my money – I also **lost my passport.** (*not* 'I lost also my passport.')
- At the end of the street you'll **see a supermarket** on your left. (*not* '... see on your left a supermarket.')

For the position of words like **also** and **often** before the verb, see Unit 106.

b) *Place* and *time*

We usually say the *place* (**where?**) before the *time* (**when? / how often? / how long?**):

	place	*time*	
Tom walks	**to work**	**every morning.**	(*not* 'Tom walks every morning to work.')
She has been	**in Canada**	**since April.**	
We arrived	**at the airport**	**early.**	

Here are some more examples:

- I'm going **to Paris on Monday.** (*not* 'I'm going on Monday to Paris.')
- Don't be late. Make sure you're **here by 8 o'clock.**
- Why weren't you **at home last night**?
- You really shouldn't go **to bed so late.**

It is often possible to put the time at the beginning of the sentence:

- **On Monday** I'm going to Paris.
- **Every morning** Tom walks to work.

Note that you *cannot* use **early** or **late** at the beginning of the sentence in this way.

There is more information about word order in Unit 106.

UNIT 105   Exercises

105.1   *In this exercise you have to decide whether the word order is right or wrong. Correct the sentences which are wrong.*
Examples: I like children very much.   RIGHT
Tom walks every morning to work.   WRONG – ...to work every morning.

1   Jim doesn't like very much football.   ....
2   Ann drives every day her car to work.   ....
3   When I heard the news, I phoned Tom immediately.   ....
4   Maria speaks very well English.   ....
5   After eating quickly my dinner, I went out.   ....
6   You watch all the time television. Can't you do something else?   ....
7   Jim smokes about 20 cigarettes every day.   ....
8   I think I'll go early to bed tonight.   ....
9   You should go to the dentist every six months.   ....
10   When I heard the alarm, I got immediately out of bed.   ....
11   Did you learn a lot of things at school today?   ....
12   How many people do you know who go on Sundays to church?   ....

105.2   *Now you have to put the parts of a sentence in the correct order. The first nine sentences are like those in section a.*
Example: (children / very much / I like)   I like children very much.

1   (he won / easily / the game)   He won ....
2   (again / please don't ask / that question)   Please ....
3   (football / every week-end / does Ken play?)   Does ....
4   (quietly / the door / I closed)   I ....
5   (his name / after a few minutes / I remembered)   ....
6   (a letter to her parents / Ann writes / every week)   ....
7   (at the top of the page / your name / please write)   ....
8   (some interesting books / we found / in the library)

....
9   (opposite the park / a new hotel / they are building)

....

The next six sentences are like those in section b.

10   (to the bank / every Friday / I go)   I go ....
11   (home / why did you come / so late?)   Why ....
12   (around the town / all morning / I've been walking)

....
13   (recently / to the theatre / have you been?)   ....
14   (to London / for a few days next week / I'm going)

....
15   (on Saturday night / I didn't see you / at the party)

....

UNIT 106 Word order (2) – adverbs with the verb

a) We put some adverbs (for example **always, also, probably**) with the verb in the middle of a sentence:

- Tom **always goes** to work by car.
- We were feeling very tired. We **were also** hungry.
- Your car **has probably been** stolen.

b) Study these rules for the position of adverbs in the middle of a sentence. (They are only general rules, so there are exceptions.)

i) If the verb is one word (**goes, cooked** etc.), we usually put the adverb *before* the verb:

	adverb	verb	
Tom	always	goes	to work by car.

- I cleaned the house and **also cooked** the dinner. (*not* 'cooked also')
- Jack **hardly ever watches** television and **rarely reads** newspapers.
- She **almost fell** over as she came down the stairs.

Note that these adverbs (**always/often/also** etc.) go before **have to**:
- We **always have to** wait a long time for the bus.

But adverbs go *after* **am/is/are/was/were**:
- We were feeling very tired. We **were also** hungry.
- Why are you always late? You're **never** on time.
- The traffic **isn't usually** as bad as it was this morning.

ii) Sometimes a verb is two or more words (**can remember, doesn't smoke, has been stolen** etc.). We usually put the adverb after the first part of the verb:

	verb 1	adverb	verb 2	
I	can	never	remember	his name.
Ann	doesn't	usually	smoke.	
	Are you	definitely	going	to the party tomorrow?
Your car	has	probably	been	stolen.

- My parents **have always lived** in London.
- Jack can't cook. He **can't even boil** an egg.
- The house **was only built** a year ago and it's **already falling** down.

In negative sentences **probably** goes before the negative. So we say:
- I **probably** won't see you.   *or*   I will **probably not** see you.
  (*but not* 'I won't probably see you.')

c) We also use **all** and **both** in these positions:

- We **all felt** ill after the meal.
- Jack and Tom **have both applied** for the job.
- We **are all going** out for a meal this evening.
- My parents **are both** teachers.

UNIT 106　Exercises

106.1　*In this exercise you have to decide whether the underlined words are in the right position or not. Correct the sentences which are wrong.*
Examples: Tom goes always to work by car.　WRONG — Tom always goes...
　　　　　I cleaned the house and also cooked the dinner.　RIGHT......

1　I have a good memory for faces but I <u>always</u> forget names.　..................
2　Those tourists over there <u>probably</u> are American.　..................
3　Tom gets <u>hardly ever</u> angry.　..................
4　We <u>both</u> were astonished when we heard the news.　..................
5　I <u>soon</u> found the keys I had lost.　..................
6　I did some shopping and I went <u>also</u> to the bank.　..................
7　Tom has <u>always</u> to hurry in the morning because he gets up so late.　..................
8　The baby is very good. She <u>seldom</u> cries during the night.　..................
9　I <u>usually</u> am very tired when I get home from work.　..................
10　I <u>usually</u> have a bath when I get home from work.　..................

106.2　*This time you have to re-write the sentences to include the word in brackets.*
Example: Ann doesn't smoke. (usually)　Ann doesn't usually smoke.......

1　Have you been arrested? (ever)　Have ....
2　I don't have to work on Saturdays. (usually)　I ....
3　Does Tom sing when he's in the bath? (always)　..
4　I'll be late home this evening. (probably)　..
5　We are going away tomorrow. (all)　..
6　(Don't take me seriously.) I was joking. (only)　I ....
7　Did you enjoy the party? (both)　..
8　(I've got a lot of housework to do.) I must write some letters. (also)

　　I ....

106.3　*Now you have to put the words in brackets into the sentences in the correct order.*
Example: I ....can never remember....... his name.　(remember / never / can)

1　I .... sugar in my tea.　(take / usually)
2　'Where's Jim?'　'He .... home early.'　(gone / has / probably)
3　Ann .... very generous.　(is / always)
4　Ann and Tom .... in Manchester.　(both / were / born)
5　Tim is a good pianist. He .... very well.　(sing / also / can)
6　Our television set .... down.　(often / breaks)
7　We .... a long time for the bus.　(have / always / to wait)
8　My sight isn't very good. I .... with glasses.　(read / can / only)
9　I .... early tomorrow.　(probably / leaving / will / be)
10　I'm afraid I .... able to come to the party.　(probably / be / won't)
11　If we hadn't taken the same train, we .... each other.
　　(never / met / might / have)

UNIT 107 Still and yet
Any more / any longer / no longer

a) Still and yet

We use **still** to say that a situation or action is continuing. **Still** usually goes in the middle of the sentence with the verb (see Unit 106b for the exact position):

  – It's 10 o'clock and Tom is **still** in bed.
  – 'Have you given up smoking?' 'No, I **still** smoke.'
  – Are you **still** living in the same house or have you moved?
  – When I went to bed, Ann was **still** working.
  – Do you **still** want to go to the party or have you changed your mind?

We use **yet** when we ask if something has happened or when we say that something has not happened. We use **yet** mainly in questions and negative sentences. **Yet** usually goes at the end of the sentence:

  – I'm hungry. Is dinner ready **yet**?
  – Have you finished writing that letter **yet**?
  – It's 10 o'clock and Tom hasn't got up **yet**. (*or* ... isn't up **yet**.)
  – We don't know where we're going for our holidays **yet**.

We often use **yet** with the *present perfect* ('**Have** you **finished** writing that letter yet?'). See also Unit 15b.

Now compare **still** and **yet** in these sentences:

  – Jack lost his job a year ago and he **is still** unemployed.
    Jack lost his job a year ago and **hasn't found** another job **yet**.
  – Is it **still raining**?
    Has it **stopped** raining **yet**?

Still is also possible in *negative* sentences:

  – He said he would be here an hour ago and he **still hasn't** come.

This is similar to 'he hasn't come yet'. But **still ... not** shows a stronger feeling of surprise or impatience. Compare:

  – She has**n't** written to me **yet**. (but I expect she will write soon)
  – She **still** has**n't** written to me. (she should have written before now)

b) We use **not ... any more**, **not ... any longer** and **no longer** to say that a situation has changed. **Any more** and **any longer** go at the end of the sentence:

  – Mr Davies doesn't work here **any more** (*or* **any longer**). He left about six months ago.
  – We were good friends once but we aren't friends **any more** (*or* **any longer**).

No longer goes in the middle of the sentence (see Unit 106b):

  – We are **no longer** friends.
  – She **no longer** loves him.

We do not normally use **no more** in this way:

  – He is **no longer** a student. (*not* 'He is no more a student.')

UNIT 107 Exercises

107.1 *In this exercise you have to ask some questions about a friend, Dave. You haven't seen Dave for a very long time. When you last saw him:*

1 he was living in Harrow Road
2 he was single
3 he was working in a factory
4 he had a beard
5 he wanted to be a politician
6 he smoked a lot

You meet someone who has met Dave recently. Ask questions about Dave using **still.**

1 *Is he still living in Harrow Road?*
2 .... single?
3 ....
4 ....
5 ....
6 ....

107.2 *This time you have to write sentences with* **yet.**
Example: It's still raining. (stopped)   *It hasn't stopped raining yet.*..................

1 George is still here. (gone)   He ....
2 The concert is still going on. (finished)   It ....
3 The children are still asleep. (woken up)   ....
4 Ann is still on holiday. (come back) ....
5 Jack is still up. (gone to bed) ....
6 We're still waiting for him to reply to our letter. (replied)

....

7 I'm still thinking about what colour to paint the wall. (decided)

....

107.3 *In this exercise you have to use* **still** *and* **not ... any more.**
Example: Tom used to play tennis and football.   (still / tennis but ...)
   He still plays tennis but he doesn't play football any more...................

1 Jack used to have long hair and a beard.   (still / long hair but ...)
   He .... but ....
2 She was in hospital and she was on the danger list.   (still / hospital but ...)
   .... but ....
3 She used to believe in God and go to church on Sundays.   (still / God but ...)

....

4 I was feeling tired and sick.   (still / tired but ...)

....

5 He was a good player and he was the best in the team.   (still / good player but ...)

....

6 I used to like George and Ken.   (still / George but ...)

Now use **no longer** *instead of* **not ... any more** *in sentences 1–4.*

7 (1)   *He no longer has a beard.*..........
8 (2)   ....
9 (3) She ....
10 (4) ....

UNIT 108   Quite and rather

a)   Quite = less than 'very' but more than 'a little':
  – I'm surprised you haven't heard of him. He's **quite famous**. (= less than very
    famous but more than a little famous)
  – It's **quite cold**. You'd better wear your coat.
  – Tom lives **quite near** me, so we see each other **quite often**.
  Quite goes before **a/an**:
  quite a nice day   **quite an** old house   **quite a** long way
  We also use **quite** with some verbs, especially **like** and **enjoy**:
  – I **quite like** tennis but it's not my favourite sport.
  For another meaning of **quite** see section c.

b)   **Rather** is similar to **quite** but we use **rather** mainly with negative words and negative ideas:
  – It's **rather cold**, so you'd better wear your coat.
  – 'What was the examination like?'   '**Rather difficult**, I'm afraid.'
  – Let's get a taxi. It's **rather a long way** to walk.
  Quite is also possible in these examples.
  We often use **quite** with a *positive* idea and **rather** with a *negative* idea:
  – She is **quite intelligent** but **rather lazy**.
  When we use **rather** with *positive* words (**nice/interesting** etc.), it means 'unusually' or
  'surprisingly'. For example: **rather nice** = unusually nice / surprisingly nice / nicer than
  expected:
  – These oranges are **rather nice**. Where did you get them?
  – Ann didn't like the book but I thought it was **rather interesting**. (= more
    interesting than expected)
  Rather can go before or after **a/an**:
  a rather interesting book   *or*   **rather an** interesting book

c)   **Quite** can also mean 'completely'. For example:
  'Are you sure?'   'Yes, **quite sure**.' (= completely sure)
  Quite means 'completely' with a number of adjectives, especially:

sure	right	true	unnecessary	different	amazing
certain	wrong	safe	extraordinary	impossible	amazed

  – She was **quite different** from what I expected. (= completely different)
  – Everything they said was **quite true**. (= completely true)
  We also use **quite** (= 'completely') with some verbs:
  – I **quite agree** with you. (= I completely agree)
  – They **haven't quite finished** their dinner yet.
  – I **don't quite understand** what you mean.

UNIT 108   Exercises

108.1 *Re-write these sentences to include* **quite**.
Example: They live in an old house.   *They live in quite an old house*

1 Tom's got a good voice.   ....
2 They bought an expensive camera.   ....
3 It was a nice day.   ....
4 We had to walk a long way.   ....
5 It was a frightening experience.   ....
6 There was a strong wind.   ....
7 You've made a lot of mistakes.   ....
8 I've had a tiring day.   ....

108.2 *Complete these sentences using the words in brackets. Each time use* **quite** *with the positive word and* **rather** *with the negative word.*
Example: Carol is ...*quite intelligent*.... but ......*rather lazy*.......... .   (intelligent / lazy)

1 The weather is .... but ....   (warm / windy)
2 Jill's flat is .... but ....   (clean / untidy)
3 The water in the pool was .... but ....
   (warm / dirty)
4 The concert was .... but ....   (good / long)
5 The film was .... but ....   (exciting / frightening)
6 The car goes .... but it's ....   (well / noisy)
7 He is .... but he's ....   (a hard worker / slow)
8 Jim lives .... me but it's .... to get to his house.
   (near / difficult)
9 Tom's plan was .... but ....   (interesting /
   complicated)
10 It's .... but it's .... work.   (a well-paid job / hard)
11 I was .... with the hotel but Jim was ....
    (pleased / disappointed)

108.3 *Complete these sentences using* **quite** *with one of the following words:*
different   amazing   impossible   right   safe   sure   unnecessary   ~~true~~

1 We didn't believe them at first, but what they said was   *quite true* ....
2 You needn't have done that. It was   ....
3 I'm afraid I can't do what you ask. It's   ....
4 I couldn't agree with you more. You are   ....
5 You won't fall. The ladder is   ....
6 You can't compare the two things. They are   ....
7 I think I saw him go out but I'm not   ....
8 I couldn't believe what had happened. It was   ....

217

UNIT 109　Although/though/even though
In spite of / despite

a) Study this example situation:

 Last year Jack and Jill spent their holidays by the sea. It rained a lot but they enjoyed themselves. You can say:

> **Although it rained** a lot, they enjoyed themselves.
> (=It rained a lot *but* they ...)

or: In spite of / Despite } the rain, they enjoyed themselves.

b) After **although** we use a *subject + verb*:
- **Although she smokes** 40 cigarettes a day, she is quite fit.
- **Although it rained** a lot, we enjoyed our holiday.
- I didn't get the job **although I had** all the necessary qualifications.

After **in spite of** (or **despite**) we use a *noun*, a *pronoun* (**this/that/what** etc.) or -ing:
- **In spite of the rain**, we enjoyed our holiday.
- I didn't get the job **despite my qualifications.**
- She wasn't well, but **in spite of this** she went to work.
- **Despite what** I said last night, I still love you.
- I'm not tired **in spite of working** hard all day.

Note that we say 'in spite **of** ', but **despite** (without **of**).
You can also say **in spite of / despite　the fact (that) ...**:
- **In spite of the fact (that)** I was tired, I couldn't sleep.
- She's quite fit **despite the fact (that)** she smokes 40 cigarettes a day.

Compare **although** and **in spite of / despite**:
- **Although the traffic was** bad, I arrived on time.
  In spite of the traffic, I arrived on time.
- I couldn't sleep **although I was** very tired.
  I couldn't sleep **despite being** very tired.

c) Sometimes we use **though** instead of **although**:
- I didn't get the job **though** I had all the necessary qualifications.

In spoken English we often use **though** at the end of a sentence:
- The house isn't very nice. I like the garden **though**. (= but I like the garden)
- I see him every day. I've never spoken to him **though**. (= but I've never spoken to him)

Even though is a stronger form of **although**:
- **Even though** I was really tired, I couldn't sleep.

218

UNIT 109   Exercises

109.1 *Complete these sentences. Each time use* **although** + *a sentence from the box.*

I didn't speak the language	~~he has a very responsible job~~
I had never seen him before	we don't like her very much
it was quite cold	he had promised to be on time

1 Although he has a very responsible job, he isn't particularly well-paid.
2 Although .... , I recognised him from a photograph.
3 I didn't wear a coat ....
4 We thought we'd better invite her to the party ....
5 .... , I managed to make myself understood.
6 He was late ....

109.2 *Complete these sentences with* **although** *or* **in spite of**.
Example: ...Although......... it rained a lot, we enjoyed our holiday.

1 .... all my careful plans, a lot of things went wrong.
2 .... I had planned everything carefully, a lot of things went wrong.
3 I love music .... I can't play a musical instrument.
4 .... being very tired, we carried on walking.
5 The heating was full on, but .... this the house was still cold.
6 Keith decided to give up his job .... I advised him not to.

109.3 *Read these sentences and then write a new sentence with the same meaning. Use the word(s) in brackets in your sentences.*
Example: I couldn't sleep although I was tired.   (despite)
   I couldn't sleep despite being tired. (or despite the fact (that) I was tired).

1 Although he's got an English name, he is in fact German.   (despite)
   Despite ....
2 In spite of her injured foot, she managed to walk to the village.   (although)

   ....
3 I decided to accept the job although the salary was low.   (in spite of)
   I decided ....
4 We lost the match although we were the better team.   (despite)

   ....
5 In spite of not having eaten for 24 hours, I didn't feel hungry.   (even though)

   ....

109.4 *Now use the words in brackets to make a sentence with* **though** *at the end.*
Example: The house isn't very nice. (like / garden)   I like the garden though.

1 She's very nice. (don't like / husband)   I ....
2 It's quite warm. (a bit windy)   It ....
3 We didn't like the food. (ate)   We ....

219

UNIT 110   Even

a) Study this example:

> Our football team lost yesterday. We all played badly. Bill is our best player but yesterday **even Bill** played badly.
>
> We use **even** to say that something is unusual or surprising. We say **even Bill** ... because he is a good player and it is unusual for him to play badly. If he played badly, it must have been a bad day for the team.

- These photographs aren't very good. **Even I** could take better photographs than these. (I'm certainly not a good photographer, so they must be bad.)
- It's a very rich country. **Even the poorest people** own cars. (so the rich people must be very rich)
- He always wears a coat – **even in summer**.
- Nobody would lend him the money – **not even his best friend**. (*or* **Even** his best friend wouldn't lend him the money.)

b) Very often we use **even** with the verb in the middle of a sentence (see Unit 106b for the exact position):

- Don has travelled all over the world. He has **even** been to the Antarctic. (It's especially unusual to go to the Antarctic, so he must have travelled a lot.)
- He always wears a tie. He **even** wears a tie in bed!
- They are very rich. They **even** have their own private jet.

Here are some examples with **not even**:

- I can't cook. I can't **even** boil an egg. (so I certainly can't cook, because boiling an egg is very simple)
- They weren't very friendly to us. They did**n't even** say hello.
- He's very fit. He's just run five miles and he's **not even** out of breath.

c) You can use **even** with *comparatives* (**hotter** / **more surprised** etc.):

- It was very hot yesterday but today it's **even hotter**.
- I got up at 6 o'clock but Jack got up **even earlier**.
- I knew I didn't have much money but I've got **even less** than I thought.
- I was surprised to get a letter from her. I was **even more surprised** when she appeared at my door the next day.

d) You can use **even** with **if, when** and **though**:

- I'll probably see you tomorrow. But **even if** I don't, we're sure to see each other before the week-end.
- He never shouts **even when** he's angry. (you expect people to shout when they are angry)
- He has bought a car **even though** he can't drive.

For **if** and **when** see Unit 9d. For **even though** see Unit 109.

UNIT 110 Exercises

110.1 *In this exercise you have to complete a conversation. Use* **even** *or* **not even**.
Example: A: We lost the match. The whole team played badly.
B: Really? ...Even...... Bill?   A: Yes, *even Bill played badly.*

1 A: Everyone was on time for work this morning.
   B: Really? ....Sue?   A: Yes, ...
2 A: Everyone makes mistakes sometimes.
   B: Really? ....you?   A: Yes, ...
3 A: The whole country is going on strike.
   B: Really? ....the police?   A: Yes, ...
4 A: Nobody knows where Peter has gone.
   B: Really? Not ....his wife?   A: No, ...
5 A: Everybody passed the examination.
   B: Really? ....George?   A: Yes, ...

110.2 *Make sentences with* **even**. *Use the words in brackets.*
Example: He wears a tie all the time. (in bed) *He even wears a tie in bed.*

1 They painted the whole room white. (the floor)
   They .... white.
2 He has to work every day. (on Sundays) He ....
3 You could hear the noise from a long way away. (from the next street)
   ....
4 They have the window open all the time. (when it's freezing)
   ....

In these sentences you have to use **not even**.
Example: She didn't say anything to me. (hello) *She didn't even say hello.*

5 I can't remember anything about her. (her name) I ....
6 There isn't anything in this town. (a cinema) There ....
7 I haven't eaten anything today. (a piece of bread) ....
8 He didn't tell anyone where he was going. (his wife)
   ....
9 I don't know anyone in our street. (the people next door)
   ....

110.3 *Complete these sentences with* **even** + *a comparative.*
Example: It was very hot yesterday but today it's *even hotter.* .

1 We found a very cheap hotel but the one Jack found was ....
2 That's a very good idea, but I've got an .... one.
3 The shop is always quite crowded but today it's .... than usual.
4 This church is 500 years old but the house next to it is ....
5 I did very little work for the examination but you did ....

221

UNIT 111

As (reason) – '**As** I was feeling tired, I went to bed early.'

As (time) – 'I watched her **as** she opened the letter.'

a) As (*reason*)

As often means 'because':

- **As** I was feeling tired, I went to bed early. (= because I was feeling tired)
- **As** they live near us, we see them quite often.
- **As** tomorrow is a public holiday, all the shops will be shut.
- **As** we had nothing better to do, we watched television the whole evening.

But we also use **as** to say that two things happened at the same time. See the next sections.

b) As (*time*): *two things happening together*

You can use **as** when two things happen at the same time or over the same period of time:

- I watched her **as** she opened the letter.
- **As** they walked along the street, they looked in the shop windows.
- Turn off the light **as** you go out, please.

We use **as** especially for two *short* actions happening at the same time:

- George arrived **as** I left. (= he arrived and I left at the same time)
- We all waved goodbye to Tom **as** he drove away in his car.

You can also use **just as** (= exactly at that moment):

- George arrived **just as** I left.
- **Just as** I sat down, the phone rang.

We also use **as** when two *changes* happen over the same period of time:

- **As the day went on,** the weather got worse.
- I began to enjoy the job more **as I got used to it.**

c) As (*time*): *one thing happening during another*

You can say that you did something **as** you were doing something else (= in the middle of doing something else).

When we use **as** in this way, both actions are usually quite short:

- The man slipped **as he was getting off the train.**
- Jill burnt herself **as she was taking the cakes out of the oven.**
- The thief was seen **as he was climbing over the wall.**

You can also use **just as**:

- **Just as we were going out,** it started to rain.
- I had to leave **just as the conversation was getting interesting.**

For the *past continuous* (**was getting** / **were going** etc.) see Unit 12.

Note that we use **as** only if two actions happen *together*. Do *not* use **as** if one action follows another:

- **When** I got home, I had a bath. (*not* 'as I got home')

UNIT 111 Exercises

111.1 *In this exercise you have to join a sentence from box A with a sentence from box B. Begin each of your sentences with* **as** *(reason).*

A ~~tomorrow is a public holiday~~	B I walked in
there isn't anything to eat in the house	I had to walk home
it was a nice day	we came in very quietly
we didn't want to wake anyone up	~~the shops will be shut~~
the door was open	let's go out for a meal
I didn't have enough money for a taxi	we decided to go for a walk

1 *As tomorrow is a public holiday, the shops will be shut.*
2 As ....
3 ....
4 ....
5 ....
6 ....

111.2 *From each pair of sentences make one sentence with* **as** *(time).*
Example: She opened the letter. I watched her.   *I watched her as she opened the letter.*

1 We posed for the photograph. We smiled.
   We smiled ....
2 He explained what I had to do. I listened carefully.
   I ....
3 The two teams ran onto the pitch. The crowd cheered.
   The crowd ....
4 She passed me in the street. She didn't look at me.

   ....

In the following sentences use **just as.**
Example: I sat down. Just at that moment the phone rang.
   The phone rang just as I sat down.

5 We arrived at the beach. Just at that moment it started to rain.
   It started ....
6 I took the photograph. Just at that moment you moved.

   ....

In these sentences, one thing happens during another.
Example: Jill was taking the cakes out of the oven. She burnt herself.
   Jill burnt herself as she was taking the cakes out of the oven.

7 Tom was climbing out of the window. He fell.
   Tom fell ....
8 We were driving along the road. A dog ran out in front of the car.
   A dog ....
9 She was getting out of the car. She dropped her bag.

   ....

UNIT 112 Like and as

a) Like = similar to / the same as / for example:
- What a beautiful house! It's **like a palace**. (*not* 'as a palace')
- 'What does George do?' 'He's a teacher, **like me**.' (*not* 'as me')
- Why do you always talk about boring things **like your job**?
- Be careful! The floor has been polished. It's **like walking** on ice.
- It's raining again. I hate weather **like this**.

Like is a *preposition*. So it is followed by a *noun* ('like **a palace** / like **your job**'), a *pronoun* ('like **me** / like **this**') or **-ing** ('like **walking**'). You can also say ' **like** (someone/something) **-ing**':
- 'What's that noise?' 'It sounds **like a baby crying**.'

b) We use **as** (not 'like') before a *subject + verb*:
- Don't move anything. Leave everything **as it is**.

Compare **like** and **as** in these sentences:
- You should have done it **like this**. (like + *pronoun*)
- You should have done it **as I showed** you. (as + *subject + verb*)

But we use **such as** (= for example) without a verb:
- Some sports, **such as motor-racing**, can be dangerous.

Note that we say **as usual**:
- You're late **as usual**.

c) **As** + *subject + verb* can have other meanings. For example:
- Do **as you are told**! (= Do what you are told.)
- They did **as they promised**. (= They did what they promised.)

You can also say **as you know / as we expected / as I said** etc.:
- **As you know**, it's Tom's birthday next week. (= you know this already)
- Ann failed her driving test, **as we expected**.

d) **As** can also be a *preposition* (which means you can use it with a *noun*), but the meaning is different from **like**.

We use **like** when we *compare* things:
- She looks beautiful – **like a princess**. (she isn't really a princess)
- Everyone is ill at home. Our house is **like a hospital**. (it isn't really a hospital)

We use **as** + *noun* to say what something *really is or was* (especially when we talk about someone's job or how we use something):
- A few years ago I worked **as a bus driver**. (I really was a bus driver)
- Sue has just found a job **as a shop assistant**.
- During the war this hotel was used **as a hospital**. (so it really was a hospital)
- We haven't got a car, so we use the garage **as a workshop**.
- The news of her death came **as a great shock**. (it really was a shock)

UNIT 112   Exercises

112.1 *Complete these sentences with* **like** *or* **as**. *The sentences in this exercise are like those in sections a, b and c.*
Examples: This house is beautiful. It's ......like...... a palace.
           Ann failed her driving test ......as........ we expected.

  1 Do you think Ann looks .... her mother?
  2 He really gets on my nerves. I can't stand people .... him.
  3 Why didn't you do it .... I told you to do it?
  4 'Where does Bill work?'   'He works in a bank, ... most of his friends.'
  5 He never listens. Talking to him is .... talking to a wall.
  6 .... I said yesterday, I'm thinking of going to Canada.
  7 Tom's idea seemed a good one, so we did .... he suggested.
  8 It's a difficult problem. I never know what to do in situations .... this.
  9 I'll phone you tomorrow evening .... usual, okay?
10 This coffee is terrible. It tastes .... water.
11 Suddenly there was a terrible noise. It was .... a bomb exploding.
12 She's a really good swimmer. She swims .... a fish.

112.2 *This time you have to choose* **like** *or* **as** *(preposition – see section d).*
Examples: She looks beautiful this evening – ......like...... a princess.
           A few years ago I worked ......as....... a bus driver.

  1 He's been learning English for a few years but he still speaks .... a beginner.
  2 My feet are really cold. They're .... blocks of ice.
  3 Margaret once had a part-time job .... a tourist guide.
  4 We don't need all the bedrooms in the house, so we use one of them .... a study.
  5 His house is full of lots of interesting things. It's .... a museum.
  6 Have you ever worked .... a labourer on a building site?
  7 The news that he was getting married came .... a complete surprise to me.
  8 He's 35 but he sometimes behaves .... a child.

112.3 *In this exercise there are sentences of all types. Put in* **like** *or* **as**.

  1 Your English is very fluent. I wish I could speak .... you.
  2 You needn't take my advice if you don't want to. You can do .... you like.
  3 He wastes too much time doing things .... sitting in cafés all day.
  4 There's no need to change your clothes. You can go out .... you are.
  5 The weather's terrible for the middle of summer. It's .... winter.
  6 He's decided to give up his job .... a journalist and become a teacher.
  7 I think I prefer this room .... it was, before we decorated it.
  8 When we asked Jack to help us, he agreed immediately, ... I knew he would.
  9 While we were on holiday, we spent most of our time doing energetic things .... sailing, water-skiing and swimming.
10 Ann's been working .... a waitress for the last few weeks.

UNIT 113　As if

a) You can use **as if** to say how someone or something **looks/sounds/feels** etc.:
- The house **looked as if** nobody was living in it.
- Ann **sounds as if** she's got a cold, doesn't she?
- I've just come back from holiday but I feel tired and depressed. I don't **feel as if** I've had a holiday.

Compare:
- You look **tired**. (**look** + *adjective*)
  You look **as if you haven't slept**. (**look** + **as if** + *subject* + *verb*)
- Tom sounded **worried**. (**sound** + *adjective*)
  Tom sounded **as if he was** worried. (**sound** + **as if** + *subject* + *verb*)

You can use **as though** instead of **as if**:
- Ann sounds **as though** she's got a cold.

b) You can also say **It looks/sounds/smells as if** (or **as though**):
- Tom is very late, isn't he? **It looks as if** he isn't coming.
- We took an umbrella because **it looked as if** it was going to rain.
- Do you hear that music next door? **It sounds as if** they are having a party, doesn't it?
- **It smells as though** someone has been smoking in here.

After **It looks/sounds/smells,** many people use **like** instead of **as if / as though**:
- It looks **like** Tom isn't coming.

c) You can also use **as if** with other verbs to say how someone does something:
- He **ran as if** he was running for his life.
- After the interruption, she **carried on talking as if** nothing had happened.
- When I told them my plan, they **looked at me as if** I was mad.

d) After **as if** we sometimes use the *past* when we are talking about the *present*. For example:
- I don't like Norman. He talks as if he **knew** everything.

The meaning is *not* past in this sentence. We use the past ('as if he **knew**') because the idea is *not real*: Norman does *not* know everything. We use the past in the same way in **if** sentences and after **wish** (see Unit 37).

When you use the past in this way, you can use **were** instead of **was**:
- Harry's only 50. Why do you talk about him **as if he were** (*or* **was**) an old man?
- They treat me **as if I were** (*or* **was**) their own son. (I'm not their son.)

UNIT 113   Exercises

113.1 *Use the sentences in the box to make sentences with* **as if.**

she had hurt her leg	he hadn't washed for ages	~~you need a good rest~~
she was enjoying it	she was going to throw it at him	he was half-asleep
you've seen a ghost	they hadn't eaten for a week	I'm going to be sick

1 Tom looks very tired. You say to him: You look *as if you need a good rest*.
2 When you talked to Jack on the phone last night, he had difficulty speaking. And he said some strange things. He sounded ....
3 Carol had a bored expression on her face during the concert.
   She didn't look ....
4 You could smell him from a long way away. He badly needed a bath.
   He smelt ....
5 Your friend comes into the room looking absolutely terrified. His face is white.
   You say: What's the matter? You look ....
6 You've just eaten a whole box of chocolates. Now you are feeling ill.
   You say: I feel ....
7 When you saw Sue, she was walking in a strange way.
   She looked ....
8 They were extremely hungry and ate their dinner very quickly.
   They ate their dinner ....
9 Ann and Tom were having an argument. She was very angry. Suddenly she picked up a plate. She looked ....

113.2 *Now you have to make sentences beginning* **It looks/sounds as if ...**

~~he isn't going to come~~	you had a good time	there's been an accident
we'll have to walk home	it's going to rain	they are having an argument

1 Tom hasn't arrived yet and it's late.   You say: *It looks as if he isn't going to come.*
2 The sky is full of black clouds.   You say: It ....
3 You hear two people shouting at each other next door.   You say: It sounds ....
   ....
4 There is an ambulance, some policemen and two damaged cars at the side of the road.
   You say: ....
5 You and your friend have just missed the last bus home.   You say: ....
   ....
6 Sue and Dave have just been telling you about all the interesting things they did on holiday.   You say: ....

113.3 *These sentences are like the ones in section d. Complete each sentence.*
   Example: Norman doesn't know everything, but he talks *as if he knew everything.*

1 I'm not a child, but sometimes you talk to me .... a child.
2 She doesn't know me, so why did she smile at me ....
3 He's not my boss, but sometimes he acts ....

227

UNIT 114 At/on/in (time)

a) **At** We use **at** with times:

     at 5 o'clock   **at** 11.45   **at** midnight   **at** lunchtime

         – Tom usually leaves work **at five o'clock.**

But we usually leave out **at** when we ask (At) **what time ...?**:

         – **What time** are you going out this evening?

We also use **at** in these expressions:

at night	I don't like going out **at night.**
at the week-end / at week-ends	Will you be here **at the week-end?**
at Christmas / at Easter (public holiday periods)	We give each other presents **at Christmas.**
at the moment / at present	Mr Benn is busy **at the moment / at present.**
at the same time	Ann and I arrived **at the same time.**
at the age of ...	Tom left school **at the age of 16 / at 16.**

b) **On** We use **on** with dates and days:

     on 12 March   **on** Friday(s)   **on** Christmas Day (*but* 'at Christmas')

         – They got married **on 12 March.**

We also say:

     on Friday morning(s)   **on** Sunday afternoon(s)   **on** Monday evening(s)
     on Saturday night(s) etc.

         – I usually go out **on Monday evenings.**

c) **In** We use **in** for longer periods of time (for example: months/years/seasons):

     in April   **in** 1968   **in** (the) winter
     in the 18th century   **in** the 1970s   **in** the Middle Ages

         – They got married **in 1968.**

We also say:

     in the morning(s) / **in** the afternoon(s) / **in** the evening(s)

         – I'll see you **in the morning.** (*but* 'I'll see you **on Friday morning.**')

d) We do not use **at/on/in** before **last** and **next**:

         – I'll see you **next** Friday.
         – They got married **last** March.

e) **In** + a period of time = a time in the future:

         – The train will be leaving **in a few minutes.** (= a few minutes from now)
         – Jack's gone away. He'll be back **in a week.** (= a week from now)
         – They are getting married **in six months.** (= six months from now)

You can also say 'in six months' **time**', 'in a week's **time**' etc.:

         – They are getting married **in six months' time.**

We also use **in** to say how long it takes to do something:

         – I learnt to drive **in four weeks.** (= it took me four weeks to learn)

228

UNIT 114 Exercises

114.1 *In this exercise you have to complete the sentences. Each time use* **at, on** *or* **in** *with one of the phrases from the box.*

the 1920s	1917	~~the 15th century~~	about five minutes	the same time
Saturdays	night	the age of five	21 July 1969	the moment

1 Columbus discovered America *in the 15th century.*...
2 The first man landed on the moon ....
3 In Britain football matches are usually played ....
4 You can see the stars .... if the sky is clear.
5 In Britain children have to start school ....
6 Jazz became popular in the United States ....
7 It's difficult to listen when everyone is speaking ....
8 The Russian Revolution took place ....
9 Tom isn't here .... He'll be back ....

114.2 *Put in the correct prepositions:* **at, on** *or* **in.**
Examples: The concert starts ......*at*...... 7.45.   I learnt to drive ......*in*...... four weeks.

1 The course begins .... 7 January and ends .... 10 March.
2 I went to bed .... midnight and got up .... 6.30 the next morning.
3 We travelled overnight to Paris and arrived .... 5 o'clock .... the morning.
4 Mozart was born in Salzburg .... 1756.
5 Are you doing anything special .... the week-end?
6 Hurry up! We've got to go .... five minutes.
7 I haven't seen Ann for a few days. I last saw her .... Tuesday.
8 I'll phone you .... Tuesday morning .... about 10 o'clock, okay?
9 I might not be at home .... the morning. Can you phone .... the afternoon instead?
10 Tom's grandmother died .... 1977 .... the age of 79.
11 Jack's brother is an engineer but he's out of work .... the moment.
12 The price of electricity is going up .... October.
13 .... Sunday afternoons I usually go for a walk in the country.
14 There are usually a lot of parties .... New Year's Eve.
15 I like walking round the town .... night. It's always so peaceful.
16 Do you fancy going to the cinema .... Friday night?
17 Tom doesn't see his parents very often these days – usually only .... Christmas and sometimes .... the summer for a few days.
18 I've been invited to a wedding .... 14 February.
19 I'm just going out to do some shopping. I'll be back .... half an hour.
20 Carol got married .... 17, which is rather young to get married.
21 Ann works hard during the week, so she likes to relax .... week-ends.
22 It was quite a short book and easy to read. I read it .... a day.
23 The telephone and the doorbell rang .... the same time.
24 Mary and Henry always go out for a meal .... their wedding anniversary.
25 Mr Davis is 63. He'll be retiring from his job .... two years' time.

UNIT 115 For, during and while

a) For and during

We use **for** + a period of time to say *how long* something goes on:

for **six years**   for **two hours**   for **a week**

- I've lived in this house **for six years**.
- We watched television **for two hours** last night.
- Ann is going away **for a week** in September.
- Where have you been? I've been waiting **for ages**.
- Are you going away **for the week-end?**

You cannot use **during** in this way:

- It rained **for three days** without stopping. (*not* 'during three days')

We use **during** + *noun* to say *when* something happens (*not* how long):

during **the film**   during **our holiday**   during **the night**

- I fell asleep **during the film**.
- We met a lot of interesting people **during our holiday**.
- The ground is wet. It must have rained **during the night**.
- I'll phone you some time **during the afternoon**.

b) During and while

We use **during** + *noun*. We use **while** + *subject* + *verb*. Compare:

		noun
I fell asleep	**during**	**the film.**
		subject + verb
I fell asleep	**while**	**I was watching** television.

Compare **during** and **while** in these examples:

- We met a lot of interesting people **during our holiday**.
  We met a lot of interesting people **while we were** on holiday.
- Robert suddenly began to feel ill **during the examination**.
  Robert suddenly began to feel ill **while he was doing** the examination.

Here are some more examples of **while**:

- We saw Ann **while we were waiting** for the bus.
- **While you were** out, there was a phone call for you.
- Tom read a book **while I watched** television.

When you are talking about the future, use the *present* (*not* 'will') after **while**:

- I'm going to London next week. I hope to see Tom **while I'm** there.
- What are you going to do **while** you **are** waiting?

See also Unit 9a.

For **while -ing** see Unit 67b. For **for** and **since** see Unit 19b.

UNIT 115　Exercises

115.1 *In this exercise you have to put in* **for** *or* **during**.
Examples: It rained ......*for*...... three days without stopping.
I fell asleep .*during*.... the film.

1 I waited for you .... half an hour and then decided that you weren't coming.
2 He hasn't lived in Britain all his life. He lived in India .... four years.
3 Production at the factory was seriously affected .... the strike.
4 I felt really ill last week. I couldn't eat anything .... three days.
5 When we were at the theatre last night, we met Ann .... the interval.
6 Sue was very angry after our argument. She didn't speak to me .... a week.
7 We usually go out at week-ends, but we don't often go out .... the week.
8 Jack started a new job a few weeks ago. Before that he was out of work .... six months.

115.2 *This time you have to put in* **while** *or* **during**.
Examples: We met a lot of people ....*while*.... we were on holiday.
We met a lot of people ..*during*... our holiday.

1 I met Tom .... I was waiting for the bus.
2 .... we were in Paris, we stayed at a very comfortable hotel.
3 .... our stay in Paris, we visited a lot of museums and galleries.
4 The phone rang three times .... we were having dinner last night.
5 I had been away for many years. .... that time, many things had changed.
6 What did she say about me .... I was out of the room?
7 Jack read a lot of books and magazines .... he was ill.
8 I went out for dinner last night. Unfortunately I began to feel ill .... the meal.
9 Many interesting suggestions were made .... the meeting.
10 Please don't interrupt me .... I'm speaking.
11 There were many interruptions .... the Prime Minister's speech.
12 Can you lay the table .... I get the dinner ready?

115.3 *Now use your own ideas to complete these sentences.*
Examples: I fell asleep while *I was reading the newspaper.*.........................
I didn't sleep very well. I kept waking up during *the night.*.........................

1 I fell asleep during ....
2 The lights suddenly went out while ....
3 I hurt my arm while ....
4 The students looked bored during ....
5 Can you wait here while .... ?
6 It rained a lot during ....
7 I fell off my chair during ....
8 It started to rain while ....
9 She burnt herself while ....

231

UNIT 116   By and until
            By the time ...

a) **By** (+ *a time*) = not later than:
- I posted the letter today, so they should receive it **by Monday**. (= *on or before* Monday, on Monday *at the latest*)
- We'd better hurry. We have to be at home **by 5 o'clock**. (= at or before 5 o'clock, at 5 o'clock at the latest)
- Where's Ann? She should be here **by now**. (= now or before now; so she should have already arrived)

You cannot use **until** with this meaning:
- Tell me **by Friday** whether or not you can come to the party. (*not* 'Tell me until Friday')

We use **until** (or **till**) to say how long a situation continues:
- 'Shall we go now?'   'No, let's wait **until** (or **till**) it stops raining.'
- I was tired this morning, so I stayed in bed **until half past ten**.

Compare **until** and **by** in these sentences:
- Tom will be away **until Monday**. (so he'll come back on Monday)
- Tom will be back **by Monday**. (= he'll be back on or before Monday, on Monday at the latest)
- I'll be working **until 11 o'clock**. (so I'll stop working at 11 o'clock)
- I'll have finished my work **by 11 o'clock**. (= I'll finish my work at or before 11 o'clock, at 11 o'clock at the latest)

b) You can also say **by the time (something happens)**, ... Study these examples carefully:
- It's not worth going shopping now. **By the time we get to the shops**, they will be shut. (= they will shut between now and the time we get there)
- (*from a letter*) I'm flying to the United States this evening. So **by the time you receive this letter**, I'll probably be in New York. (= I will arrive in New York between now and the time you receive this letter.)

When you are talking about the past, you can use **By the time (something happened)**, ...
- Tom's car broke down on the way to the party last night. **By the time he arrived**, most of the guests had left. (= It took him a long time to get to the party and most of the guests left during this time.)
- I had a lot of work to do yesterday evening. **By the time I finished**, I was very tired. (= It took me a long time to do the work and I became more and more tired during this time.)
- It took them a long time to find a place to park their car. **By the time they got to the theatre**, the play had already started.

You can also use **by then** or **by that time**:
- Tom finally arrived at the party at midnight. But **by then** (*or* **by that time**), most of the guests had left.

232

UNIT 116   Exercises

116.1 *Make sentences with* **by**.
Example: I have to be at home not later than 5 o'clock.   *I have to be at home by 5 o'clock.*

1 I have to be at the airport not later than 10.30.
   I have to be at the airport ....
2 Let me know not later than Saturday whether you can come to the party.
   Let me know ....
3 Please make sure that you are here not later than 2 o'clock.
   Please ....
4 If you want to do the examination, you have to enter not later than 3 April.
   If ....
5 If we leave now, we should be in London not later than lunchtime.
   If ....

116.2 *In this exercise you have to put in* **by** *or* **until**.
Examples: Tom has gone away. He'll be away ....*until*..... Monday.
            Sorry, but I must go. I have to be at home ......*by*........ 5 o'clock.

1 I've been offered a job. I haven't decided yet whether to accept it or not. I have to decide
   .... Thursday.
2 I think I'll wait .... Thursday before making a decision.
3 A: I hear you're writing a book. Have you finished it yet?
   B: Not quite, but I hope to finish it .... the end of this month.
4 A: I'm going out now. I'll be back at 4.30. Will you still be here?
   B: I don't think so. I'll probably have gone .... then.
5 I'm moving into my new flat next week. I'm staying with some friends .... then.
6 A: Do you think I'll still be unemployed this time next year?
   B: No, of course not. I'm sure you'll have found a job .... that time.

116.3 *Read these situations and then complete the sentences using* **By the time** ....
Example: Tom was invited to a party but he got there much later than he intended.
            By the time he got to the party............ , most of the guests had left.

1 I had to catch a train but it took me longer than expected to get to the station.
   .... , my train had left.
2 I saw two men who looked as if they were trying to steal a car. So I called the police. But
   it was some time before the police arrived.
   .... , the two men had disappeared.
3 A man escaped from the prison last night. It was a long time before the guards discovered
   what had happened.
   .... , the escaped prisoner was miles away.
4 I intended to go shopping after finishing my work. But I finished my work much
   later than expected.
   .... , it was too late to go shopping.

233

UNIT 117   In/at/on (position) (1)

a) In   Study these examples:

   OOOOXOOOO

in a room / in a building   in the water   in a row / in a line
in a garden / in a park   in the sea   in a queue
in a town / in a country   in a river

- There's no-one **in the room / in the building / in the shop.**
- The children are playing **in the garden / in the park.**
- When we were **in Italy,** we spent a few days **in Venice.** (*not* 'at Venice')
- Robert lives **in a small village in the mountains.**
- She keeps her money **in her bag / in her purse.**
- What have you got **in your hand / in your mouth?**
- Look at that girl swimming **in the water / in the sea / in the river!**
- When I go to the cinema, I prefer to sit **in the front row.**
- Have you read this article **in the newspaper?**

Note that we say:

> (sit) **in an armchair** (*but* 'on a chair')   **in the street**
> **in a photograph / in a picture / in a mirror**   **in the sky**

- 'Where did you meet Tom?'   'In the street.' (*not* 'on the street')
- Who is the woman **in that photograph?** (*not* 'on that photograph')
- It was a lovely day. There wasn't a cloud **in the sky.**
- Don't sit **in that armchair.** It's broken.

b) At   Study these examples:

at the top (of the page)

at the bus-stop
at the door
at the window

at the end
of the street

at the back

at the front

at the bottom (of the page)

- Who is that man standing **at the bus-stop / at the door / at the window?**
- Turn left **at the traffic lights.**
- If you leave the hotel, please leave your key **at reception.**
- Write your name **at the top / at the bottom**   of the page.
- Jack's house is the white one **at the end of the street.**
- I couldn't see very well because I was standing **at the back.**
  (See also section e.)

c) On   Study these examples:

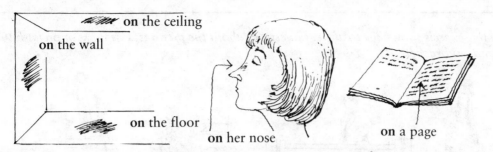

on the ceiling

on the wall

on the floor

on her nose

on a page

- Don't sit **on the floor / on the ground / on the grass!**
- There's a dirty mark **on the wall / on the ceiling / on your nose.**
- Have you seen the notice **on the notice-board?**
- The book you are looking for is **on the top shelf / on the table.**
- There's a report of the football match **on page 7** of the newspaper.
- Don't sit **on that chair.** It's broken. (*but* 'sit **in an armchair**')

Note that we say:

> **on the left / on the right** (*or* **on** the left- / right-**hand side**)
> **on the ground floor / on** the first **floor / on** the second **floor** etc.

- In Britain we drive **on the left.** (*or* **... on the left-hand side**)
- Our flat is **on the second floor** of the building.

We use **on** with small islands:

- Tom spent his holidays **on a small island** off the coast of Scotland.

We also say that a place is **on the coast / on a river / on a road:**

London is **on the river Thames.**
Portsmouth is **on the south coast** of England.

We say that a place is **on the way** to another place:

- We stopped at a pretty village **on the way** to London.

d) In/at/on the corner   We say '**in the corner** of a room', but '**at the corner** (*or* **on the corner**) of a **street**':

- The television is **in the corner** of the room.
- There is a telephone box **at/on the corner** of the street.

e) In/at/on the front   In/at/on the back
We say '**in the front / in the back**   of a **car**':

- I was sitting **in the back** (of the car) when we crashed.

We say '**at the front / at the back**   of a **building/hall/cinema/group of people**' etc.:

- The garden is **at the back of the house.**
- Let's sit **at the front** (of the cinema). (*but* '**in the front row**')

We say '**on the front / on the back**   of a **letter / piece of paper**' etc.:

- Write your name **on the back of this piece of paper.**

Do the exercises on the next pages and then study Unit 118.

UNIT 117   Exercises

117.1 *In this exercise you have to answer questions about the pictures. Use* **in**, **at** *or* **on** *with the words in brackets.*

1   Where's the label? (bottle) .... the bottle.
2   Where's the man standing? (gate) ....
3   Where's Tom sitting? (armchair) ....
    Where's the picture? (wall) ....
4   Where's Ann standing? (top / stairs) ....
    And where's the cat? (bottom / stairs) ....
5   What's George doing? (looking / mirror)   He's ....
6   Tom lives in this building. Where's his flat exactly? (second floor) ....
7   Where is the dog? (back / car) ....
8   Tom is in the cinema. Where's he sitting? (back) ....
                                or: (back row) ....
9   Where's the post office? (left) .... And the bank? (right) ....
10 Where's the notice? (door) ....
11 Where is the girl standing? (corner) ....
12 Where is the man standing? (corner) ....

117.2 *Complete these sentences. Each time use* **in**, **at** *or* **on** *with one of the phrases from the box.*

the front row	~~New York~~	the west coast
the third floor	the back of the class	the Swiss Alps
my way to work	the back of the envelope	the window
the right	the front page of the newspaper	

1 The headquarters of the United Nations is *in New York* .
2 In most countries people drive ....
3 I usually buy a newspaper .... in the morning.
4 Last year we had a lovely skiing holiday ....
5 San Francisco is .... of the United States.
6 She spends all day sitting .... and watching what is happening outside.
7 I have to walk up a lot of stairs every day. My flat is .... and there is no lift.
8 I read about the accident. There was a report ....
9 We went to the theatre last night. We had seats ....
10 I couldn't hear the teacher very well. She had a quiet voice and I was sitting
....
11 When you send a letter, it is a good idea to write your name and address
....

117.3 *Complete these sentences with* **in**, **at** *or* **on**.
Examples: Turn left .....*at*......... the traffic lights.
You'll find the cups ....*on*..... the top shelf.

1 It can be dangerous when children play football .... the street.
2 I'll meet you .... the corner (of the street) at 10 o'clock.
3 We got stuck in a traffic jam .... the way to the airport.
4 There was an accident .... the crossroads this morning.
5 Look at those beautiful horses .... that field!
6 I can't find Tom .... this photograph. Is he .... it?
7 .... the end of the street there is a path leading to the river.
8 I wouldn't like an office job. I couldn't spend the whole day sitting .... a desk.
9 Do you take sugar .... your coffee?
10 Ann's brother lives .... a small village .... the south coast of England.
11 You'll find the sports results .... the back page of the newspaper.
12 Sue and Dave got married .... Manchester four years ago.
13 Paris is .... the river Seine.
14 Mr Boyle's office is .... the first floor. When you come out of the lift, it's the third door .... your left.
15 We normally use the front entrance to the building but there's another entrance .... the back.
16 If you want to get away from modern life, you should go and live .... a small island in the middle of the ocean.
17 The man the police are looking for has a scar .... his right cheek.
18 I wasn't sure whether I had come to the right flat because there was no name .... the door.

UNIT 118   In/at/on (position) (2)

a) We say that someone is **at** an event. For example: '**at** a party / **at** a concert / **at** a conference / **at** a football match':
- Were there many people **at the party / at the meeting?**
- I saw Jack **at the football match / at the concert** on Saturday.

b) We say:

at home	**at** university	**at** the seaside	**in** bed	**on** a farm
at work	**at** a station	**at** sea (on a voyage)	**in** hospital	
at school	**at** an airport		**in** prison	

- I'll be **at work** until 5.30 but I'll be **at home** all evening.
- Julia is studying medicine **at university.**
- We'll be arriving at 9.30. Can you meet us **at the station**?
- Tom's father is **in hospital.**
- Have you ever worked **on a farm**?

c) You can often use **in** or **at** with buildings. You can stay **in a hotel** or **at a hotel**; you can eat **in a restaurant** or **at a restaurant.**
We usually say **at** when we say where an event takes place (for example: a concert, a film, a meeting, a sports event etc.):
- We went to a concert **at the Royal Festival Hall.**
- The meeting took place **at the company's headquarters.**
- 'Where were you last night?'   '**At the cinema.**' / '**At the theatre.**'

We say **at someone's house**:
- I was **at Tom's house** last night. (*or* I was **at Tom's** last night.)

We use **in** when we are thinking about the building itself:
- The rooms **in** Tom's house are very small.
- I enjoyed the film but it was very cold **in** the cinema.

d) We usually say **in** with towns and villages:
- Tom's parents live **in Nottingham.** (*not* 'at Nottingham')

But you can use **at** when the town or village is a point on a journey:
- Do you know if this train stops **at** Nottingham?
- We stopped **at** a pretty village on the way to London.

e) We say **arrive IN** a country or town:
- When did he **arrive in Britain / in London**?

We say **arrive AT** with other places (buildings etc.) or events:
- What time did he **arrive at school / at work / at the hotel / at the party**?

We say **arrive home** (without a preposition):
- When did he **arrive home**?

UNIT 118   Exercises

118.1 *Complete these sentences. Use* **in**, **at** *or* **on** *with one of the words or phrases from the box.*

bed	sea	the National Theatre	a farm	hospital
school	prison	the airport	the cinema	~~the station~~

1 My train arrives at 11.30. Can you meet me *at the station* ?
2 I didn't feel very well when I woke up, so I stayed ....
3 Are they showing any good films .... this week?
4 Many people are .... for crimes that they did not commit.
5 I like the countryside and the fresh air. I think I'd like to work ....
6 Did you get on well with your teachers when you were .... ?
7 We went to see a play .... when we were in London.
8 Linda was injured in a road accident a few days ago. She is still ....
9 It was a very long voyage. We were .... for ten weeks.
10 Our flight was delayed. We had to wait .... for four hours.

118.2 *Complete these sentences with* **in** *or* **at**.
Example: Were there many people ....*at*....... the concert?

1 I didn't see you .... the party on Saturday. Where were you?
2 It was a very slow train. It stopped .... every little station.
3 He speaks quite good French. He studied .... Paris for a year.
4 Tom's ill. He wasn't .... work today. He was .... home .... bed.
5 The exhibition .... the art gallery finished on Saturday.
6 There will be a public meeting .... the Town Hall next week to discuss the plan to build a new road.
7 I haven't seen Ken for some time. I last saw him .... Dave's wedding.
8 Paul is a student .... London University.
9 Don't phone tomorrow evening. I won't be .... home. I'll be .... Ann's.
10 It's always too hot .... Ann's house. She has the heating on too high.

118.3 *Complete these sentences with a preposition if a preposition is necessary.*
Example: What time did you arrive ....*at*...... the station?

1 After many years away, he arrived back .... England a month ago.
2 The train from London arrives ....platform 4.
3 What time do you expect to arrive .... London?
4 What time do you expect to arrive .... the hotel?
5 What time do you usually arrive .... home in the evening?
6 What time do you usually arrive .... work in the morning?
7 We arrived .... the town with nowhere to stay.
8 When we arrived .... the cinema, there was a long queue outside.
9 It's a strange feeling when you first arrive .... a foreign country.
10 I arrived .... home feeling very tired.

UNIT 119   To, been to, into
By car / in my car

a) **To**   We say **go/come/travel** (etc.) **to** a place or event. For example:

go to America	**come to** England	**return to** Italy
fly to Moscow	**walk to** work	**drive to** the airport
go to the bank	**go to** a party	**go to** a concert
be sent to prison	**be taken to** hospital	**go to** bed

We say **get to** (*but* **arrive in/at** – see Unit 118e):
   – What time did you **get to** London / work / the party?
We say **go home / come home / get home** etc. (with no preposition):
   – I'm tired. Let's **go home**.   – What time did you **get home** last night?

b) **Been to**   **I have been to** (a place) = I have visited a place; I went there but now I have come back (see also Unit 13d):
   – Have you ever **been to Japan**?
   – I've **been to Rome** four times.
   – Ann has never **been to a football match** in her life.
   – Jack has got plenty of money. He has just **been to the bank**.

c) **Into**   'Go **into** / come **into**' etc. = **enter** (a room / building etc.):
   – I opened the door and **went into the room**.
   – Don't wait outside! **Come into the house**.
   – The man the police were chasing **ran into a shop**.
   – A bird **flew into the room** through the window.

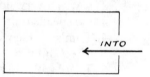

d) **By car / in my car**   We use **by ...** to say how we travel:

by car	**by train**	**by plane**	**by boat/ship**	**by bus**	**by bicycle**
also:	**by road**	**by rail**	**by air**	**by sea**	**by Underground**

   – 'How did you go to Paris?'   '**By plane**.'
   – Tom usually goes to work **by bicycle / by car / by bus / by train**.
But we say '**on foot**':
   – Did you come here **by car** or **on foot**?
But you cannot use **by** if you say '**my car / the train / a taxi**' etc. We say '**in my car**' (*not* 'by my car'), '**on the train**' (*not* 'by the train').

We use **in** for cars and taxis:
in my car   **in Tom's** car   **in the** car   **in a** car   **in a** taxi
We say **get in(to) / get out of** a car or taxi:
He **got into** the car and drove off. (*or* He **got in** the car ...)
We use **on** for bicycles and public transport (buses, trains etc.):
on my bicycle   **on the** bus   **on the** 6.45 train   **on a** big ship
We say **get on / get off** a bicycle, bus or train:
Quick! **Get on** the train. It's ready to leave.

240

UNIT 119   Exercises

119.1 *Complete these sentences with* **to, into, on** *or* **by**. *If no preposition is necessary, leave the sentence as it is.*
  Examples: When are you going ......*to*........ Spain?
         Tom usually goes ....*to*...... work ......*by*....... car.

  1 I'm tired. I'm going .... bed.
  2 What time are you going .... home?
  3 I decided not to go .... car. I went .... my bike instead.
  4 We went .... a very good party last night. We didn't get .... home until 3 a.m.
  5 I saw Jane this morning. She was .... a bus which passed me.
  6 Sorry I'm late. I missed the bus, so I had to come .... foot.
  7 The easiest way to get around London is .... Underground.
  8 I must go .... the bank today to change some money.
  9 I had lost my key but I managed to climb .... the house through a window.
  10 Marcel has just returned .... France after two years in England.
  11 I didn't feel like walking, so I came home .... a taxi.

119.2 *In this exercise you have to use* **been to**. *Write questions asking someone if they have been to these places.*
  Example: (Australia)   Have you been to Australia? ....

  1 (London)   Have ....   4 (Moscow)   ....
  2 (Sweden)   ....   5 (Rome)   ....
  3 (Ireland)   ....   6 (the United States)   ....

  Now choose four of these places and say whether you have been to them. Answer in the way shown.
  Example: (Australia)   I've been to Australia once / twice / many times etc. ....
         or I've never been to Australia. ....

  7 I've ....   9 ....
  8 ....   10 ....

119.3 *In this exercise you have to write sentences using* **get** *into/out of/on/off.*
  Example: You were walking home. A friend passed you in his car. He saw you, stopped and offered you a lift. He opened the door. What did you do?
         I got into the car......... .

  1 You were waiting for your bus. At last your bus arrived. The doors opened. What did you do then?   I got ....
  2 You drove home in your car. You arrived at your house and parked the car. What did you do then?   I ....
  3 You were travelling by train to Bristol. When the train arrived at Bristol, what did you do?   ....
  4 You needed a taxi. After a few minutes a taxi stopped for you. You opened the door. What did you do then?   ....
  5 You were riding your bike. There was a big hill and you didn't have the energy to cycle up it. What did you do?   .... and pushed it up the hill.

UNIT 120   On time / in time
           At the end / in the end

a) **On time** and **in time**

On time = punctual, not late. If something happens **on time**, it happens at the time which was planned:

- The 11.45 train left **on time**. (= it left at 11.45)
- A: I'll meet you at the corner at 7.30.
  B: Okay, but please be **on time**. (= don't be late / be there at 7.30)
- The conference was very well organised. Everything began and finished **on time**.

In time (for something / to do something) = soon enough for something / soon enough to do something:

- Will you be home **in time for dinner**? (= soon enough for dinner)
- I've sent Jill her birthday present. I hope it arrives **in time** (for her birthday). (= soon enough for her birthday)
- I must hurry. I want to get home **in time to see** the football match on television. (= soon enough to see the football match)

The opposite of **in time** is **too late**:

- I got home **too late** to see the football match.

Note the expression **just in time**:

- We got to the station **just in time** to catch the train.
- A dog ran across the road in front of the car, but I managed to stop **just in time** (to avoid hitting the dog).

b) **At the end** and **in the end**

At the end (of something) = at the time when something ends. For example:

at the end of the month   at the end of January
at the end of the film   at the end of the course
at the end of the match   at the end of the concert

- I'm going away **at the end of January / at the end of the month**.
- **At the end of the concert**, there was tremendous applause.
- All the players shook hands **at the end of the match**.

You cannot say 'in the end of something'.
The opposite of **at the end** is **at the beginning**:

  at the beginning of the concert   **at the beginning** of January

In the end = finally. We use **in the end** when we say what the final result of a situation was:

- We had a lot of problems with our car. **In the end** we sold it and bought another one.
- He got more and more angry. **In the end** he just walked out of the room.
- Tom couldn't decide where to go for his holidays. He decided to go to Italy **in the end**.

242

UNIT 120   Exercises

120.1 *Complete these sentences with* **on time** *or* **in time**.
  Example: The bus was late this morning, which is unusual. It's usually .on time................

  1 George is usually late for work but this morning he arrived ....
  2 I washed your shirt this morning but it should be dry .... for you to wear it this evening.
  3 We had to get on the train without tickets because we didn't get to the station .... to buy them.
  4 It's a very good train service. The trains always run ....
  5 Our car is being repaired. I hope it's ready .... for our holidays.
  6 Our best player was injured in the last match. We hope he will be fit .... to play in the next game.
  7 Please don't be late for the meeting. We want to begin ....
  8 We plan to go to America in two weeks' time, but we're still waiting for our visas. I hope they arrive ....
  9 I like to get up .... to have a big breakfast before going to work.

120.2 *In this exercise you have to make sentences with* **just in time**.
  Example: A dog ran across the road in front of the car. You saw it at the last moment.
      (I / manage / stop / time)   I managed to stop just in time...........................

  1 Tom was going to sit on the chair you had painted. You said, 'Don't sit on that chair!' so he didn't. (I / stop / him / time)   I ....
  2 You were walking home without an umbrella. Just after you got home, it started to rain very heavily. (I / get / home / time)   ....
  3 You thought you were going to miss the beginning of the film, but it began just as you sat down in the cinema. (I / get / the cinema / time / beginning / film)
      ....

120.3 *Complete these sentences with* **at** *or* **in**.
  Example: The players shook hands ....at...... the end of the match.

  1 It took John a long time to find a job after he left school. .... the end he found a job as a waiter.
  2 'When do you get paid?' '.................... the end of the month.'
  3 Are you going away .... the beginning of August or .... the end?
  4 I couldn't decide what to get Ann for her birthday. .... the end I didn't get her anything at all.
  5 We waited ages for a taxi. We gave up .... the end and walked home.
  6 .... the end of the course the students usually have a party.
  7 I'll be moving to a new address .... the end of September.
  8 His illness got worse and worse. .... the end he had to go into hospital for an operation.
  9 Tom didn't want to lend us the money at first but .... the end he agreed.

UNIT 121   Noun + preposition ('reason **for**', 'cause **of**' etc.)

Study this list of *nouns + preposition*. Sometimes other prepositions are possible – a good dictionary will give you more information.

---

a **cheque FOR** (a sum of money):
 – They sent me a **cheque for** £50.

a **demand** / a **need FOR** something:
 – The firm closed down because there wasn't enough **demand for** its product.

a **reason FOR** something:
 – The train was late but no-one knew the **reason for** the delay.

a **rise** / an **increase** / a **fall** / a **decrease IN** something:
 – There has been an **increase in** road accidents recently.

an **advantage** / a **disadvantage OF** something:
 – The **advantage of** living alone is that you can do what you like.
but we say '**there is an advantage in** doing something':
 – There are many advantages **in** living alone.

a **cause OF** something:
 – Nobody knows what the **cause of** the explosion was.

a **photograph** / a **picture OF** someone/something:
 – He always keeps a **photograph of** his wife in his wallet.

damage TO something:
 – The accident was my fault, so I paid for the **damage to** the other car.

an **invitation TO** a party / a wedding etc.:
 – Did you get an **invitation to** the party?

a **reaction TO** something:
 – I was surprised at his **reaction to** what I said.

a **solution TO** a problem / an **answer TO** a question / a **reply TO** a letter / a **key TO** a door:
 – Do you think we'll find a **solution to** this problem?
 – The **answer to** your question is 'No'!

an **attitude TO/TOWARDS** someone/something:
 – His **attitude to/towards** his job is very negative.

a **relationship** / a **connection** / **contact WITH** someone/something:
 – Do you have a good **relationship with** your parents?
 – Police want to question a man in **connection with** the robbery.
but: a **relationship** / a **connection** / **contact** / a **difference BETWEEN** two things:
 – Police have said that there is no **connection between** the two murders.
 – There are some **differences between** British English and American English.

UNIT 121 Exercises

121.1 *In this exercise you have to read a sentence and then complete another sentence with the same meaning.*
Example: What caused the explosion?   What was the cause *of the explosion* ?

1 We're trying to solve the problem.   We're trying to find a solution ....
2 Ann gets on well with her brother.   Ann has a good relationship ....
3 Prices have increased a lot.   There has been a big increase ....
4 I don't know how to answer your question.   I can't think of an answer ....
5 Nobody wants to buy shoes like these any more.
   There is no demand ....
6 I think that being married has some advantages.
   I think that there are some advantages ....
7 The number of people without jobs has fallen this year.
   There has been a fall ....
8 I don't think that a new road is necessary.
   I don't think that there is any need ....

121.2 *Complete these sentences with the correct preposition.*
Example: There are some differences **between** British English and American English.

1 I've just received an invitation .... a wedding next week.
2 The cause .... the fire in the hotel last night is still unknown.
3 Ann showed me a photograph .... the hotel where she stayed during her holiday.
4 Money isn't the solution .... every problem.
5 The company has rejected the workers' demands .... an increase .... pay.
6 The two companies are completely independent. There is no connection ....
   them.
7 When I opened the envelope, I was delighted to find a cheque .... £500.
8 Have you seen this picture .... the town as it looked 100 years ago?
9 Sorry I haven't written to you for so long. The reason .... this is that I've been ill
   recently.
10 The advantage .... having a car is that you don't have to rely on public transport.
11 There are many advantages .... being able to speak a foreign language.
12 There has been a sharp rise .... the cost of living in the past few years.
13 The front door is locked. Have you got the key .... the back door?
14 Bill and I used to be good friends but I don't have much contact .... him now.
15 I've never met Carol but I've seen a photograph .... her.
16 It wasn't a serious accident. The damage .... the car was only slight.
17 Tom's reaction .... my suggestion was not very enthusiastic.
18 What were George's reasons .... giving up his job?
19 The fact that he got a job in the company has no connection .... the fact that his
   father is the managing director.
20 When he left home, his attitude .... his parents seemed to change.
21 I wrote to Jim last week, but I still haven't received a reply .... my letter.

UNIT 122   Preposition + noun ('**by** mistake', '**on** television' etc.)

Students often use the wrong preposition before the words in this unit. So study this list and the examples carefully:

---

to **pay BY cheque** (*but* 'to **pay IN cash**' *or* 'to **pay cash**'):
    – Did you **pay by cheque** or **in cash**?

(to do something) **BY accident / BY mistake / BY chance**:
    – We hadn't arranged to meet. We met **by chance**.

a **play BY Shakespeare** / a **painting BY Rembrandt** / a **novel BY Tolstoy** etc.:
    – Have you read any books **by Agatha Christie**? (= any books **written** by
      Agatha Christie?)

(to be / to fall) **IN love WITH** someone:
    – Have you ever been **in love with** anyone?

IN (my) **opinion**:
    – **In my opinion** the film wasn't very good.

(to be) **ON fire**:
    – Look! That car is **on fire**.

(to be) **ON the telephone / ON the phone**:
    – You can't phone me. I'm not **on the phone**. (= I haven't got a phone)
    – I've never met her but I've spoken to her **on the phone**.

ON television / ON the radio:
    – I didn't watch the match **on television**. I listened to it **on the radio**.

(to be / to go) **ON a diet**:
    – I've put on a lot of weight. I'll have to go **on a diet**.

(to be / to go) **ON strike**:
    – There are no trains today. The railway workers are **on strike**.

(to be / to go) **ON holiday / ON business / ON a trip / ON a tour / ON an excursion /
ON a cruise / ON an expedition** etc.
    – Tom's away at the moment. He is **on holiday** in France.
    – Did you go to Paris **on business** or **on holiday**?
    – One day I'd like to go **on a world tour**.
  but you can also say 'go **to a place FOR a** holiday / **FOR my** holiday(s)':
    – Tom has gone to France **for a** holiday.
    – Where are you going **for your** holidays this year?

(to go / to come) **FOR a walk / FOR a swim / FOR a drink** etc.:
    – She always goes **for a walk** with her dog in the morning.
    – After work we went to a café **for a drink**.

(to have something) **FOR breakfast / FOR lunch / FOR dinner**:
    – What did you have **for lunch**?

UNIT 122   Exercises

122.1 *Complete these sentences. Each time use a preposition with one of the words or phrases from the box.*

mistake	business	a diet	breakfast	a swim	strike
the phone	television	~~a drink~~	Shakespeare	cheque	love

1 After work we went to a café *for a drink* .
2 The factory has closed because the workers have gone ....
3 I didn't intend to take your umbrella. I took it ....
4 I got up late this morning and had to rush. All I had .... was a cup of coffee.
5 I feel lazy this evening. Is there anything worth watching .... ?
6 They fell .... with each other almost immediately and were married in a few weeks.
7 It was an extremely hot day, so we went .... in the river.
8 Jim's job involves a lot of travelling. He often goes to other towns ....
9 I didn't have any money on me, so I paid ....
10 George has put on a lot of weight recently. I think he should go ....
11 It's difficult to contact Sue because she's not ....
12 *Hamlet* and *Macbeth* are plays ....

122.2 *Complete these sentences with the correct preposition.*
Example: We hadn't arranged to meet. We met ....*by*.... chance.

1 I'm hungry. What's .... dinner this evening?
2 .... my opinion, violent films shouldn't be shown .... television.
3 I think I need a bit of exercise. Shall we go .... a walk?
4 Do you know any songs .... the Beatles?
5 I mustn't eat too much. I'm supposed to be .... a diet.
6 There was panic when people realised the building was .... fire.
7 The weather was terrible when we were .... holiday in Scotland.
8 Next month I'm going to Scotland .... a short holiday.
9 Where did you go .... your holidays last year?
10 I won't be at work next week. I'll be .... holiday.
11 We're going .... holiday with some friends of ours in September.
12 I wouldn't like to go .... a cruise. I think I'd get bored.
13 The shop assistant wouldn't accept my cheque and insisted that I paid .... cash.
14 Ann reads a lot of books .... American women writers.
15 Did you hear the news this morning .... the radio?
16 It was only .... accident that I found out who the man really was.
17 When we went to Rome, we went .... a tour around the city.
18 I wouldn't like his job. He spends most of his time talking .... the telephone.
19 What's that music? I can't remember the title but I know it's .... Beethoven.
20 When I was 14, I went .... a trip to France organised by my school.
21 Ann liked the dress, but .... my opinion it didn't suit her.

UNIT 123   Adjective + preposition (1)

Study these groups of *adjectives + preposition*. Sometimes other prepositions are possible –
a good dictionary will give you more information.

**nice/kind/good/generous/mean/stupid/silly/intelligent/clever/sensible/(im)polite / rude /
unreasonable OF** someone (to do something):
  - Thank you. It was very **nice/kind of you** to help me.
  - It's **stupid of her** to go out without a coat. She'll catch cold.
but: (to be) **nice/kind/good/generous/mean/(im)polite/rude/(un)pleasant/
(un)friendly/cruel TO** someone:
  - She has always been very **nice/kind to** me. (*not* 'with me')
  - Why were you so **rude/unfriendly to** Ann?

angry/annoyed/furious { ABOUT something
                          { WITH someone FOR doing something:
  - What are you so **angry/annoyed about**?
  - They were furious **with me for** not inviting them to the party.

delighted/pleased/satisfied/disappointed WITH something:
  - I was **delighted/pleased with** the present you gave me.
  - Were you **disappointed with** your examination results?

bored / fed up WITH something:
  - You get **bored / fed up** with doing the same thing every day.

surprised/shocked/amazed/astonished AT/BY something:
  - Everybody was **surprised/shocked** at/by the news.

excited/worried/upset ABOUT something:
  - Are you **excited about** going on holiday next week?
  - Ann is **upset about** not being invited to the party.

afraid/frightened/terrified/scared OF someone/something:
  - 'Are you **afraid of** dogs?' 'Yes, I'm **terrified of** them.'

proud/ashamed OF someone/something:
  - I'm not **ashamed of** what I did. In fact I'm quite **proud of** it.

jealous/envious/suspicious OF someone/something:
  - Why are you always **so jealous of** other people?
  - He didn't trust me. He was **suspicious of** my intentions.

aware/conscious OF something:
  - 'Did you know they were married?' 'No, I wasn't **aware of** that.'

good/bad/excellent/brilliant/hopeless AT (doing) something:
  - I'm not very **good at** repairing things.

married/engaged TO someone:
  - Linda is **married to** an American. (*not* 'with an American')

UNIT 123   Exercises

123.1   *In this exercise you have to say how you feel about George in each situation.*
Example: George has kept you waiting for hours. (annoyed)   *I'm annoyed with him.*

1   George hasn't been eating well recently. (worried)   I'm .... him.
2   George has been telling lies about you. (angry)   I'm .... him.
3   George is much better at everything than you are. (jealous)   ....
4   George is big, strong, aggressive and violent. (afraid)   ....
5   You've had enough of George. (fed up)   I'm ....
6   *(ladies only)* But George is your husband. (married)   .... !

123.2   *Complete these sentences with the correct preposition.*
Example: I was delighted ......*with*...... the present you sent me.

1   It's very nice .... you to let me use your car. Thank you very much.
2   Why are you always so rude .... your parents? Can't you be nice .... them?
3   It wasn't very polite .... him to leave without saying thank you.
4   I can't understand people who are cruel .... animals.
5   Why do you always get so annoyed .... little things?
6   The people next door are annoyed .... us .... making so much noise last night.
7   We enjoyed our holiday but we were rather disappointed .... the hotel.
8   I was surprised .... the way he behaved. It was quite out of character.
9   She doesn't often go out at night. She's afraid .... the dark.
10   I've been trying to learn Spanish but I'm not very satisfied .... my progress.
11   Jill starts her new job on Monday. She's quite excited .... it.
12   I was shocked .... what you said. You should be ashamed .... yourself.
13   Did you know that Linda is engaged .... a friend of mine?
14   I had never seen so many people before. I was astonished .... the crowds.
15   Bill has been doing the same job for too long. He's bored .... it.
16   These days everybody is aware .... the dangers of smoking.
17   Are you still upset .... what I said to you yesterday?
18   She's quite nice but I wouldn't like to be married .... her.
19   Mr Davis spends a lot of time gardening. His garden is very well-kept and he's very proud .... it.

123.3   *Now you have to write sentences about yourself. Are you good at these things or not?*
Use: **brilliant / very good / quite good / not very good / hopeless.**
Examples: (repairing things)   *I'm hopeless at repairing things.*
            (tennis)   *I'm not very good at tennis*

1   (repairing things)   ....
2   (tennis)   ....
3   (remembering people's names)   ....
4   (telling jokes)   ....
5   (languages)   ....

249

UNIT 124 Adjective + preposition (2)

Study this list of *adjectives + preposition*:

---

sorry ABOUT something:
- I'm **sorry about** the noise last night. We were having a party.

but: **sorry FOR doing something:**
- I'm **sorry for shouting** at you yesterday.

But it is more usual to say: **I'm sorry I ...**:
- I'm **sorry I shouted** at you yesterday.

(to **feel** / to **be**) **sorry FOR** someone:
- I feel **sorry for** George. He has got no friends and no money.

impressed BY/WITH someone/something:
- I wasn't very **impressed by/with** the film.

famous FOR something:
- The Italian city of Florence is **famous for** its art treasures.

responsible FOR something:
- Who was **responsible for** all that noise last night?

different FROM (*or* **TO**) someone/something
- The film was quite **different from** (*or* **to**) what I expected.

interested IN something:
- Are you **interested in** art and architecture?

capable/incapable OF something:
- I'm sure you are **capable of** passing the examination.

fond OF someone/something:
- Mary is very **fond of** animals. She has three cats and two dogs.

full OF something:
- The letter I wrote was **full of** mistakes.

short OF something:
- I'm a bit **short of** money. Can you lend me some?

tired OF something:
- Come on, let's go! I'm **tired of** waiting.

keen ON something:
- We stayed at home because Ann wasn't very **keen on** going out in the rain.

similar TO something:
- Your writing is **similar to** mine.

crowded WITH (people etc.):
- The city centre was **crowded with** tourists.

UNIT 124 Exercises

124.1 *In this exercise you have to complete the sentences. Each time use the most suitable word in the box with the correct preposition.*

different	full	~~sorry~~	responsible	interested
short	similar	tired	capable	impressed

1 I don't feel ....**sorry for**............ George. All his problems are entirely his own fault.
2 I can't stop to talk to you now. I'm a bit .... time.
3 'Do you want to watch the football match on television?' 'No, thanks. I'm not
   .... football.'
4 Your shoes are .... mine but they're not exactly the same.
5 My new job is a completely new experience for me. It's quite ....
   what I did before.
6 Man is now .... destroying the whole world with nuclear weapons.
7 We've got plenty of things to eat. The fridge is .... food.
8 I wasn't very .... the service in the restaurant. We had to wait ages
   before getting our food.
9 Can't we have something different to eat for a change? I'm ....
   having the same thing day after day.
10 The editor is .... what appears in his newspaper.

124.2 *Complete these sentences with the correct preposition.*
Example: Sorry ...**about**... the noise last night. We were having a party.

1 I'd rather not go to an Indian restaurant. I'm not very keen .... Indian food.
2 Ann is very fond .... her younger brother.
3 This part of town is always very lively at night. It's usually crowded .... people.
4 In the cupboard I found a box full .... old letters.
5 I felt sorry .... the children when we went on holiday. It rained every day and
   they had to spend most of the time indoors.
6 He said he was sorry .... the situation but that there was nothing he could do.
7 Britain certainly isn't famous .... its food.
8 They looked bored. I don't think they were interested .... what I was saying.
9 That man's very honest. He isn't capable .... telling a lie.
10 The man we interviewed for the job was quite intelligent but we weren't very impressed
   .... his appearance.
11 Travelling is great at first but you get tired .... it after a while.
12 Do you know anyone who might be interested .... buying an old car?
13 Our house is similar .... theirs – I think ours is a bit larger.
14 Bill and I come from the same town but my accent is different .... his.
15 The police are responsible .... maintaining law and order.
16 We're short .... staff in our office at the moment. There aren't enough people to
   do the work that has to be done.
17 I'm sorry .... the smell in this room. It's just been painted.

UNIT 125   Verb + preposition (1)

Study this list of *verbs + preposition*:

---

apologise (TO someone) **FOR** something (see also Unit 60a):
  - When I realised I was wrong, I **apologised to** him **for** my mistake.

apply FOR a job / a place at university etc.:
  - I think this job would suit you. Why don't you **apply for** it?

believe IN something:
  - Do you **believe in** God? (= Do you believe that God exists?)
  - I **believe in** saying what I think. (= I believe that it is a good thing to say what I think.)

belong TO someone:
  - Who does this coat **belong to**?

care ABOUT someone/something (= think someone/something is important):
  - He is very selfish. He doesn't **care about** other people.
care FOR someone/something:
  i) = like something (usually in questions and negative sentences):
      - Would you **care for** a cup of coffee? (= Would you like ...?)
      - I don't **care for** hot weather. (= I don't like ...)
  ii) = look after someone:
      - She is very old. She needs someone to **care for** her.
take care OF someone/something (= look after):
  - Have a nice holiday. **Take care of** yourself!

collide WITH someone/something:
  - There was an accident this morning. A bus **collided with** a car.

complain (TO someone) **ABOUT** someone/something:
  - We **complained to** the manager of the restaurant **about** the food.

concentrate ON something:
  - Don't look out of the window. **Concentrate on** your work!

consist OF something:
  - We had an enormous meal. It **consisted of** seven courses.

crash/drive/bump/run INTO someone/something:
  - He lost control of the car and **crashed into** a wall.

depend ON someone/something:
  - 'What time will you arrive?' 'I don't know. It **depends on** the traffic.'
  You can leave out **on** before question words (**when/where/how** etc.):
  - 'Are you going to buy it?' 'It **depends** (on) **how much** it is.'

die OF an illness:
  - 'What did he **die of**?' 'A heart attack.'

UNIT 125 Exercises

125.1 *In this exercise you have to complete the sentences. Each time use one of the following words with the correct preposition:* **belong** **applied** ~~**apologised**~~ **die** **concentrate** **believe** **crashed** **depends**

1 When I realised that I had taken the wrong umbrella, I immediately *apologised for* my mistake.
2 I was driving along when the car in front of me stopped suddenly. Unfortunately I couldn't stop in time and .... the back of it.
3 'Does this bag .... you?' 'No, it isn't mine.'
4 Don't try and do two things at once. .... one thing at a time.
5 Ken is still unemployed. He has .... several jobs but hasn't had any luck yet.
6 'Are you playing tennis tomorrow?' 'I hope so, but it .... the weather.'
7 If you smoke, there is a greater chance that you will .... lung cancer.
8 I don't .... ghosts. I think people only imagine that they see them.

125.2 *Complete these sentences with a preposition (if a preposition is necessary).* *Example:* There was an accident this morning. A bus collided ....*with*.... a car.

1 He loves complaining. He complains .... everything.
2 Our neighbours complained .... us .... the noise we made last night.
3 She hasn't got a job. She depends .... her parents for money.
4 You were very rude to Tom. Don't think you should apologise .... him?
5 Are you going to apologise .... what you did?
6 Tom and I ran .... each other in town yesterday afternoon.
7 He decided to give up sport in order to concentrate .... his studies.
8 I don't believe .... working hard. It's not worth it.
9 A football team consists .... 11 players.
10 It is terrible that some people are dying .... hunger while others eat too much.
11 As I was going out of the room, I collided .... someone who was coming in.
12 There was an awful noise as the car crashed .... the tree.
13 Do you belong .... a political party?
14 I don't know whether I'll go out tonight. It depends .... how I feel.

125.3 *In this exercise you have to put in the correct preposition after* **care**. *Example:* He's very selfish. He doesn't care ....*about*.... other people.

1 Are you hungry? Would you care .... something to eat?
2 He doesn't care .... the examination. He's not worried whether he passes or fails.
3 Please let me borrow your camera. I promise I'll take good care .... it.
4 I don't care .... money. It's not important to me.
5 Don't worry about arranging our holiday. I'll take care .... that.
6 'Do you like this coat?' 'No, I don't care .... the colour.'

UNIT 126 Verb + preposition (2)

Study this list of *verbs + preposition*:

> **dream ABOUT** someone/something:
> – I **dreamt about** you last night.
> **dream OF** being something / doing something (= imagine):
> – I often **dream of** being rich.
>   *also:* '(I) **wouldn't dream** (of doing something)':
> – 'Don't tell anyone what I said.'   'No, I **wouldn't dream of it**.'
>
> **happen TO** someone/something:
> – A strange thing **happened to** me the other day.
> – What **happened to** that gold watch you used to have?
>
> **hear ABOUT** something (= be told about something):
> – Did you **hear about** the fight in the club on Saturday night?
> – Have you **heard about** Jane? She's getting married.
> **hear OF** someone/something (= know that someone/something exists):
> – 'Who is Tom Madely?'   'I have no idea. I've never **heard of** him.'
> – Have you **heard of** a company called 'Smith Electrics'?
> **hear FROM** someone (= receive a letter / telephone call from someone):
> – 'Have you **heard from** Ann recently?'   'Yes, she wrote to me last week.'
>
> **laugh/smile AT** someone/something:
> – I look stupid with this haircut. Everyone will **laugh at** me.
>
> **listen TO** someone/something:
> – We spent the evening **listening to** records.
>
> **live ON** money/food:
> – George's salary is very low. It isn't enough to **live on**.
>
> **look AT** someone/something (= look in the direction of):
> – Why are you **looking at** me like that?
>   *also:* **have a look AT, stare AT, glance AT**
> **look FOR** someone/something (= try to find):
> – I've lost my keys. Can you help me **look for** them?
> **look AFTER** someone/something (= take care of):
> – She's very old. She needs someone to **look after** her.
> – You can borrow this book if you promise to **look after** it.
>
> **pay** (someone) **FOR** something:
> – I didn't have enough money to **pay for** the meal.
>   *but:* **pay a bill / a fine / £50 / a fare / taxes** etc. (no preposition).
>
> **rely ON** someone/something:
> – You can **rely on** Jack. He always keeps his promises.

UNIT 126   Exercises

126.1 *Complete these sentences. Each time use one of the following words with a preposition:*
rely   listen   ~~look~~   live   laughing   glanced   paid   happened

1   She's very old and can't live alone. She needs someone to ...*look after*...... her.
2   I haven't seen Harry for ages. I wonder what's .... him.
3   You must .... this record. You'll love it.
4   I .... the newspaper to see if there was anything interesting in it.
5   When you went to the theatre with Paul, who .... the tickets?
6   It's not a very good bus service. You can't .... it.
7   What are you .... ? I don't understand what's funny.
8   It's a very cheap country. You can .... very little money there.

126.2 *Complete these sentences with a preposition (if a preposition is necessary).*
Example: She smiled ......*at*...... me as she passed me in the street.

1   Don't listen .... what he says. He's stupid.
2   What happened .... the picture that used to be on that wall?
3   A: You wouldn't go away without telling me, would you?
    B: Of course not. I wouldn't dream .... it.
4   I dreamt .... Ann last night. We were dancing together at a party when she suddenly hit me. Then I woke up.
5   The accident was my fault, so I had to pay .... the damage.
6   I didn't have enough money to pay .... the bill.
7   You know that you can always rely .... me if you need any help.
8   The man sitting opposite me on the train kept staring .... me.
9   She doesn't eat very much. She lives .... bread and eggs.

In these sentences put in the correct preposition after **hear**.

10   'Did you hear .... the accident last night?'   'Yes, Ann told me.'
11   Jill used to write to me quite often but I haven't heard .... her for a long time now.
12   A: Have you read any books by James Hudson?
     B: James Hudson? No, I've never heard .... him.
13   Thank you for your letter. It was nice to hear .... you again.
14   'Do you want to hear .... our holiday?'   'No, tell me later.'
15   The town I come from is very small. You've probably never heard .... it.

In these sentences put in the correct preposition after **look**.

16   When I looked .... my watch, I couldn't believe that it was so late.
17   Who looked ....you when you were ill?
18   The police are still looking .... the seven-year-old boy who disappeared from his home last week. Nobody knows where the boy is.
19   When we went out for the evening, a neighbour of ours looked .... the children.
20   I'm looking .... Tom. Have you seen him anywhere?

UNIT 127 Verb + preposition (3)

Study this list of *verbs + preposition*:

search (a person / a place / a bag etc.) **FOR** someone/something:
- I've **searched** the whole house **for** my keys but I still can't find them.
- The police are **searching for** the escaped prisoner.

shout AT someone (*when you are angry*):
- He was very angry and started **shouting at** me.

but: **shout TO** someone (*so that they can hear you*):
- He **shouted to** me from the other side of the street.

speak/talk TO someone ('with' is also possible but less usual):
- (*on the telephone*) Hello, can I **speak to** Jane, please?
- Who was that man I saw you **talking to** in the pub?

suffer FROM an illness:
- The number of people **suffering from** heart disease has increased.

think ABOUT someone/something (= *consider, concentrate the mind on*):
- You're quiet this morning. What are you **thinking about**?
- I've **thought about** what you said and I've decided to take your advice.
- 'Will you lend me the money?' 'I'll **think about** it.'

think OF someone/something (= *remember, bring to mind, have an idea*):
- He told me his name but I can't **think of** it now. (*not* 'think about it')
- That's a good idea. Why didn't I **think of** that?

We also use **think OF** when we ask for or give an *opinion*:
- 'What did you **think of** the film?' 'I didn't **think** much **of** it.'

The difference between **think OF** and **think ABOUT** is sometimes very small. Often you can use **OF** or **ABOUT**:
- My sister is **thinking of** (*or* **about**) going to Canada.
- Tom was **thinking of** (*or* **about**) buying a new car but changed his mind.
- When I'm alone, I often **think of** (*or* **about**) you.

wait FOR someone/something:
- I'm not going out yet. I'm **waiting for** the rain to stop.

write TO someone:
- Sorry I haven't **written to** you for such a long time.

We do *not* use a preposition with these verbs:

phone someone	Did you **phone your father** yesterday?
discuss something	We **discussed many things** at the meeting.
enter (= *go into a place*)	She felt nervous as she **entered the room**.

For verbs + preposition + **-ing** see Unit 60a.

UNIT 127 Exercises

127.1 *Complete these sentences with a preposition where necessary. If no preposition is necessary, leave the sentence as it is.*
Example: He was angry and started shouting ....*at*....... me.

1 I've searched everywhere .... John but I haven't been able to find him.
2 Ken gets very jealous. He doesn't like his girlfriend talking .... other men.
3 I don't want to go out yet. I'm waiting .... the post to arrive.
4 Please don't shout .... me! Be nice to me.
5 We passed Tom as we were driving along. I shouted .... him but he didn't hear.
6 Ann doesn't write .... her parents very often but she phones .... them at least once a week.
7 Can I speak .... you a moment? There's something I want to ask you.
8 Sally is often not well. She suffers .... severe headaches.
9 The police have been searching the countryside .... the missing girl.
10 She's a bit lonely. She needs someone to talk ....
11 I don't want to discuss .... what happened last night. I want to forget about it.
12 We're going out for a meal tonight. I must phone .... the restaurant to reserve a table.

In these sentences you have to use the correct preposition (of or about) after think. Remember that sometimes you can use either of or about.

13 Before you make a final decision, think carefully .... what I said.
14 I don't know what to get Ann for her birthday. Can you think .... anything?
15 You're selfish. You only think .... yourself.
16 'I've finished the book you lent me.' 'Oh, have you? What did you think .... it?'
17 We're thinking .... going out for a meal tonight. Would you like to come?
18 I don't really want to go out to dinner with Tom tonight. I'll have to think .... an excuse.
19 When he asked her to marry him, she said that she wanted to go away and think .... it for a while.
20 She is rather homesick. She's always thinking .... her family back home.
21 I don't think much .... this coffee. It's like water.

127.2 *Complete these sentences with one of the following words. Use a preposition if necessary.*
phoned   ~~shouted~~   discussed   entered   wrote   waited

1 He got angry and .*shouted at*. me.
2 I .... Ann last week but she hasn't replied to my letter yet.
3 I .... Tom yesterday but there was no answer. He must have been out.
4 We .... the problem but we didn't reach a decision.
5 We .... Jim for half an hour but he never arrived.
6 The children stopped talking when the teacher .... the room.

257

UNIT 128 Verb + object + preposition (1)

Study this list of *verbs + object + preposition*:

> **accuse** someone **OF** (doing) something (see also Unit 60b):
> — Tom **accused** Ann **of** being selfish.
> — Three students were **accused of** cheating in the examination.
>
> **ask** (someone) **FOR** something:
> — I wrote to the company **asking** them **for** more information about the job.
> *but:* '**ask** (someone) **a question**' (no preposition)
>
> **blame** someone/something **FOR** something:
> — Everybody **blamed** me **for** the accident.
> *or:* **blame** something **ON** someone/something:
> — Everybody **blamed** the accident **on** me.
> We also say: '(someone is) **to blame for** something':
> — Everybody said that **I was to blame for** the accident.
>
> **borrow** something **FROM** someone:
> — I didn't have any money. I had to **borrow** some **from** a friend of mine.
>
> **charge** someone **WITH** (an offence / a crime):
> — Three men have been arrested and **charged with** robbery.
>
> **congratulate** someone **ON** (doing) something (see also Unit 60b):
> — When I heard that he had passed his examination, I phoned him to **congratulate** him **on** his success.
>
> **divide/cut/split** something **INTO** (two or more parts):
> — The book is **divided into** three parts.
> — **Cut** the meat **into** small pieces before frying it.
>
> **do** something **ABOUT** something (= do something to improve a bad situation):
> — The economic situation is getting worse and worse. The government ought to **do** something **about** it.
>
> **explain** (a problem / a situation / a word etc.) **TO** someone:
> — Can you **explain** this word **to** me? (*not* 'explain me this word')
> *also:* '**explain** (**to** someone) **that/what/how/why** ...' (note the word order):
> — Let me **explain to you what** I mean.
>
> **invite** someone **TO** (a party / a wedding etc.):
> — Have you been **invited to** any parties recently?
>
> **leave** (a place) **FOR** (another place):
> — I haven't seen her since she **left** home **for** work this morning.
>
> **point/aim** something **AT** someone/something:
> — Don't **point** that knife **at** me! It's dangerous.

UNIT 128   Exercises

128.1 *Complete these sentences with a preposition.*
Example: I didn't have any money, so I had to borrow some ...**from**..... a friend of mine.

1 You're always asking me .... money. Why don't you ask someone else for a change?
2 I've been invited .... the wedding but unfortunately I can't go.
3 When I saw Dave, I congratulated him .... passing his driving test.
4 Be careful with those scissors. Don't point them .... me!
5 It's not very pleasant when you are accused .... something you didn't do.
6 The driver of the car was taken to the police station and later charged .... dangerous driving.
7 'Is that your own book?' 'No, I borrowed it .... the library.'
8 It's a very large house. It's divided .... four flats.
9 Mr and Mrs Roberts are on a tour of Europe at the moment. They're in Rome now, but tomorrow they leave .... Venice.
10 The roof of the house is in very bad condition. I think we ought to do something .... it.

128.2 *In this exercise you have to use the correct preposition after* **blame**. *Sometimes you have to use* **for**, *and sometimes* **on**.
Examples: Tom said that the accident was my fault. Tom blamed me **for the accident.**
Tom said that the accident was my fault. Tom blamed the accident **on me.**

1 Ann said that what happened was Jim's fault. Ann blamed Jim ....
2 You always say that everything is my fault. You always blame everything ....
3 Do you think that the economic situation is the fault of the government?
   Do you blame the government .... ?
4 I think that the increase in violent crime is the fault of television.
   I blame the increase in violent crime ....

Now re-write sentences 3 and 4 using **... to blame for ....**
Example: Tom said that **I was to blame for** the accident.

5 (3) Do you think that the government is .... ?
6 (4) I think that ....

128.3 *In this exercise you have to make sentences using* **explain**. *You ask someone to explain some things that you don't understand.*
Examples: (I don't understand this word). **Can you explain this word to me?**
(I don't understand what you mean) **Can you explain to me what you mean?**

1 (I don't understand this question.) Can you explain .... ?
2 (I don't understand the system.) Can you .... ?
3 (I don't understand how this machine works.) ....
4 (I don't understand why English food is so bad.) ....

259

UNIT 129 Verb + object + preposition (2)

Study this list of *verbs + object + preposition*:

> **prefer** someone/something **TO** someone/something (see also Unit 64):
> – I **prefer** tea **to** coffee.
>
> **protect** someone/something **FROM** (or **against**) someone/something:
> – He put sun-tan oil on his body to **protect** his skin **from** the sun. (*or* ... **against** the sun.)
>
> **provide** someone **WITH** something:
> – The school **provides** all its students **with** books.
>
> **regard** someone/something **AS** something:
> – I've always **regarded** you **as** one of my best friends.
>
> **remind** someone **OF** someone/something (= cause someone to remember):
> – This house **reminds** me **of** the one I lived in when I was a child.
> – Look at this photograph of Tom. Who does he **remind** you **of**?
> *but:* **remind** someone **ABOUT** something (= tell someone not to forget):
> – I'm glad you **reminded** me **about** the party. I had completely forgotten it.
> For '**remind** someone **to do** something' see Unit 55b.
>
> **sentence** someone **TO** (a period of imprisonment):
> – He was found guilty and **sentenced to** six months' imprisonment.
>
> **spend** (money) **ON** something:
> – How much money do you **spend on** food each week?
> Note that we usually say '**spend** (**time**) doing something':
> – I **spend a lot of time** reading.
>
> **throw** something **AT** someone/something (in order to hit them):
> – Someone **threw** an egg **at** the minister while he was speaking.
> *but:* **throw** something **TO** someone (for someone to catch):
> – Ann shouted 'Catch!' and **threw** the keys **to** me from the window.
>
> **translate** (a book etc.) **FROM** one language **INTO** another language:
> – George Orwell's books have been **translated into** many languages.
>
> **warn** someone **ABOUT** someone/something (**of** is also possible sometimes):
> – I knew she was a bit strange before I met her. Tom had **warned** me **about** her.
> – Everybody has been **warned about** the dangers of smoking.
> For '**warn** someone **against** doing something' see Unit 60b.
> For '**warn** someone **not to do** something' see Unit 55b.

For verbs + object + preposition + **-ing** see Unit 60b.

UNIT 129   Exercises

129.1 *In this exercise you have to read a sentence and then complete another sentence with the same meaning. Each time begin in the way shown.*
Example: Many people think he is one of the greatest pianists in the world.
        Many people regard *him as one of the greatest pianists in the world.*

1 I don't mind pop music but I prefer classical music.
   I prefer ....
2 He has enemies but he has a bodyguard to protect him.
   He has a bodyguard to protect .... his enemies.
3 I got all the information I needed from Tom.
   Tom provided ....
4 I bought a pair of shoes this morning – they cost £40.
   This morning I spent ....
5 Ann said to Tom, 'Don't forget your appointment with Mr Fox.'
   Ann reminded ....

129.2 *Complete these sentences with the correct preposition.*
Example: Ann shouted 'Catch!' and threw the keys ....*to*........ me from the window.

1 Do you prefer your present job .... the one you had before?
2 They wore warm clothes to protect themselves .... the cold.
3 He's written many books but most people regard his first book .... his best.
4 Do you spend much money .... clothes?
5 Do you see that girl over there? Does she remind you .... anyone you know?
6 Remind me .... the meeting tomorrow night. I'm sure to forget otherwise.
7 I love this music. It always makes me feel very happy. It reminds me .... a warm spring day.
8 When we went on our skiing holiday last year, the organisers provided us .... all the equipment we needed.
9 Before he came to Britain, many people had warned him .... the weather. So he was prepared for plenty of rain.
10 He was sentenced .... life imprisonment for the murder of a policeman.
11 Don't throw stones .... the birds! It's cruel.
12 If you don't want to eat that sandwich, throw it .... the birds. They'll eat it.
13 I couldn't understand the letter because it was in Spanish. So a friend of mine translated it .... English for me.
14 I prefer travelling by train .... driving. It's much more pleasant.
15 What do you spend most of your money .... ?
16 She got really angry. She even threw a chair .... me!
17 You remind me very much .... someone I used to know a long time ago. You are really like him in many ways.
18 Some words are difficult to translate .... one language .... another.
19 Before you go into the house, I must warn you .... the dog. He can be very aggressive sometimes.

UNIT 130 Phrasal verbs (**get up, break down, fill in** etc.)

a) We often use verbs with these words:

on	off	in	out	up	down	away
back	over	about	round	forward	through	along

We often use these words with verbs of *movement*. For example:

get on	The bus was full. We couldn't **get on.**
drive off	She got into the car and **drove off.**
come back	Tom is leaving tomorrow and **coming back** on Saturday.
turn round	When I touched him on the shoulder, he **turned round.**

But often these words (**on/off/up/down** etc.) give a special meaning to a verb. For example:
- Sorry I'm late. The car **broke down.**
- **Look out!** There's a car coming.
- It was my first flight. I was very nervous as the plane **took off.**
- I was so tired this morning that I couldn't **get up.**
- How did you **get on** in your examination yesterday?

These verbs (**break down** / **get up** / **get on** etc.) are *phrasal verbs*.

b) Sometimes a phrasal verb has an *object*. Usually there are *two possible positions* for the object. So you can say:

      object   *object*

I **turned off** the light. *or* I **turned** the light **off.**

Here are some more examples:
- Could you   { **fill in** this form? / **fill** this form **in?**
- It's warm.   { **Take off** your coat. / **Take** your coat **off.**
- The fire-brigade soon arrived and { **put out** the fire. / **put** the fire **out.**
- I think I'll { **throw away** these old newspapers. / **throw** these old newspapers **away.**
- The police got into the house by { **breaking down** the door. / **breaking** the door **down.**

Sometimes the object of a phrasal verb is a *pronoun* (**it/them/me/you/him/her/us**). These pronouns go *before* **on/off/in/out/up/down** etc.:
- They gave me a form and told me to **fill it in.** (*not* 'fill in it')
- Ann's asleep. Don't **wake her up.** (*not* 'wake up her')
- 'What shall I do with these old newspapers?' 'Throw them away.'
- Here's the money you need. Don't forget to **pay me back.**

c) Sometimes we use a *phrasal verb + preposition*. For example: **look forward to** / **keep up with** / **cut down on.** The object always comes *after the preposition*:
- Are you **looking forward to your holiday?**
- You're walking too fast. I can't **keep up with you.**
- Jack has **cut down on smoking.** He only smokes five cigarettes a day now.

UNIT 130　Exercises

130.1　*In this exercise you have to complete the sentences using a suitable phrasal verb from the box. Use the correct form of the verb each time.*

~~break down~~	clear up (= become bright –	get on
speak up (= speak louder)	for weather)	grow up
turn up (= appear/arrive)	show off (= show how good	~~fall off~~
close down	you are at something)	move in

1　Be careful on that horse! Don't ....*fall off*........ !
2　Sorry I'm late. The car ...*broke down*.... on the way here.
3　How did you .... in your interview yesterday?
4　There used to be a very good shop on the corner but it .... a year ago.
5　'We've bought a new house.' 'Oh, have you? When are you .... ?'
6　Wayne is eight years old. When he .... , he wants to be a pilot.
7　I arranged to meet Jim after work last night but he didn't ....
8　The weather's horrible, isn't it? I hope it .... later.
9　We all know how wonderful you are. There's no need to ....
10　(*on the telephone*) I can't hear you very well. Can you .... a bit?

130.2　*Complete these sentences as shown in the examples:*
Examples: He told me to fill in the form, so *I filled it in.*
　　　　　　He told me to throw away the newspapers, so *I threw them away.*

1　He told me to put out my cigarette, so I ....
2　He told me to take off my shoes, so I ....
3　He told me to turn on the heating, so ....
4　He told me to ring up Ann, so ....
5　He told me to give up smoking, so ....
6　He told me to put on my glasses, so ....
7　He told me to write down my address, so ....

130.3　*Complete these sentences using a suitable phrasal verb from the box. Where necessary use the past tense of the verb. Each time use* **it/them/me** *with the verb.*

look up	~~turn down~~	wake up	shave off
pick up	cross out	knock out	try on

1　The radio is a bit loud. Can you ....*turn it down*...... a bit, please?
2　There was a £20 note lying on the pavement, so I ....
3　The children are asleep. Don't .... !
4　If you make a mistake, just ....
5　I saw a jacket which I liked in the shop. So I went in and .... to see if it fitted me.
6　There were a few words that I didn't understand, so I .... in my dictionary.
7　He had a beard for a long time but he got fed up with it. So he ....
8　A stone fell on my head and .... I was unconscious for half an hour.

263

Appendix 1   List of present and past tenses

Present simple   **I do**   (Units 2–4)
I **work** in a bank but I **don't enjoy** it very much.
Tom **watches** television every evening.
Do you **like** parties?
We **don't go** out very often. We usually **stay** at home.

Present continuous   **I am doing**   (Units 1, 3 and 4)
Please don't disturb me. **I'm working.**
'What's Tom **doing**?'   'He's **watching** television.'
Hello, Ann. **Are** you **enjoying** the party?
We **aren't going** to the party tomorrow night.

Present perfect   **I have done**   (Units 13–21)
I've **lost** my key. **Have** you **seen** it anywhere?
'Is Tom here?'   'No, he **has gone** home.'
How long **have** they **been** married?
The house is very dirty. We **haven't cleaned** it for weeks.

Present perfect continuous   **I have been doing**   (Units 16–18)
I'm tired. **I've been working** hard all day.
You're out of breath. **Have** you **been running?**
How long **has** he **been learning** English?
I **haven't been feeling** very well recently.

Past simple   **I did**   (Unit 11)
I **lost** my key yesterday.
They **went** to the cinema but they **didn't enjoy** the film.
What time **did** you **get** up this morning?
It **was** hot in the room, so she **opened** the window.

Past continuous   **I was doing**   (Unit 12)
When I arrived, Tom **was watching** television.
This time last year I **was living** in Brazil.
What **were** you **doing** at 10 o'clock last night?
The television was on but they **weren't watching** it.

Past perfect   **I had done**   (Unit 22)
I couldn't get into the house because I **had lost** my key.
When I arrived at the party, Tom wasn't there. He **had gone** home.
They didn't come to the cinema with us because they **had** already **seen** the film.
The house was dirty because we **hadn't cleaned** it for weeks.

Past perfect continuous   **I had been doing**   (Unit 23)
I was very tired. I **had been working** hard all day.
He was leaning against a wall, out of breath. He **had been running**.

For the passive see Unit 43.
For the future see Units 4–10.

264

Appendix 2   Regular and irregular verbs

1   *Regular verbs*

The past simple and past participle of regular verbs end in **-ed**. For example:

infinitive:	clean	improve	paint	carry
past simple / past participle:	clean**ed**	improv**ed**	paint**ed**	carri**ed**

For spelling rules see Appendix 3.

For the past simple see Unit 11.
We use the past participle to make the perfect tenses (**have/has/had cleaned**) and for all the passive forms (see Units 42–4):

- I clean**ed** my room yesterday. (*past simple*)
- Your English has improv**ed**. (*present perfect* – see Units 13–21)
- The house was dirty. We hadn't clean**ed** it for a long time. (*past perfect* – see Unit 22)
- This door has just been paint**ed**. (*present perfect passive*)
- He was carri**ed** out of the room. (*past simple passive*)

When the past simple and past participle do *not* end in **-ed**, the verb is *irregular*.

2   These verbs can be *regular* or *irregular*:

infinitive	*past simple / past participle*			*infinitive*	*past simple / past participle*		
burn	burnt	*or*	burned	smell	smelt	*or*	smelled
dream	dreamt	*or*	dreamed	spell	spelt	*or*	spelled
lean	leant	*or*	leaned	spill	spilt	*or*	spilled
learn	learnt	*or*	learned	spoil	spoilt	*or*	spoiled

So you can say:
- I **leant** out of the window.   *or*   I **leaned** out of the window.
- The dinner has been **spoilt**.   *or*   The dinner has been **spoiled**.

In British English the irregular form (**burnt/learnt** etc.) is more usual.

3   *Irregular verbs*

With some irregular verbs all three forms (*infinitive*, *past simple* and *past participle*) are the same. For example, **hit**:

- Someone **hit** me as I came into the room. (*past simple*)
- I've never **hit** anyone in my life. (*past participle – present perfect*)
- George was **hit** on the head by a stone. (*past participle – passive*)

With other irregular verbs the past simple is the same as the past participle (but different from the infinitive). For example, **tell – told**:
- He **told** me to come back the next day. (*past simple*)
- Have you **told** anyone about your new job? (*past participle – present perfect*)
- I was **told** to come back the next day. (*past participle – passive*)

With other irregular verbs all three forms are different.
For example, **break – broke – broken**:
- He **broke** his arm in a climbing accident. (*past simple*)
- Somebody has **broken** the window. (*past participle – present perfect*)
- When was the window **broken**? (*past participle – passive*)

$\gg\!\!\!\rightarrow$

265

infinitive	past simple	past participle
be	was/were	been
beat	beat	beaten
become	became	become
begin	began	begun
bend	bent	bent
bet	bet	bet
bite	bit	bitten
blow	blew	blown
break	broke	broken
bring	brought	brought
build	built	built
burst	burst	burst
buy	bought	bought
catch	caught	caught
choose	chose	chosen
come	came	come
cost	cost	cost
cut	cut	cut
deal	dealt	dealt
dig	dug	dug
do	did	done
draw	drew	drawn
drink	drank	drunk
drive	drove	driven
eat	ate	eaten
fall	fell	fallen
feed	fed	fed
feel	felt	felt
fight	fought	fought
find	found	found
fly	flew	flown
forbid	forbade	forbidden
forget	forgot	forgotten
forgive	forgave	forgiven
freeze	froze	frozen
get	got	got
give	gave	given
go	went	gone
grow	grew	grown
hang	hung	hung
have	had	had
hear	heard	heard
hide	hid	hidden
hit	hit	hit
hold	held	held
hurt	hurt	hurt
keep	kept	kept
know	knew	known
lay	laid	laid
lead	led	led
leave	left	left
lend	lent	lent
let	let	let
lie	lay	lain
light	lit	lit

infinitive	past simple	past participle
lose	lost	lost
make	made	made
mean	meant	meant
meet	met	met
pay	paid	paid
put	put	put
read /riːd/	read /red/	read /red/
ride	rode	ridden
ring	rang	rung
rise	rose	risen
run	ran	run
say	said	said
see	saw	seen
seek	sought	sought
sell	sold	sold
send	sent	sent
set	set	set
sew	sewed	sewn/sewed
shake	shook	shaken
shine	shone	shone
shoot	shot	shot
show	showed	shown
shrink	shrank	shrunk
shut	shut	shut
sing	sang	sung
sink	sank	sunk
sit	sat	sat
sleep	slept	slept
speak	spoke	spoken
spend	spent	spent
split	split	split
spread	spread	spread
spring	sprang	sprung
stand	stood	stood
steal	stole	stolen
stick	stuck	stuck
sting	stung	stung
stink	stank	stunk
strike	struck	struck
swear	swore	sworn
sweep	swept	swept
swim	swam	swum
swing	swung	swung
take	took	taken
teach	taught	taught
tear	tore	torn
tell	told	told
think	thought	thought
throw	threw	thrown
understand	understood	understood
wake	woke	woken
wear	wore	worn
win	won	won
write	wrote	written

Appendix 3   Spelling

Nouns, verbs and adjectives can have the following endings:

noun + **-s/-es** (plural)	books	ideas	matches
verb + **-s/-es** (after **he/she/it**)	works	enjoys	washes
verb + **-ing**	working	enjoying	washing
verb + **-ed**	worked	enjoyed	washed
adjective + **-er** (*comparative*)	cheaper	quicker	brighter
adjective + **-est** (*superlative*)	cheapest	quickest	brightest
adjective + **-ly** (*adverb*)	cheap**ly**	quick**ly**	brightly

When we use these endings, there are sometimes changes in spelling. These changes are listed below.

> *Vowels* and *consonants*
> **a   e   i   o   u**   are *vowel* letters.
>
> The other letters (**b   c   d   f**   etc.) are *consonants*.

1   Nouns and verbs + -s/-es

The ending is **-es** when the word ends in **-s/-ss/-sh/-ch/-x**:
match/matches   bus/buses   box/boxes
wash/washes   miss/misses   search/searches
Note also:
potato/potatoes   tomato/tomatoes
do/does   go/goes

2   Words ending in -y (**baby, carry, easy** etc.)

If a word ends in a *consonant* + **y** (**-by/-ry/-sy** etc.):

> **y** changes to **ie** before **-s**:
> baby/babies   lorry/lorries   country/countries   secretary/secretaries
> hurry/hurries   study/studies   apply/applies   try/tries
>
> **y** changes to **i** before **-ed**:
> hurry/hurried   study/studied   apply/applied   try/tried
>
> **y** changes to **i** before **-er** and **-est**:
> easy/easier/easiest   heavy/heavier/heaviest   lucky/luckier/luckiest
>
> **y** changes to **i** before **-ly**:
> easy/easily   heavy/heavily   temporary/temporarily

y does *not* change before **-ing**:
hurr**ying**   stud**ying**   appl**ying**   tr**ying**

y does *not* change if the word ends in a *vowel* + **y** (**-ay/-ey/-oy/uy**):
play/plays/played   enjoy/enjoys/enjoyed   monkey/monkeys
Exception: day/daily
Note also: pay/**paid**   lay/**laid**   say/**said**

$\ggg\!\!\rightarrow$

3 Verbs ending in -ie (**die, lie, tie**)

If a verb ends in **-ie, ie** changes to y before **-ing:**
lie/ly**ing**   die/dy**ing**   tie/ty**ing**

4 Words ending in -e (**smoke, hope, wide** etc.)

Verbs

If a verb ends in **-e,** we leave out **e** before **-ing:**
smoke/smok**ing**   hope/hop**ing**   dance/danc**ing**   confuse/confus**ing**
Exceptions: be/be**ing**
        verbs ending in -ee: see/see**ing**   agree/agree**ing**

If a verb ends in **-e,** we add **-d** for the *past* (of regular verbs):
smoke/smoke**d**   hope/hope**d**   dance/dance**d**   confuse/confuse**d**

Adjectives and *adverbs*

If an adjective ends in **-e,** we add **-r** and **-st** for the *comparative* and *superlative*:
wide/wide**r**/wide**st**   late/late**r**/late**st**   large/large**r**/large**st**

If an adjective ends in **-e,** we *keep* **e** before the adverb ending **-ly:**
polite/polite**ly**   extreme/extreme**ly**   absolute/absolute**ly**

If an adjective ends in **-le** (**terrible, probable** etc.), we leave out **e** and add **-y** for the adverb:
terrib**le**/terrib**ly**   probab**le**/probab**ly**   reasonab**le**/reasonab**ly**

---

5 Doubling consonants (**stop/stopping/stopped,   hot/hotter/hottest** etc.)

Sometimes a verb or an adjective ends in *consonant–vowel–consonant*. For example:
stop plan rob hot thin wet prefer begin

We double the final consonant (**-pp-, -nn-** etc.) of these words before **-ing, -ed, -er** and **-est:**
stop/sto**pp**ing/sto**pp**ed   plan/pla**nn**ing/pla**nn**ed   rob/ro**bb**ing/ro**bb**ed
hot/ho**tt**er/ho**tt**est   thin/thi**nn**er/thi**nn**est   wet/we**tt**er/we**tt**est

If the word has more than one syllable (**prefer, begin** etc.), we double the final consonant only if the final syllable is stressed:
preFER/prefe**rr**ing/prefe**rr**ed   perMIT/permi**tt**ing/permi**tt**ed
reGRET/regre**tt**ing/regre**tt**ed   beGIN/begi**nn**ing

If the final syllable is *not* stressed, we do *not* double the final consonant:
VISit/visiting/visited   deVELop/developing/developed
LISten/listening/listened   reMEMber/remembering/remembered

Exception: In British English verbs ending in **-l** have **-ll-** before **-ing** and **-ed** (whether the final syllable is stressed or not):
travel/trave**ll**ing/trave**ll**ed   cancel/cance**ll**ing/cance**ll**ed

We do *not* double the final consonant if the word ends in two consonants (**-rt, -rn, -ck** etc.):
start/starting/started   turn/turning/turned   thick/thicker/thickest

We do *not* double the final consonant if there are two vowel letters before it (**-oil, -eed, -ain** etc.):
boil/boiling/boiled   need/needing/needed   explain/explaining/explained
cheap/cheaper/cheapest   loud/louder/loudest   quiet/quieter/quietest

Note that we do *not* double **y** or **w** at the end of words. (At the end of words **y** and **w** are not consonants; they are part of the vowel sound.):
stay/staying/stayed   grow/growing   new/newer/newest

Appendix 4   Short forms (**I'm/you've/didn't** etc.)

In spoken English we usually say 'I'm/you've/didn't' etc. (= I am / you have / did not). We also use these short forms in *informal* written English (for example, in letters to friends). When we write short forms, we use an *apostrophe* (') for the missing letter or letters:

I'm = I **am**   you've = you **have**   didn't = did **not**

Short forms of auxiliary verbs (am/is/are/have/has/had/will/shall/would):

'm = am 's = is *or* has 're = are 've = have 'll = will *or* shall 'd = would *or* had	I'm I've I'll I'd	he's he'll he'd	she's she'll she'd	it's it'll	you're you've you'll you'd	we're we've we'll we'd	they're they've they'll they'd

's can be is or has:
- He's ill. (= He **is** ill.)
- He's gone away. (= He **has** gone away.)

'd can be would or had:
- I'd see a doctor if I were you. (= I **would** see)
- I'd never seen her before. (= I **had** never seen)

We use some of these short forms after question words (**who/what/how** etc.) and after that/there/here:

who's	what's	where's	that's	there's
who'll	what'll	when's	that'll	there'll
who'd	how's	here's		

- **Who's** that girl over there? (= who **is**)
- **What's** happened? (= what **has**)
- I think **there'll** be a lot of people at the party. (= there **will**)

Sometimes we use short forms (especially **'s**) after a noun:
- **John's** going out tonight. (= John **is** going)
- **My friend's** just got married. (= My friend **has** just got)

You can*not* use these short forms ('m/'s/'ve etc.) *at the end of a sentence* (because the verb is stressed in this position):
- 'Are you tired?'   'Yes, I **am**.' (*not* 'Yes, I'm.')
- Do you know where he **is**? (*not* 'Do you know where he's?')

Short forms of auxiliary verbs + **not** (isn't/didn't etc.):

isn't	(= is not)	haven't	(= have not)	wouldn't	(= would not)
aren't	(= are not)	hasn't	(= has not)	shouldn't	(= should not)
wasn't	(= was not)	hadn't	(= had not)	mightn't	(= might not)
weren't	(= were not)	can't	(= cannot)	mustn't	(= must not)
don't	(= do not)	couldn't	(= could not)	needn't	(= need not)
doesn't	(= does not)	won't	(= will not)	daren't	(= dare not)
didn't	(= did not)	shan't	(= shall not)		

Note that you can say:
he **isn't** / she **isn't** / it **isn't**   *or*   he's **not** / she's **not** /it's **not**
you **aren't** / we **aren't** / they **aren't**   *or*   you're **not** / we're **not** / they're **not**

Appendix 5   American English

There are a few grammatical differences between British and American English:

Unit 13 In American English the *past simple* is often used to give new information or to announce a recent happening:
  – I **lost** my key. Can you help me look for it?

The *past simple* is used with **just** and **already**:
  – I'm not hungry. I **just had** lunch.
  – 'Don't forget to post the letter.'   'I **already posted** it.'

Unit 15b Americans use the *past simple* with **yet**:
  – I **didn't tell** them about the accident **yet**.

Unit 24a In American English the forms I **have** / I **don't have** / **do you have**? are more usual than 'I've got / I haven't got / have you got?':
  – We **have** a new car.
  – **Do** you **have** any change?

Unit 35c Americans often use the infinitive (without **to**) in structures with **insist/suggest** etc.:
  – They **insisted** that we **have** dinner with them.
  – Jim **suggested** that I **buy** a car.
This structure is also used in British English.

Unit 75a Americans say '**the** hospital':
  – The injured man was taken to **the** hospital.

Unit 104d Americans say '**on** a team':
  – He's the best player **on** the team.

Unit 108a **Quite** is not often used with this meaning in American English. In American English **quite** usually means 'completely' as in section c.

Unit 114d Americans say '**on** the week-end / **on** week-ends'.

Unit 124 In American English 'different **than**' is also possible. 'Different **to**' is *not* used.

Unit 127 Americans say **write someone** (without **to**):
  – Please **write me** soon and tell me how you are.

Appendix 2.2 These verbs (**burn, learn** etc.) are normally regular in American English: burned, learned etc.

Appendix 2.4 The past participle of **get** is **gotten** in American English:
  – Your English has **gotten** much better since I last saw you.

Appendix 3.5 Note the American spelling of these words:
    traveling, traveled   canceling, canceled

Index

The numbers in the index refer to units, not pages.

Index

divide (*into*) 128
do/does (in present simple questions and negatives) 2b, 49b
dream
   dream of -ing 60a
   dream about/of 126
during 115

each (*of*) 82
each other 81c
-ed clauses 93
either (*of*) 83
   not ... either 51c
   either ... or 83e
elder 102b
eldest 104c
encourage 55c
end (*in the end* and *at the end*) 120b
engaged (*to*) 123
enjoy (*-ing*) 53a, 56a
enough 99
enter (no preposition) 127
envious (*of*) 123
even 110
   even if/when 110d
   even though 109c, 110d
ever (with the present perfect) 14a
every 87
everyone/everybody/everything 87
excited (*about*) 123
   excited and *exciting* 94
expect
   I expect so / I don't expect so 51d
   expect + infinitive 55a
expected (*it is expected that*) 45a
experience (countable and uncountable) 69c
explain 54d, 128

fail (+ infinitive) 54a
famous (*for*) 124
fancy (*-ing*) 53a
farm (*on a farm*) 118b
fast 97b
fed up (*with*) 123
feel
   feel like 60a
   feel + adjective 95c
few (*of*) 82, 86
   few and *little* 86a
   few and *a few* 86d
finish (*-ing*) 53a
fire (*on fire*) 122

first
   it's the first time I've ... 14b
   the first/second + infinitive 100b
fond (*of*) 124
for 115
   for with the present perfect 14c, 16b, 18, 19
   for and *since* 19b
   for and *during* 115a
forget (+ infinitive) 54
forgive (*for*) 60b
frightened (*of*) 123
front (*in/at/on the front*) 117e
full (*of*) 124
furious (*about/with/for*) 123
furniture (uncountable) 69d
further 102a
future 4–10
   present tenses for the future 4
   going to 5
   will 6–7
   will and *shall* 7b
   will and *going to* 8
   when and *if* sentences 9
   will be doing (future continuous) 10
   will have done (future perfect) 10d

generous 100d, 123
geographical names with and without *the* 76
gerund *see* -ing
get
   get in the passive 44d
   get something done 46b
   get someone to do something 55b
   get used to 62
   get + adjective 95c
   get in/out/on/off 119d
give (in passive sentences) 44a
give up (*-ing*) 53a
glad (+ infinitive) 100c
go
   go -ing 61
   go on holiday / go for a walk etc. 122
   go on -ing 53a
going to 5, 8
   going to and *will* 8
   was/were going to 5c
gone to and *been to* 13d
good
   good at 123
   good of someone to do something, (be) good to someone 123
   good and *well* 97a
   it's no good -ing 61

Index

Index